*For the Man in the Seat Next to Me,
my lovely husband, Richard*

PROLOGUE

Trains are wonderful....To travel by train is to see nature and human beings, towns and churches and rivers, in fact to see life!
Agatha Christie

HOW IT CAME
TO PASS

When I did my first Interrail trip, I was foot loose and fancy free. By the time I did my fifth Interrail trip, I was also foot loose and fancy free. There was, however, the small matter of four decades and a lot of water under the bridge that divided these two Interrail trips.

My first four interrail trips were all a month long and I was in my teens and twenties. By the time I did my fifth trip in 2023, I'd waved off my third child to university and retired from the teaching profession after thirty-five years at the chalk face, hence I was footloose and fancy free again! It would be my first three-month trip and was booked to celebrate my 60th Birthday.

My first Interrail trip was in 1982, when it was a rite of passage for university students. I was still a teenager (just!) and it was before the advent of Ryan Air and well before the smart phone came on the scene, both of which would change the face of travel.

I travelled with a mad Welsh woman called Jessica, who I'd met in my first year at university. "Is it wise to go with her?" asked a fellow student. "She's unhinged!" She was unhinged, I had to admit, but I wasn't ready to go solo and she wanted to interrail so off we went.

Jessica had the advantage of speaking some Welsh. Now you might be wondering why speaking Welsh was an advantage whilst travelling around Europe on a train so let me explain. As we were young women, we got lots of unwanted attention from randy men. They'd sidle up to us and try and engage us in conversation. "Sprechen Sie, Deutsch?", "Parlez vous, Francais?", "You speak English?". It was relentless and very tedious! Jessica would speak Welsh to them which totally confused them! Probably the worst incident, however, was when we were flashed at! There were no words in Welsh to stop that happening!

We headed south, through the familiar territory of the Low Countries, Germany, Austria, Italy and Greece before going behind the Iron Curtain and hopping between the capital cities of eastern Europe. We were armed with our small, booklet style Interrail; a Thomas Cook Train Timetable which, amazingly, had the timetables for trains throughout Europe and even included Morocco in north Africa; a backpack; and a Youth Hostel Association Membership Card.

There was no booking.com for easy planning or google to answer a multitude of questions. The local tourist office and our paperback "Let's Go Guide" were our best friends.

The contrast between east and west Europe was much starker in the early eighties, when the west operated on free market capitalist principles and the east was controlled by communism, than today. I remember a frisson of fear going down my spine when I saw trains to Moscow waiting to depart from Bucharest. It would be the equivalent of going to North Korea now. I couldn't, of course, have boarded that train because travel to the Soviet Union was not allowed. In 1991, I made it to Moscow as the Soviet Union was collapsing and then travelled by train on to the wonderful Saint Petersburg but, ironically, by the time I did my 2023 Interrail trip, the doors to Moscow had been firmly shut again by a FCDO "Advice Against All Travel" edict.

Travelling around Europe in the eighties was much harder

than today. For Eastern Europe we had to get visas and for Western Europe there was no euro covering countless countries so we had to change currencies every time we crossed a border. This meant we handled about eleven currencies with all the stresses and strains of using up and changing currency every time we crossed a border.

In 1982 Eastern Europe had been in the midst of the dark days of communist rule and food was rationed. Once we left Greece, we couldn't get food so had to rely on the little we had taken with us, which wasn't much as we hadn't anticipated not being able to feed ourselves. We eyed people who had large straw bags full of baguettes but when we went into shops, the shelves were devoid of food and only sold cleaning products. The only food we could find that wasn't rationed was a few 'biscuits' sold by a vendor at a train station. When we bit into them, however, we were very disappointed as they tasted awful. I'd never eaten a mixture of dirt and concrete but, if I had, I imagined this was what it would taste like.

In the end, we were forced to sightsee during the day and travel on by train at night so we could reach the appropriately named Hungary before we starved. The trains were totally full so we ended up sleeping on the dirty, narrow floors of the train corridors for three nights in a row. One night, we could only lie down near a foul-smelling toilet. The thought of it still makes me gag to this day. I'm still an intrepid traveller but I would have drawn the line at that by my 2023 Interrail trip. It's amazing what you do when you're nineteen years old!

Whilst Hungary was part of the Soviet Block, it had a government that worked towards economic reform, limited political liberalisation and greater trade with the west. In 1982, that translated into crusty bread and chocolate for two starving students. I still remember the elation of crossing the border on our way to Budapest and a decent meal!

I had been particularly shocked by the poverty of Romania where it was etched onto the faces of the people. They wore rags and rode on the rickety old trams which were well past their sell by date. They were always full so people just clung on to the sides or rode on the roof. Whilst I'd notched up quite a bit of travel in western Europe and America with my Mum, Dad and brother, it is was my first foray outside the western world and, as a consequence, I was shocked.

Whenever we came to a border in eastern Europe, the train would come to a standstill for about thirty minutes and officious looking guards would take rods over and under the train to check for stowaways. They would also lift up all the carriage seats and shine torches inside to check no one was hiding in there.

They were also looking for people smuggling contraband. Two men of sub-Saharan appearance asked my friend and I if we would take jeans over the border in our backpacks. They were probably on the guards' radar but two nineteen-year-old western students were likely to have jeans amongst their luggage. American Jeans were a scarce commodity in the Soviet Block. America epitomised the evil of capitalism so they could not be imported and went for a pretty penny on the thriving black market. I would love to have helped the guys out but I didn't fancy ringing my Mum and Dad from a communist jail. My Mum worried about me constantly and thought I was in mortal danger whenever I left the country as it was. I made sure she didn't know half of what I got up to!

Whilst in Yugoslavia Jessica and I were, inadvertently, caught smuggling ourselves by a guard. When a guard came to do an inspection, he told us we had too much money. It was in the days when you cashed Stirling travellers' cheques in exchange for the local currency and if you had any cash left over you changed it at a bureau de change in the next country. I take my credit card and the ATM for granted now but, thinking about it, how did I ever cope with that malarky?!

We only had a about £20 each but as poor students, back in the eighties, that was a significant amount. He told us we could only take the equivalent of £10 over the border. We asked him what we were supposed to do with the surplus cash. "Spend it in the restaurant car," he told us abruptly.

"Okay," we said. "We'll go later". We hid about £14 worth in our bras just in case he returned. The full amount would have been too suspicious.

Thirty minutes later, he was back. He started to get very aggressive and menacing at this point and marched us down to the restaurant car. He stood over us while we had overpriced coffee and dry biscuits which was all that was on offer. He then checked our money belts and let us return to the compartment. Luckily, he didn't twig that some of the money had mysteriously disappeared. He was probably too busy returning to the restaurant car to get his cut of what those unsuspecting travellers had been forced to spend!

Looking back, I was able to visit places that I later saw change for ever, over the years. Eastern Europe was to be transformed out of all recognition once the Berlin Wall fell so I was pleased to have seen it before, as well as after.

I visited Dubrovnik in 1982 on my Interrailing trip and then headed out to the beautiful island of Korcula. It was before Dubrovnik was, sadly, bombed during the break-up of Yugoslavia in the nineties. It was also before it was used as 'King's Landing' in Game of Thrones. When I visited thirty-seven years later in 2019, Dubrovnik had become one of the theme parks of Europe, along with such places as Barcelona and Venice. It was heaving and cruise passengers who were pouring in by the thousands. It was a bigger invasion than the Battle of the Blackwater! There was a tour group on every corner! They had the look of robots programmed to follow their guide through every twist and turn. It is a jewel in the crown of Balkans but one couldn't help thinking the experience was being ruined. "Give me 1982 over 2019 any day!" I thought.

The next year, in 1983, I went Interrailing with Welsh Jessica around France, Spain and Portugal. Jessica was studying Drama at university with modules in 'How to be a Drama Queen' and 'The Art of Moaning and Groaning'. "You're a glutton for punishment! I'd rather stick pins in my eyes than spend a month with that woman," said someone at university. They did have a point but I'd concluded that she could be funny and frustrating in equal measure and, again, I didn't want to Interrail on my own.

Jessica and I had a different approach to travel which was a further complication. She was more interested in beaches, cafes and nightclubs; and I was more interested in history, culture and landscapes. She thought our route the year before had been "too heavy". I agreed to countries with miles of holiday beaches as a compromise but I had no intention of spending the trip sitting on them for too long!

After expensive France, the countries of Spain and Portugal were a treat for two poor students. I'd worked during the summer to fund my trip but I could only dream of the kind of resources I would have at my disposal by 2023. Mind you, it was all relative. Looking back at my diary, I'd recorded that a double room was two to three pounds. By 2023, a double room was, on average, seventy-five pounds. We ate like royalty and enjoyed free port wine at the Oporto Port Wine Cellars.

Portugal and northwest Spain were particularly poor for western European countries. In many ways, I was reminded of our trip Eastern Europe the year before. In one town we visited women were washing clothes in communal stone baths which was more like a scene from a developing country.

In 1986, I went on my first solo Interrail trip. For several years, I'd gone to work on an American Summer Camp in Vermont. There hadn't been a train in sight because, compared to Europe, America is pretty much a train free zone. Their preferred method of transport is the huge gas guzzling vehicles on the extensive network of freeways. I had had such a wonderful time but when very long university holidays had been replaced by long school holidays, I decided to get myself an Interrail Pass and head for Scandinavia, an area I hadn't yet explored. My grandmother was very against me going to Scandinavia because the Chernobyl nuclear disaster cloud had

9

floated across Scandinavia in the spring of that year. I wasn't about to change my plans to please granny, having done my own risk assessment, but she had threatened to cut me out of her will so my Mum had to drop post cards from a previous trip to Greece onto the mat when she visited her that summer. She never twigged. Years after she died and left me a bob or two, I even visited Chernobyl itself!

I ended up travelling through Denmark and then north through Norway, across the Arctic Circle, down through Finland and finally, across to Sweden by ferry where I met up with a Swedish woman who I'd met at university. My overriding impression of the trip, besides its beautiful cities and stunning scenery, was how expensive alcohol was throughout Scandinavia. At £3 for a pint, and trust me, that was bloody expensive in 1986, I had to become teetotal for the duration of the trip!

Morocco was on the Interrail Pass in the eighties. I was desperate to go but, very annoyingly, women on their own were advised not to go to Morocco. We'd received this advice so often that it was hard to ignore. I eyed it longingly. I'd never been to Africa and the idea of exotic Kasbahs and souks was very enticing!

When, therefore, my boyfriend of over a year and I were planning an Interrail trip in 1988, I made sure Morocco was on the itinerary. Of course, I may have failed to mention the bit about Morocco being a bit adventurous. The extent of Richard's travel abroad, when I rescued him from the gutter of travel in 1986, was a five-day trip to Belgium with his university. Talk about boring!

Being the travel guru in the relationship, he let me get on and do all the organising and it wasn't long before we were setting off for our month through France, Switzerland, Spain and Portugal. He loved it! I had slipped Morocco in at the end of the trip, as I didn't want him dumping me and heading for home at an earlier stage in the trip!

Morocco was a horrific culture shock for him and he still

groans when the trip is mentioned. The trains were fine. They were old SNCF trains. As we travelled across Morocco, we had good views of the countryside from the train. The train was the only place we met ordinary Moroccans. One man on a train advised us not to lend our Walkman music player to a young woman who had asked to borrow it. We had no intention of letting her anywhere near it but we felt touched by his genuine concern for us.

The main problem was the cities. They were chaotic and if you strayed from the very centre, the streets were littered with rubbish, including, dead cats and rats. During one meal, starving stray cats spat angrily at us as they eyed our food. We felt desperately sorry for the poor creatures but it was a scary experience.

We arrived in Tangiers from Spain and got a double room. We checked with the Thomas Cook Train Timetable that there hadn't been a time change in the absence of mobiles which you can set to change the time display when you change time zones. It reliably informed us that there was no time difference between Spain and Morocco. When we settled down to sleep, it was still very noisy. A band went up the street with loud drumbeats ringing out and a man got his prayer mat out and was praying to Mecca right outside our door. "It's rather late!" I moaned to Richard. Unfortunately, it wasn't as late as we thought. When we went down to reception early the next morning to get our train, we had to knock up the night porter to let us out. "What time is it?" we asked.

"5:00 AM," he said. When we looked shocked, he continued, laughing, "Oh, Thomas Cook Train Timetable!" We obviously weren't the first people to get caught out by this big fat misprint!

I initially loved Marrakesh. We got a room in a traditional hotel with a flower strewn courtyard on the main square full of fortune tellers and snake charmers. This was the exotic Morocco I'd come to experience. Unfortunately, however, we got lost in the maze of the souk and started to get hounded by aggressive men who wanted to be our guide. In the end, we were forced to pay for a guide just so he would keep the others at bay. 'The others' were not happy and one kicked me hard on my ankle. At this point, feeling very distressed, we told our guide, in no uncertain terms, that we wouldn't be doing any shopping so he wouldn't get his commission until he dealt with 'the others'. He directed us into a café and sent some heavies out to deal with 'the others'. We never saw them again.

Eventually, we did some shopping for the famous leather goods that drew travellers to the souk and our guide, who was a Berber in a long white robe, was more than happy with his commission. We made sure he helped us find our way out before we paid him his fee, as I think we would still have been there now!

That night, we ate at a stall on the square. The meal included an array of colourful salad and we really enjoyed it. It wasn't until we were paying and observed them putting our plates in a large bucket of dirty water to wash them that we realised that the decision to eat there may not have been wise. It took about four hours before we were doubled up with pain that took days to subside.

By the time I decided to interrail in 2023, boyfriend Richard had long since turned into husband Richard and, much to Richard's relief, Morocco was no longer part of the Interrail Pass, having been replaced by Turkey.

I have always planned to return to Morocco to give the country another chance and see the spectacular Atlas Mountains but I think I will have to go with my daughter who wants to see Morocco because, as I tell her, her dad would have to be bound, gagged, blind folded and chucked in the back of a van in order to get him back to Morocco.

Over the years, I'd re-visited most of the places I'd been to on my Interrail trips, particularly those I had loved and wanted to dwell in for longer in than was possible on an Interrail whistle stop tour.

A GREAT BARGAIN!

About eleven months before my 2023 trip, as I was trundling along on a South American chicken bus, feeling every bump in the road, I read a report about an Interrail sale. They were giving 50% off in celebration of their 50th birthday. The interrail pass had started life in 1972 when it had offered those up to the age of twenty-one, a rail pass covering twenty-one countries. Luckily, they'd removed the age restrictions long before because, whilst I still felt twenty-one in my head, that ship had long since sailed!

I contacted Richard back in the U.K. and asked him to buy us each a pass in the short window during which they were being offered. Hence, for the grand total of €600 each, we splashed the cash on a first class pass and I dreamed of luxury as the South American chicken bus bounced into yet another pothole in the road.

PREPARATION!

As the trip approached, I'd read up on how to operate the modern day Interrail Pass which was very different to the circa 1980s pass! It felt like a minefield of electronic menus, QR codes and expensive seat reservations that didn't exist back in the 1980s. "It seemed much simpler back in the eighties," I moaned as I started my research for the trip. Of course, that wasn't entirely true. If my sixty-year-old self had described Facebook and all its advantages as a wealth of information, help and support at your fingertips to my nineteen-year-old self, it would have seemed like something out of a science fiction film!

Back in the day, you just had a small paper booklet that you recorded journeys in. The ticket collector then stamped or clipped the pass. Simple. It was so simple that we were able to change the handwritten dates to give ourselves extra time. A number one could easily be changed to a seven as it was only recorded numerically. Dreadful, I know, but we were poor as a church mouse students. I'd never do anything like that these days, of course! And with the electronic pass, that is an easy thing to say anyway because they are tamper proof! The other advantage is that the paper copy can be lost or misplaced but the electronic copy is always there in the electronic cloud so can be downloaded onto a different devise, for example, if your mobile malfunctions or is stolen.

I'd joined two Facebook pages to get help and advice-

'Interrail and Eurrail' as well as 'Interrailing for the Older Crowd'. Specialist travel Facebook pages had become my lifeblood since I'd retired and become a full-time traveller. They put one in touch with a wealth of experts on everything from whether it's safe to drink the tap water to the likelihood of getting charged a shed load of cash because my carry-on bag is 1 inch bigger than the EasyJet website dimensions.

"Don't worry," said one of the old hands on the Interrail Facebook Pages. "Once you download the electronic app and start using it, you'll find it really easy. It's much better than a paper pass." A paper pass was still an option but the general consensus seemed to be that the electronic pass was by far superior.

I had done little train travel since my four epic one month Interrail trips in the 1980s, if you don't count the commuter train from our local station in Essex, where we had lived most of that time, into London. Unlike Richard who became a robot commuter for many years, I was an occasional C2C passenger, travelling up to London for work related conferences, theatre trips and to visit London's museums and other wonderful sights. The 1960s slam door trains with a reputation for poor punctuality, earnt the line the nickname of The Misery Line. Things improved dramatically between 2000 and 2003 when the line had a makeover and introduced a fleet of brand spanking new trains but they remained overcrowded and unreliable so were hardly an advert for train travel.

On a school trip I ran in 1992, we travelled by train from Mumbai up to Rajasthan. Indian trains are an experience in themselves and having travelled on Indian roads, I felt that that travelling by rail would be kinder to my risk assessment which is always a headache when you are responsible for other people's children. After a long overnight train journey that had been delayed the night before by drunks on the line, we opened the train windows to let some fresh air in, only to find black deposits were flying in through the window. I caught one between my fingers and it dissolved into a black powder that blackened my hands. "Could it be soot?" I said, thinking aloud. It was! As the long train went around a huge bend, I could see the steam train that was pulling us. Commercial trains had long since disappeared in Britain, so it was a thrilling sight and felt as if we were on the journey of a bygone era!

On finishing work as a teacher and becoming a full-time traveller, I mainly travelled by bus in developing countries but there were some notable exceptions. On a trip to Southeast Asia in 2022, I used the new Chinese built high speed line in Laos to travel from Luang Namtha to Luang Prabang. It took just two hours and we were herded onto the train by Chinese officials with loud speakers. I'd done the equivalent in reverse by bus and that had taken nine hours! In a country that is still very poor, it was like going from Victorian Times to The Space Age. Deep down, I preferred to see Laos as it really was so when I travelled the whole length of the famous Unification Line from Ho Chi Minh City to Hanoi, I was pleased to see it was a far more authentic experience with rundown old trains that were dirty and grimy. It was the perfect way to see life in the paddy fields of Vietnam.

Just before Richard and I set off to interrail in 2023, we spent a month travelling around Tunisia. We hired a car to see most of the country but we did do one journey by train from Tunis to Sousse. Our interrail trip was just around the corner and very much on our mind so we were hoping for a good experience to whet our appetites. It was, of course, far from that! Having started life in the 1980s as an SNCF train in France, where it had clearly been condemned (you only needed to look at the state of the toilets to see why!) it had got a stay of execution in Tunisia. The train was delayed by an hour and there was nowhere to sit on the platform. We didn't want to go back into the station because we were unsure of the reliability of the information we'd been given verbally, in the absence of any kind of electronic boards giving train times or details of delays. Once the train got going, the average speed was 24 kilometres an hour. It did speed up a few times in the countryside but in urbanl areas, it was painfully slow. Okay, it only cost seven dinars each which was about £2 but much of the time, I was convinced I could have jogged faster than the train went. The train tracks were dumping grounds for rubbish. In one town, everyone dumped stuff over a long white wall. A carpet was draped over it, having not quite made it over the wall. The colourful and noisy locals on the train more than made up for all the downsides. They took us under their wings as we neared our stop with a running commentary on how many more stops to our destination. As the sun set, we were treated to a beautiful sky, streaked with orange and bright gold brush strokes. Then, as the sun exited stage right, a huge full moon rose up over the Mediterranean. All thoughts of the disgusting, stinking rubbish strewn tracks were banished!

PART ONE

The train is a small world moving through a larger world.
Elisha Cooper

ON OUR WAY!

In spite of being a regular traveller, I still felt nervous in the days and hours leading up to the trip. On the day of our departure, we awoke early and activated the pass. Facebook Group Members had been very explicit about not doing this before the day of travel, just in case you fell ill or had a family emergency because once it's activated, it's activated and there is no going back. You can do a dummy run without activating it but it's not the same as putting it into practice and that was what I was champing at the bit to do, if only to reduce the stress of getting this technological mystery up and running so we could travel around Europe for three months, as planned. We successfully seemed to generate a ticket and QR code, as if by magic, but I had no idea whether it was going to work. I'd got navigating Ryan Air down to a fine art, but this was a whole new ball game!

We had a four-egg omelette to use up the last of our supplies for breakfast and headed off to the station at 9:00 AM. I dropped a bag of cut flowers with some life still left in them over a friend's gate and we made our way through Beverley town centre where typically British clouds hung low and oppressively over us, and where there was a dampness in the air.

Richard had decided the night before that he needed a new pair of headphones. It's an important piece of kit on a train trip but his timing wasn't great! As we headed though the town centre in search of headphones, our large backpacks got some funny looks in gentile, middle class Beverley, a posh market town, which was to be our launch pad.

BEVERLEY TRAIN STATION

We had about 30 minutes to spare at the station so, keen to get the reassurance of someone on the ground that we had got the right ticket and the right QR code, we headed straight for the ticket office.

The general consensus on Facebook was that station staff were really helpful to Mobile Interrail Pass Virgins with I.T. special needs in the modern era. "The station staff checked our passes for us and showed us how they work," said one novice. I took comfort from this. Big mistake! The ticket office was deserted and no one appeared in order to help us so we proceeded onto the platform but it soon became clear that we needed to be on the opposite platform. What wasn't clear was how we got there. The overpass was locked and bolted and there was no helpful information giving any suggestions, such as 'clamber down onto the train tracks to cross' or 'take a running jump and pole vault over'. It wasn't an auspicious start!

We returned to the ticket office, which was still like the Marie Celeste. "Hello! Is anyone there?" I called out to try and attract attention.

"She's probably in the loo," said the woman in the taxi booth opposite, in the kind of tone that suggested that she spent a lot of her time in the loo. I called out again, as if this was true, she'd been in the loo for a long time.

It was at this point that I realised we weren't going to get a "nice friendly member of station staff to help"! A short, stocky woman, about my age, came raging into the ticket office like an angry bull. "There's no need to shout," she snarled at me, having turned into a rottweiler.

"I was just trying to get some attention" I told her, in as neutral a tone as possible.

"I was in the toilet" she snapped at me, "I have a right to go to the toilet,"

"Yeah, and I have a right to see a sign that says, 'On the loo! Back in 5 minutes!'" I thought. "Too much to ask?" I gave up, sensing that any request for help would not be well received. The train was racing southwards and we were still on the opposite side of the platform.

"You call this customer service?" I shouted over my shoulder as we left. "I'm composing my complaint as we speak!"

"Like I care," she spat back and disappeared out of the ticket office again, no doubt to return to the loo to finish the Sun Crossword!

Now, I'm no wilting Violet, as you can probably gather, but even Richard, who has a much higher tolerance level when it comes to the fools of this world, said, "Wow, she was rude!"

I consoled myself with the fact that I was off to swan around Europe for three months in first class and poor Snotty Sue (her name was conveniently on her name badge for complaint purposes) was going to be stuck doing a job that she clearly hated.

We went up the road and crossed the level crossing in order to access the opposite platform. Here, a young woman took a photo for us under the Beverley Train Station sign in order to mark the start of our momentous journey for posterity and I still had five minutes before the train arrived to fill in an online complaint form about Snotty Sue!

When the 11.06 AM rolled into the station, we should have proudly boarded first class, the first time we'd been in first class in our lives. Sadly, it was a Sprinter Train with no 1st class. All were second class carriages! What a let down!

A GREEN AND PLEASANT LAND!

The aristocrats, if such they could be called, generally hated the whole concept of the train on the basis that it would encourage the lower classes to move about and not always be available.
Terry Pratchett

I n the spirit of "things can only get better", we travelled to Hull where we appeared to turn around and go back in the same direction we'd come. Richard who's a local, assured me we weren't just returning to Beverley. "Hull is a spur so we just have to get back to the main line."

As we chugged along the Humber Estuary and under the Humber bridge, the kind of ticket inspector who restores one's faith in humanity came to check our tickets. She gave us a warm smile and having zapped our QR codes, assured us all was in order. In addition, she advised us how to navigate our change at Doncaster. "This train gets in at platform 3. The Kings Cross train goes from platform 3 or platform 1 which is on the other side. There are no stairs negotiate." She was the total opposite of Snotty Sue and I could feel my blood pressure going down as we spoke. I half expected the sun to come out and for there to be a wall to wall blue sky and lambs frolicking in the fields but perhaps that was too much to ask for. One step at a time!

Our tickets said we were in carriage thirteen of a long train with sixteen carriages. Thanks to my Facebook buddies, I'd worked out how to reserve seats for free. We boarded carriage thirteen, only to be faced with large red stickers announcing we were in Standard Class. "Oh, for the love of God!" I moaned to Richard. Hearing my cry of anguish, a ticket inspector directed us through the glass doors, where we found the World of First Class. The next problem was that there was a man was sitting in our seats. "I'll move," he immediately told us and we at last sank into the large, comfortable first class seats. I quickly posted a photo on my personal Facebook Page to brag about being in 1st Class and started the hash tag #Did I mention I was travelling in 1st Class? so I could use it throughout the trip and drive them all mad with envy!

"You get a hot meal delivered to your seat!" said the good people on Facebook Interrail. I think my expectations, however, were rather too high. In the end, I had a pot of porridge and Richard had a bacon roll, both washed down with a cuppa. Better than nothing but not the bacon, sausage and egg that I'd envisaged! I think you have to get the train in Edinburgh or Newcastle to get the full English!

On our way to London, we stopped in Peterborough. "Where it all began," I reminded Richard. It was here where we'd met and fallen in love thirty-seven years earlier. As I've said, at this point the extent of Richard's foreign travels was a five-day university trip to Belgium! Meeting a "travel addict" as he called me had done wonders for his travel miles, but I wasn't sure he always saw it that way!

As we sped south, the weather remained on a continuous loop of wet, damp and miserable. Thick grey clouds hung like a huge duvet over the agricultural landscape. I'd travelled the route we were taking hundreds of times by car but I had to admit that even with the grim weather, the different perspective was well worth giving up the gas guzzler for a while and letting the train take the strain. We whizzed past numerous deer from roe deer to smaller monk jack. Perhaps the higher elevation on a train made them easier to spot.

We arrived at King's Cross at 1 PM. I'd originally factored in four hours for delays and to get across London to the Eurostar Terminal. This was until I realised St Pancreas International was right next to Kings Cross!

We had two and a half hours until our Eurostar to Paris. A long wait but news of train delays that were constantly in the media in the build-up to our trip had made me nervous. Luckily, Kings Cross and St Pancreas are grande dames of railway architecture so we could admire their impressive buildings. Kings Cross is solid and stocky, whereas St Pancreas is elegantly decorative. A modern fan like structure illuminated the inside concourse of Kings Cross where we whiled away some time buying boiled sweets for the journey.

We joined a long queue to check in for our 3:30 PM Eurostar to Paris. Our interrail pass ticket didn't work at the barriers. "You can only use that in Europe," said the staff member. I'd loaded St Pancras International to Paris onto my pass and had assumed it would work. It was rather nerve racking but, in the end, it turned out we had to use our seat reservations that were attached to our passes through the input of the pass numbers on purchase of the reservations. We scanned the barcode on the reservations and proceeded to security which looked suspiciously like airport security but without the need to put liquids in a separate bag.

The departure lounge was very crowded and boarding was chaotic with swarms of people heading for the platforms up two escalators. Thankfully, once on the Eurostar, first class was an oasis of calm. I posted another photo and got some good-natured moans and groans from Facebook Friends! Afterall, they are used to my photos of rickety old buses!

"Enjoy free Wi-Fi for the entire journey," said the tic-a-tape. It didn't work for the entire journey, in actual fact! We had a meal delivered to our seats that was similar to an aeroplane meal, but, if possible, even smaller. We got a bottle of wine but there was "a problem with the water" so there was no coffee. I was flagging so I could really have done with a shot of caffeine.

As you leave London, you go through a long tunnel. This reminded us of our last Eurostar trip when our young daughter, Helen, asked, as we emerged from the tunnel, ten minutes after leaving the station in London, "Are we in France?". I messaged her to let her know we were having a laugh at her expense. She wasn't impressed.

In those days, the Eurostar Terminal was at Waterloo Station. It was widely believed that this station was chosen to wind up the French by reminding them of our glorious victory on the fields of Flanders!

The dirty Eurostar windows reminded me of the windows on South American buses! For someone like me, who likes to see the world go by, this was very frustrating.

Once through the channel tunnel proper, we raced through the French countryside at speeds up to 200km/h. The weather, at long last, improved. The heavy blanket of cloud lifted and there was a hint of blue sky and sunshine!

It's funny how everything changes after crossing a border. French countryside, farms and villages were distinctly different to their English equivalents.

Before we knew it, we were rolling into the suburbs of Paris. It was only just over two hours from London to Paris, but it felt like a long journey from Yorkshire. We normally launched ourselves from London when going abroad as we'd lived near there for most of our lives but as the Interrail Pass offered an outward/ inward journey we'd decided to maximise our U.K. travel days and set off from Beverley, Richard's family hometown. One has to get one's money's worth!

Once in Paris, we had to negotiate the Paris Metro to get to the People's Hostel – Paris Bercy. Friends had visited in January and reported that prices were rocketing so I had booked a twin room with a balcony for two nights at what seemed like an astronomical €150 per night.

It turned out to be a wise move. It was in the 11th Arrondissement. Not a great location if you want to do the rock star sights like the Eiffel Tower, Louvre and Arc de Triomphe but we'd done all those places countless times before, including on two previous Interrail trips, so I'd worked out an itinerary of gardens and squares we hadn't visited in the past, figuring that the gardens would be beautiful in the spring so long as it wasn't pissing it down with rain.

We settled into our spacious room that was minimalist but light, clean and modern with crisp white linen. The best bit was the balcony, looking out over a wide, typically Parisian boulevard. I was dispatched to get alcohol and crisps and we sat on the balcony in order to decompress after a long day.

I'd had to get a box of wine because, typically, the wine being sold was all French wine and in bottles with corks. We didn't have a cork screw so I got a box of rose which was great value for money, in spite of the prospect of lugging it around in my backpack until I'd drunk all five litres!

PARIS

We were up early to enjoy our one day in Paris. 8 AM to be precise! I ventured down to the communal kitchen. This was one step too far for Richard. Our twin room with a balcony felt like a four-star hotel but there were also multiple occupancy rooms that made it a hostel. I think we were about 35 years older than the average clientele! There were free eggs and bread in the 'Free Box' which is always worth checking as you'd be amazed what people leave behind. I rustled something up using these goodies and made tea which we had on our balcony. There were large signs that said "no food and alcohol in the rooms" but I figured that didn't include the balcony and no one batted an eyelid as I made my way back to our room with breakfast.

Google Maps said the circular walk I'd planned would add up to two hours walking, not including stops. Google Maps, of course, is a notorious liar! Richard calculated that we'd walked for eight hours, not including stops, by the end of the day. As I pointed out, using Google Maps offline can lead to a few detours.

We walked in a westerly direction and then crossed the River Seine. Whilst there was still plenty of clouds, there was also lots of blue sky and sunshine too, so things weren't as bad as they could have been and my 'Gardens and Squares Tour' was still very much on the agenda!

We watched large barges pass under the bridge from where

there were views of plenty of modern, funky architecture; a box balanced on a bigger box, fluorescent panels and a bit of brutalism decorated this grittier end of the city.

We passed Gard D' Austerlitz, named after a battle that Napoleon had actually won rather than lost! It was obviously a thing to name stations after battles, back in the day! Nearby was the first stop on our tour, The Jardin de Plant. Spring flowers provided a splash of colour against a backdrop of pink and white blossom. A rather handsome palace sat at the end of the gardens and ancient botanical greenhouses to the side.

Gasping for coffee, we found a cafe just outside the gates of the gardens. I balked at the €4.30 cost of a cafe crème, but it soon became clear that that this was cheap for Paris. It wasn't unusual for a simple coffee to cost a bank busting €6, which we refused to pay, by the way! My 1982 diary reminded me I'd been flabbergasted by a £1 cost of a cup of coffee on my first ever visit to Paris.

Opposite the café, refuse collectors were collecting huge piles of rubbish. Before our arrival, there had been violent protests and strikes every other day in France. Nothing new there, then! We were relieved to hear that they'd been called off when we arrived at our hostel, obviously in honour of our visit. The French love a good fight with the authorities, so it was no surprise that there were still some peaceful protests going on around Paris.

We walked around the Pantheon which started life as a church in the 18th century but then became a mausoleum for the great and the good of Paris. It is here that Victor Hugo is buried. The second garden of the day was the pretty Luxembourg Gardens. The gardens were created in the 17th century when the Palais du Luxembourg, a royal palace, was built. Here we indulged in a bit of sitting around on the deck chairs provided before wandering through an avenue of box trees. The rose garden was beautiful, as was the English garden which played host to my favourite statue, a stag and fawns. We looped round and walked back towards the palace, which is now home to the French Senate.

We retraced our steps back towards the Pantheon which was now bathed in blue sky and sunshine. At a traditional restaurant, Richard had a Caesar salad and I had a French onion soup. It's always good to eat the local cuisine and France is certainly famous for its cuisine! We had a ring side seat in order to observe banner waving protesters with loud speakers going up the street and other diners who, in the great French tradition, were enjoying a long lunch.

After eating, we walked down to the river and past poor old Notre Dame. Repair and restoration were in full swing. I still had vivid memories of watching flames licking through its roof in 2019. As its spire collapsed, I headed off to bed, worried that I'd wake up to find this mediaeval gem had been entirely lost to the world. Thankfully, a significant amount was saved, including the iconic towers, but it seemed it would be many years before I would visit the interior of Notre Dame again. An interesting exhibition showed the extent of the damage and the mammoth task of bringing it back to life.

We walked through the medieval streets of the Marais District and headed for Place de Vosges. We were starting to flag and feel our age, so it didn't help that we overshot and ended up in Bastille Square, scene of all the recent violent protests.

"If you avoid that Bastille area," the hotel receptionist had told us, "you'll be fine."

There were no fireworks being thrown by protestors or tear gas being chucked back by the police, but peaceful protesters were out in force, milling around in the middle of the square, and the police were on standby around the edge of the square.

We back tracked and wandered around the attractive Place de Vosges, an elegant square that is the oldest in Paris. It was laid out in the early 17th century and became a model for other squares in Paris. It was originally called Place Royale because it was created by King Henri IV. The original inhabitants were posh aristocrats who enjoyed a good party in the splendid surroundings of the square. There were tournaments, state receptions, court weddings and even a few duels when the alcohol flowed!

We had to brace ourselves for the walk back to the hostel, past the railway arches of Viaduct Des Arts, where fancy artists create works of art in workshops in the former arches of the disused railway. We stopped at a supermarket near the hotel. Richard was so exhausted that he walked around like a zombie before going to sit on a bench outside. We had quiche and salad on the balcony, washed down by beer and wine. "We've done nearly 30,000 steps today!" groaned Richard.

Free hostel croissants and bread for breakfast were a bonus. Checkout was 10:30 AM, so after two exhausting days, we had a lazy start. As we had breakfast on the balcony, we watched a street market being set up. We had a bird's eye view of the market that stretched for about one kilometre along the length of the boulevard. Red and white awnings were being put up to the soundtrack of clanking metal bars. Large white vans were parked in two serried rows, either side of the street; and from these, the stalls were being filled with colourful fruit and veg, and knickers for a euro. The locals soon started to arrive to bag a bargain, pulling trolleys to fill. It reminded us of the summer we spent in Bayeux where Saturday market was in a class of its own. Sadly, this market didn't have any live chickens and ducks!

We had coffee at a cafe bar at the end of the street for the bargain price of €3.50! It's all relative! It was a classic Parisian glass box street café. Then we set off to walk the Parisian highline, the original highline! New York just copied the concept!

The weather was rather grey and miserable, but it wasn't raining and the spring flowers along the elevated walkway brought some colour to the proceedings. We made our way through Jardin de Reuilly where the trees were deep pink with the spring blossom which was at its peak. We followed the path through the middle of two apartment blocks, clearly designed to allow the line to run between them and then past elegant 19th Century buildings and over viaducts. It was a popular dog walking spot. One small terrier was a reluctant participant. It plonked itself down in a flower bed and refused to move. On our way back, we encountered its patient owner waiting while his furry friend continued to drag its heels.

OFF TO ORLEANS!

Nowhere can I think so happily as in a train.
A.A.Milne

B ack at the hotel, we collected our bags from the storage
locker and walked to Gare d' Austerliz. Here, we caught
the train to Orleans. We had our tickets checked on the
way to the platform and were pleased to find the train had
a first class. We settled into first class and before the train
started to move, a young man came in and asked something
I didn't fully understand, but guessed it was "Are these
seats free?" It turned out that Mathurin Legrand spoke fluent
English. There were no seats in second class, so he'd ventured
into first class. Who could blame him?! He'd checked with the
guards and they said it was fine. He was travelling with his
wife, who didn't immediately appear.

He stored his luggage and sat down. He said he was an
engineer who lived in Grenoble. He and his wife had lived in
Paris, where they still owned a flat. They now rented out the
small flat in Paris and rented a much bigger flat in Grenoble.

We chatted about the protests and pension reforms in
France. When I expressed concern that his wife hadn't
appeared, he went off to find her. When Cecile came back with
him, I joked that we'd started to think that Mathurin had an
imaginary wife! They both lived in the USA for a period of time,

hence their good English. In addition, Cecile had also lived in Australia. We spent much of the journey comparing travel notes!

From Orleans train station, we walked through the centre of Orleans to our one bed apartment. Passing the cathedral, some blue sky started to appear. Check-in was a late 5:00 PM but they said we could check in at 4:00 PM and drop our bags earlier, which we did.

We walked back to the centre and had two coffees at "The Green Café", which should have been called "The Expensive Café" because two medium sized coffees came to €9! I noticed, as we left, seething at the size of the bill, that vegetable soup was cheaper. Perhaps that was a way to go. Give up coffee and start drinking soup instead!

We walked down to the Carrefour Express but decided to look for a larger supermarket. Opposite was a covered market. This was full of artisan products, but with very limited kitchen supplies, we needed something simple like tuna pasta.

I asked a woman if there was a larger supermarket in town. She said there wasn't so we returned to the Carrefour Express. They had pasta but no pasta sauce! We ended up with noodles, sweet and sour sauce, and frozen seafood; and returned to prepare it for dinner. It tasted as bland as it sounded!

On our return, we were greeted by a woman who opened the door of the apartment for us and went back upstairs without saying a word. Later, when I couldn't work out how to turn on the hot water tank, I went upstairs and knocked on the door. A man came down and pulled off a cap. He pressed a button and a red light came on. He then disappeared back upstairs again, without saying a word. They spoke very little English but did give me their son's WhatsApp so he could liaise with me in English.

Reviews for the apartment were interesting:
"It was full of antiques. Who needs an upright piano in a rental apartment?"
One man called it 'clutter'.

"You can see it's French vintage from the photos," responded the owner, rather defensively.

Some guests, particularly those from the New World, loved the look. I have to say, we were with those from the Old World. It looked like a junkyard, and this look was extended to the courtyard outside. It was, however, reasonably priced, so it was swings and roundabouts!

BLOIS

We caught the 11:42 AM train to Blois. The train had spacious first class seats in a very quiet carriage. This was good news because Facebook had indicated that regional trains in France didn't have first class carriages. Once we cleared the suburbs of Orleans, we sped across flat agricultural land dotted with farmhouses. The rapeseed oil fields were starting to bloom, creating a blaze of bright yellow and the clouds were clearing.

By the time we got off in Blois, the sun was shining. We walked downhill and past the Chateau. I popped into the tourist office to ask if the scaffolding was still on the Chambord Chateau. We'd visited Chenonceau Chateau on a pre-kids trip to the Loire Valley with another married couple. Chenonceau is a beautiful, romantic chateau that looks as if it's come straight out of a Disney Princess movie. As it's possible to visit a Chateau on every day of the year in the Loire Valley, it is best to be selective and Chambord seemed to me to be the perfect choice for a Chateau visit on this occasion.

Chambord is another big daddy of chateaux, all conical towers and classic French gardens. Unfortunately, however, a quick internet search suggested it would be covered in scaffolding until spring 2023. The first woman I spoke to at the tourist office didn't understand what I meant by 'scaffolding'. She called a colleague and with the help of a photo of Chambord, she explained that there was still scaffolding on the

exterior. "You can still enjoy the interior," she assured me.
"No," I said, "I will probably only visit once, and I want to see it in all its glory".

We went to the front of the Blois Chateau, from where you could see to the courtyard with an elegant Renaissance staircase and stone reliefs of porcupine, some with crowns on their backs as it's a royal symbol. The equestrian statue of Louis XII on the outside façade was impressive.

We made our way down steep steps into town and through a market to the medieval Quartier des Arts. It was full of classic half-timbered buildings and the ghosts of silversmiths, weavers, blacksmiths, potters and glass blowers.

At the bottom of the hill, we got our first glimpse of the famous Loire River and crossed it on an ancient stone bridge. Clouds of seagulls swirled around, diving for fish in the fast-flowing river. On the South Bank of the Loire, we found a restaurant and had the dish of the day, beef bourguignon for €14. We added a veal terrain starter and a coffee and raspberry ice cream to make it 2 course meal for €19 each. From the restaurant, we had a good view of the spires of Nicholas Church and the towers of the cathedral which were piled up on the old town which stretched up the hill on the other bank.

We returned to the old town and climbed up to the cathedral where I was surprised to read that the French state owned eighty seven French Cathedrals. It seemed rather odd that a country so keen to separate church and state should own most of the cathedrals but I guessed it was to protect these ancient historical buildings.

A baby was being christened in a side chapel so singing rang out across the church, along with the cries of the baby, who clearly wasn't at all impressed by the attention.

We had a walk past the town hall and along a terrace with spectacular views of the Loire Valley and the old medieval stone houses below. We headed downhill for a final wander in the narrow medieval streets, chock full of 14th Century stone houses before climbing back up to the station via a quick look inside Saint Vincent de Paul Church.

There were drunks with empty wine bottles in and around the station. One sat next to me as we waited for the train on the station concourse. In fact, he nearly sat on me!

We caught the 4:43 PM train back. Richard and I suspected some other people in first class didn't have first class tickets, for example, the young man on the way to Blois and the German family on the way back. Tickets hadn't been checked whilst on the train and there were no barriers so I was getting the impression you could ride around France in first class for free! This was our 3rd journey in France and we hadn't had our passes checked once on a train! I almost wanted my pass checked to know it worked properly on the continent!

Once back in Orleans, we went to Carrefour in the shopping centre next to the station to get groceries. We decided to get fish soup in a jar and a baguette. The first bottle I picked up leaked so I replaced it and took another one. In the long queue for self-service, we observed how multicultural Orleans was – like Paris but unlike Blois. Self-service was trial and error. It was all a bit archaic compared to the U.K.

As we walked back to the apartment, I felt the bottom of the shopping bag only to discover it was damp. I then realised poisson soup was dripping down my leg. Peering into the bag, I found the lid had come off the soup and half of it had leaked all over the other groceries.

Swearing loudly, I took the groceries out and put them on the pavement. Richard had disappeared over Cathedral Square so I had to call him back. He trudged back with a "what the hell is she doing?" look and demeanour!

Picture the scene. We had to pour poisson soup from the bag, back into the glass jar to salvage our dinner plans. I'm sure we got some very strange looks but we were too busy swearing and cursing to notice. That evening we had a "small" bowl of fish soup for dinner!

A DRAB DAY IN
ORLEANS

T he weather forecast was black cloud all day. We awoke under a dark cloud so decided to hibernate for the morning and hope the weather improved. It didn't! As we left the apartment, a middle-aged man came towards us singing like an opera singer in French. He passed us and continued singing on down the street!

We walked up to explore the inside of the impressive medieval cathedral! Particularly striking amid all the bog-standard naves, transepts and statues of the Madonna, was a series of stain glass windows about Joan of Arc who, at the tender age of nineteen was burnt at the stake by the 'evil' English. One window showed bright red flames lapping at the legs of poor Joan, about to consume her in the most unimaginable way.

Whilst the headlines blame the English, it takes a bit of scratching beneath the surface to discover that the French were actually complicit in the demise of Joan of Arc. In some ways, she was like a latter-day Greta Thunberg. A teenager with a cause who ended up getting the attention of world leaders. Originally from a peasant family, she claimed to be guided by saintly visions. At the tender age of seventeen, she convinced King Charles VII that she could help him defeat the

English and it started well when she led an army and defeated them at the Battle of Orleans. This paved the way for France's victory in the Hundred Years War and she was at the side of Charles when he was crowned King of France. This remarkable peasant girl had had a meteoric rise so when she had a few defeats, it didn't take long for the old guard to turn against her. A French faction, disloyal to the crown, captured her and handed her over to the English to do their dirty work.

Joan of Arc, however, had the last laugh. She was made Patron Saint of France and you now can't move without falling over her statue or coming across streets named after her. What a rags to riches story for a young peasant girl who triumphed in a man's world. Girl Power is what I say, even if she was burnt to a crisp by my ancestors!

We walked down, yes, you've guessed it....... Rue Jeanne d'Arc, hung with huge colourful banners, including flags of Ukraine and from there we continued on to Place du Martroi where there is a huge equestrian statue of guess who......yep, Joan of Arc! Are you picking up on a theme here?

The Carrefour at the shopping centre near the station was closed but we managed to find a reasonably sized Franprix supermarket near Place du Martroi. The man at the checkout was very friendly but scanning of items, as at the Carrefour, was archaic. "It's like going back to the 1990s!" I commented to Richard. French supermarkets have an amazing array of deli style products but I feared they were not keeping up with the latest technology!

SAUMUR IN THE HEART OF THE LOIRE VALLEY

Having been bang on the day before when it was bad weather, the weather forecast was sadly lacking the next day. It said it would be sun and cloud in the morning followed by absolute sun. This was, in fact, a big fat lie. I suspected the day before that they were having a wobble because they kept putting back the time when cloud became sun and cloud. Plan A to go at 1:00 PM became Plan B to go at 11:00 AM and then went back to plan A to go at 1:00 PM. I wanted to get some photos of Orleans with some sunshine but, sadly, as we drew out of the station, the cloud still hung low over Orleans.

Whilst waiting at the station, I returned the fish soup to customer services and managed to complain in French. All those hours helping my three children with GCSE French has paid off! Okay, I had to use a few well-placed mimes of my drama in town with the fish soup but when she got on the phone to authorise the refund and used the word "explosion", I knew she had understood.

Richard and I sat in what had become our favourite seats in first class. There were more SNCF train staff in first class (about

eight!) than passengers. They were very polite and friendly, and we got a cheerful "bonjour" as they passed. They wore smart black caps with a red trim and for the first time we had our tickets checked. When the zapper went beep and the 'fat controller'
went "merci", I felt a wave of relief. We really were finally on our way!

We had to change in the evocatively named St Pierre de Corps where we had a twenty-minute wait. The advantage of taking the earlier train was that it would have been direct.

As we followed the Loire River west, around a huge bend in the river, the weather improved and became the promised sun and cloud. The Loire River is known as "the last wild river" in Western Europe which means it has had little human intervention and certainly not in the form of weirs, dams and canals. The Loire River is 1,006 kilometres long. In Medieval times when they pootled along in small wooden boats, 700 kilometres were navigable but today, the only navigable section is from Bouchemaine near Angers to the mouth at Saint-Nazaire. My favourite bit of trivia about the Loire River is to do with its source. It starts life in the Ardeche region in the southeast of the Massif Central. In 1938, so the story goes, when a schoolgirl was asked in an exam, 'Where is the source of the Loire?' she answered, 'In my grandfather's stable!' which wasn't as mad as it sounds because the Loire has several known sources, one of which runs into a stone basin on a little farm at the foot of Mount Gerbier-de-Jonc.

Orchards and vineyards lined the train line near Saumur. On the second leg, a woman gathered up her bags and darted out of first class when the ticket inspector appeared. Very suspicious, if you ask me! The inspector didn't bat an eyelid.

At the station, I got disorientated. We turned left out of the station but after about 10 minutes, I realised the blue dot was going in the wrong direction. "Oh, for God's sake!" moaned Richard. Richard is very good at letting me do all the organising and then moaning when things go wrong! Mind you I wasn't about to hand over any kind of control of our travels to Richard as I'm a self-confessed travel control freak so it's no grounds for divorce!

Once back to the station, we crossed the Loire River which was hiding behind the station. There was a substantial island with roads and buildings in the middle of the Loire so we had to cross the Loire again and turn immediately left to get to our apartment. The old town of Saumur spread up the hill behind the apartment with the impressive Chateau de Saumur as its crowning glory.

Previous guests had complained about difficulty accessing the key safe and guess what. We had difficulty accessing the key safe. The information said the penultimate box from the top, so we focused on the second one down of four boxes. No luck. We tried all of them but no luck. Luckily, in my bid to dot all the i's and cross all the t's, I had taken a photo of the Wi-Fi code so I could connect to the apartment Wi-Fi and WhatsApp the owner. "I'll be there in 10 minutes," he said. It turned out to be the 'penultimate from the bottom' not the top or 'one up from the bottom.' We explained penultimate in English. He blamed Google for the error. "I should number them," he said, as if a light bulb had just gone on.

"Now there's a thought, it's not rocket science," I thought.

The apartment was fabulous. It was spacious and light, with a contemporary feel. It was everything that our last apartment hadn't been. Most importantly, it had a balcony with a fabulous view of the Loire River, and it was only a few euros more than the last apartment. It was definitely a few more euros well spent. The sky was now completely clear and the Loire was bathed in sunshine. The low grey clouds had beat a retreat and I was rejoicing. I declared it wine o'clock and we headed for the balcony and the idyllic view.

Unfortunately, the two chairs and table on the balcony were just for decoration. There was no room for two people unless you were a toddler. Nothing, however, could dampen my spirits. We improvised by leaving the table on the balcony and pulling the chairs just inside the double doors. We still had our view of the Loire and we had the added bonus that we were out of the chilly breeze. We had bread dipped in sunflower oil (another compromise because we had no olive oil) and salt.

In the early evening, we walked up to the main square which was bathed in bright sunlight from the setting sun making it a perfect time to see its handsome light stone historic buildings. This important medieval town is in the heart of the Anjou region and its chateau was home to the Counts of Anjou before it became a royal residence for King Louis IX, also Saint Louis, as if being a king isn't enough!

Back at the apartment, we watched the sunset on the Loire. Bright sunshine that was caught in the windows of a house on the opposite bank shimmered in golden bands on the river. The image could have been an impressionist painting.

We had pizza for dinner and got an early night, hoping that the blue sky from start to finish, as predicted by the Boys at the Met Office for the next day would materialise. We really hoped it would not turn out to be another big fat lie!

BEAUTIFUL BOURGES

We got up at 6:30 AM. It was still dark but peering out, I could see the skies were clear. We were out of the door and heading for the station at 6:50 AM. It was absolutely freezing. It must have been about minus 1 degree centigrade.

As we crossed the long medieval stone bridge, we were treated to the start of the sunrise over the Loire. A band of orange appeared above the buildings along the bank of the river, in stark contrast to the midnight blue of the river and sky above. Lights were still shimmering on the water, patiently awaiting the biggest light of them all before they were extinguished.

At the station, we caught the 7:32 AM train to Bourges. It was a direct train that took just over two hours. We managed to get two
seats diagonally opposite each other with space for luggage, legs and feet because the seat directly opposite wasn't occupied so we were very contented!

As the train raced through the idyllic rural idyl, the frost sparkled on the grass after a night of sub-zero temperatures. About fifteen minutes before we were due to arrive in Bourges, a woman appeared at my seat, claiming to have booked my seat. As it was an intercity, as opposed to a TER (no seat reservations) or a TGV (seat reservations), you had the option to book but it wasn't compulsory. I persuaded her to sit diagonally opposite until I got off fifteen minutes later, with the help of a smile and a woman opposite who spoke English.

We arrived in Bourges at 9:50 AM, having had very French and very high in calories, pain au chocolat for breakfast on the train. French pastries are wonderful! There are also croissants with sweet or savoury fillings, pain aux raisins, macarons, eclairs, chausson aux pomme.........need I go on? Unfortunately, I can hear the scales groaning even if I just look at them!

It was a twenty minutes to walk to the medieval centre, past Jardin des Pres Fichaux Gardens. Once in the centre, we walked from pretty Place Gordaine up Rue Bourbonnoux that was little changed over four hundred years to the Saint-Etienne de Bourges Cathedral. Here we entered the skyscraper of a cathedral which is a UNESCO World Heritage site. Built in the 12th century, it still has some of its original stained-glass windows. The front facade with its five doorways (who needs five doors?) was a riot of carved figures. It reminded me of an elaborately decorated wedding cake. Amid all the angels, saints and kings my eye was drawn to the scene of the sinners. Rejected at the pearly gates by the security guard with a pair of weighing scales to count good deeds versus bad deeds, they were cast down to hell to be met by the devil who burnt them in a boiling pot. Twisted and writhing bodies were seen burning in hell. Any peasant gazing up at that scene as it emerged from the stone mason's hammer and chisel in the 12th century must have been scared witless! It certainly made me do a reassessment of my good deeds verses bad deeds with the conclusion that it was probably in the balance!

The side of the cathedral had impressive buttress is to support its south naves and there were typically French gardens that were still in winter hibernation. As we wandered around Jardin de l'Archeveche we were afforded attractive views of the cathedral. Then, as it was still very chilly, we ambled back down the ancient narrow cobbled streets to the main square where we had a coffee in a cosy coffee shop.

Once we'd thawed out, we walked past a classic art nouveau department store where I imagine they have sold fashion from the catwalks of Paris to stylish French ladies for over a hundred years, and on to the Palace of Jacques Coeur with its impressive towers and spires. A carved relief of a merchant looking out of a window caught my eye and a statue of the man himself stood in a square opposite.

On the other side of town, we went for a stroll through the Marais, a wetland area where channels feed allotments between two rivers. We spotted a red squirrel doing a high wire act on a telegraph wire above us. Its agility was awe-inspiring and I had the Mission Impossible theme tune playing in my head as I watched it move swiftly along the wire. Red squirrels are very rare in the U.K. because their habitats have been taken over by non-native American greys. Being lucky enough to have grown up on the Isle of Wight, a safe haven for red squirrels, I saw them all the time but even there, without the threat of the grey squirrels, their numbers have declined. It was a real treat to see this one's antics!

We returned to the main square to have dish of the day for a very reasonable €9.50. The French prefer to eat out at lunch time when it is far more reasonable with Plat du Jour and set menus on offer, as opposed to in the evening. The Bistro didn't have a drinks menu. I opted for a small rose wine but checked the price before putting in my order. I've been caught out in the U.K. and paid over £8 for a glass of wine. You can get a whole bottle of decent wine for that in a supermarket. "€2.30," said the waitress, probably rather bemused by the question!

First class on the intercity back to Saumur was crowded. Richard and I sat apart to give him more legroom. In a re-run of our outward journey, Richard had a woman approach him and say he was in her seat. Luckily, we were nearly back to our stop and she obligingly sat in a seat nearby.

Once back, we sat and had a wine overlooking the Loire River. People were jogged along the opposite bank and a rowing boat came past. We had fish soup and bread for dinner; poisson soup that had been nowhere near a pavement!

HOW THE OTHER HALF LIVE!

We had a lie-in after our very early start the day before. Mid-morning, I went off to have a look inside Saumur's Saint Peter's Church, on the main square. The organ was being played, with the organ master probably trying to get in a quick practice before the important Easter services which were just around the corner. Classical organ music filled the church as I sat and enjoyed the free concert. Large posters with the faces of Catholic priests from developing countries around the world decorated the walls. As I studied each different face, which was so zoomed in that you could see individual pores in their skin, I tried to imagine their stories. Did they have a bike to cycle to distant parishioners who lived in remote areas to administer the sacrament? Did the roof leak on their wooden shack of a church so they had to put buckets down to collect rainwater? Did they chuckle during their sermons where hundreds of devout worshipers hang on their every word?

When I returned to the apartment, Richard said a notification about train strikes the next day had popped up on his phone. My heart sank. The treat of train strikes had been looming large over this trip. As it was the Easter holidays, I'd pre-booked and paid for accommodation but if we couldn't get to the accommodation, it was non-refundable. I didn't want to over-plan for this very reason but the Loire Region is a popular place and decent accommodation gets booked up very quickly so it was a fine balance.

We walked to the station and there, I joined the queue in the ticket information office. As is so often the case, there was only one person serving and everyone ahead of me was taking an inordinate amount of time. The clock was ticking down to our 12:18 PM train. With five minutes to spare, I got to the front of the queue. The French version of Snotty Sue was far from snotty. She was, in fact, delightful. She spoke good English and explained that there would be some trains running the next day to Angers but they wouldn't know until 5:00 PM which ones. I could look up online to see which trains had been cancelled and which trains would be running. This went a long way to relieve my stress and we boarded our train feeling far more content about the situation.

Once on the train, however, another problem had cropped up. Our station wasn't on the tic-a-tape list of stops. We started to worry that in our haste to board the train, after our stressful stop at the information office, we had got on the wrong train. I'd checked the time against the platform but I hadn't checked it was stopping at our stop. I went off to find the ticket inspector. "Yes, don't worry," he assured me, "we are stopping at Onzain. There's a problem with the display."

It was a pleasant thirty-minute walk over the Loire River to Chaumont Chateau. There were attractive views of the Chaumont Sur Loire town with the Chateau perched above it from the bridge, and of the wide river. Some campervans had found a pleasant pitch beside the river to camp and enjoy the views with a glass of the strong stuff.

Once we'd got a ticket for Chaumont Chateau, we walked up a long wide path to the front of the fairy tale chateau. Round conical shaped towers and pinnacles made me feel as if a Prince Charming on his white steed was going to come and sweep me off my feet at any moment!

The staff were very helpful and spoke good English. They were keen to give us information and answer questions. The historic apartments were kitted out by the last private owners in the 19th century. The most famous owner, Catherine de Medici, seemed to have left without much of a trace. There was, however, a copy of a portrait of Catherine. She wore a bejewelled gown which the room guide and I agreed must have been very heavy and uncomfortable to wear. In addition, she wore a necklace that she had given to Mary Queen of Scots. Its journey then took a tragic turn because it was acquired by Elizabeth I when she had Mary Queen of Scots' head cut off. It was passed down the royal family and many generations later, Queen Victoria had four of the pearls placed in the crown jewels and there they remain to this day!

On the top floor there were displays of modern art, most of which didn't grab either of us. When we went up the one passage with what looked like a storage rooms leading off it, Richard commented that it was, "Just junk being stored." I pointed out, having read the information, that it was, in fact, an art installation. There was a screen image in each room and, as Richard said, a load of junk!

High in the loft rafters there was a more interesting "contemporary" art display. Photos had been taken of flowers in the garden and then digitalized into spirals and patterns, and projected onto huge screens along the length of the large space. The views from the top floor of the river were spectacular and much more to my taste than most of the 'contemporary' artwork!

Finally, we went through the private apartments that had been recreated for the 16th century by the 19th century owners.

When we had our photos taken outside the Chateau, it didn't go well with the woman who took the photos cutting off the tops of the towers, so we had to go for a re-run with a new photographer!

The stable building was an interesting structure with

its hat-shaped exercise arena. Inside the exercise arena was another art installation. This one was far more impressive than most of those in the house. They had broken rocks in half to reveal crystals inside. Hundreds were mounted on spikes to give the impression of a field of flowers.

The farmyard sadly had no animals, so we had a wander through the attractive and extensive gardens and then headed back to the station.

Once back on the train, we found there was a man sat in our favourite set of four seats facing each other in first class. Didn't he know that these seats were block booked for us for six weeks? Bloody cheek!

It was thirty minutes to Tours where I took photos of the attractive art nouveau station building. Four allegorical statues of women who represent destinations reached by train from Tours sit above a large clock and arched glass facade. We walked from the station to historic Plumereau Square, lined on one side with handsome half-timbered houses. It didn't take much imagination to picture what it would have been like five hundred years earlier. The square in 2023, however, was very different. It was buzzing with young people drinking and chatting. Richard had an artisanal beer and I had hot wine and we sat and drank them at our table on the square, feeling very old!

We had a wander around the quaint streets of the old town and then walked across town to the cathedral with Richard moaning loudly about being forced to visit yet another cathedral. A quick look at my 1988 Interrail Diary illustrated the old adage that a leopard doesn't change its spots! In Toledo, south of Madrid, Richard had enjoyed an ice lolly in the sun while I went around several ecclesiastical establishments. Four decades on, history was repeating itself with two leopards whose spots definitely hadn't changed! Perhaps this kind for compromise is the secret to a long and happy marriage!

It was a short hop then to the station but, on arrival, when we looked at the departures board we found our train was flashing. Concerningly it kept flashing on the screen and, eventually, I worked out it was delayed by one and a half hours! We'd been travelling for a week and this was our first delay!

We eventually got a train at 20:06 PM. While we waited, I got some help from a female station official to check the details of our delayed train and what trains were available on the strike day. It appeared that there was a much-reduced timetable but there was at least a timetable of sorts. We could get a train in the late afternoon from Saumur to Angers. My biggest fear had been a situation where there were no trains! Could we get a bus? It was, to be fair, only twenty minutes on the train. It would have taken eight hours, however, to walk so that was out of the question, even without heavy backpacks! I suggested hitchhiking to Richard but he didn't look impressed.

The delayed journey from Tours to Saumur was on a local train that stopped everywhere and, to add insult to injury, there was no first class! We joked about having to slum it with the peasants. Until our first class deal we were, of course, peasants ourselves and would be again when our first class Interrail Passes expired so we were keen to make the most of our opportunity to live the high life! We didn't get back to the apartment until 9:30 PM. Richard prepared a quick chicken pasta in pesto but the view of the Loire had long since faded into the darkness.

TANKS, TANKS AND MORE TANKS!

W e had a lazy start after our late return the day before. We were supposed to check out at 11:00 AM. When the cleaner came knocking at 11:30 AM doing a hoovering mime, I assured her we would only be "Cinq minute."

I'd arranged with the owner to leave our backpacks in the hallway. Unfortunately, it was back to miserable, damp weather. Unbeknownst to me, when I'd booked an apartment in Saumur, there was a tank and armoured vehicle museum – Le Musee de Blindes, only twenty five minute's walk away. This was a big bonus for tank fanatic Richard and he simply couldn't miss it.

Once at the museum, I didn't have to read any information as I had my own personal tour guide. Richard knew the history of every tank, right down to the millimetre size of every gun. He was in tank heaven and we spent two and a half hours there, finishing off with the rusting hulks of tanks yet to be restored outside. Richard got particularly excited when he found a tiger tank in bits in a marquee, something they didn't have at Bovington Tank Museum which he visits about three times a year. At Bovington, the Tiger Tank is in one piece so you can't see its guts and inner workings.

I expressed surprise that some of the tanks were made by Renault. "Yeh," said Richard. "They weren't very good. They started falling apart after a few years, a bit like their cars!" He was referring to the Renault cars we'd endured over the years. We now had a much sturdier Skoda, built by the Germans these days. I was surprised to hear that Skoda, when it was a Czechoslovak company, had also built tanks in the inter-war period. Like their car equivalents, they were taken over by the Germans when they invaded at the start of the Second World War and were turned into German panzer tanks. British Leyland Car Company produced tanks and armoured vehicles during the war. I bet they fell apart!

At the museum, we met an Australian couple from Melbourne who were driving around France for seven weeks. They were similar age to us and he was originally from Ireland. War hasn't blighted the Australian mainland, if you don't count the brief Second World War aerial bombing of Darwin one night in 1942 by the Japanese, so military museums are in short supply in Australia; however, they do like a good ANZAC Day parade, if I remember correctly from my time there.

We walked back to the main square but we were too late to get a Plat du Jour so we had to settle for a sandwich and brioche at the bakery; and a drink at the bar so we could sit on the square. I had Saumur white wine and Richard had a local artisanal beer for the purposes of immersing ourselves in local culture, of course! There were intermittent periods of sun to enjoy as we people watched on the square, a perfect place to observe the locals coming and going!

We collected our bags and walked to the station. The train was late and it was a local train that stopped at every station so it wasn't the twenty minute hop on the schedule we should have caught on a normal day; and yet again, there was no first class. There was, however, at least a train running, on this day of strikes, so we didn't complain too much.

IT WAS A RIOT!

Once in Angers, we walked right into the middle of a violent protest. The French really know how to protest! They make the British look like lightweights in that department. They've been protesting for as long as I can remember. My 'favourite' one was the tractors blockading Calais as part of a French farmers' protest. It wasn't personal but it really hacked off British travellers and lorry drivers who felt they were being targeted rather than the French port. In reality, they were just collateral damage.

More recently, there had been the Gilets Jaunes (Yellow Vest) Protests, named after the fluorescent yellow vests that the protesters wore, and now the violent protests against President Emmanuel Macron's pension reforms. To be fair to Macron, he had put the reforms in his manifesto the year before and won an election on that basis. In addition, the French retirement age was five years behind the rest of western Europe! Didn't that tell them something?

As we walked from the station down a wide central boulevard, we first heard lots of sirens and police motorbikes racing down the road, lights flashing. We next noticed crowds of young people looking excitedly and expectantly down the road. There was an explosion and red flares went off in the sky, followed by clouds of smoke.

Starting to feel anxious about what was happening, we quickly decided to get off the main street. When riot police came into view, we turned right immediately and started to flee along a side street to escape the battle zone. As we did this, Richard shouted, "tear gas!". My eyes started to sting and it penetrated the back of my throat. It was painful.

Most of the protestors couldn't have been much older than twenty years old. They'd come prepared for a fight with many wearing eye goggles so it must have been planned. It's easy to plan a riot and attract hundreds, if not thousands of people to join in these days of social media. As the tear gas cloud dispersed they ran, teenage girls squealing with exhilaration. They probably had little understanding of the serious political issues such as rising life expectancy forcing retirement at a later age. In conversations with French people I told them, "I would love to retire at sixty-four. My current age of retirement is sixty-seven and for younger people it's sixty-eight with the expectation it will go up to sixty nine to seventy years old for those the age of the teenagers protesting on the streets of Angers!"

On the steps of a neoclassical official looking building, a group of men in black with huge gas masks on looked ready for action. They had fluorescent pink arm bands. Richard thought they were anarchists but I thought they were specialist riot police. Who knows! It was so chaotic that they could have been members of the local football supporters club!

A group of firefighters were on standby. They stood huddled on a street corner assessing the situation and ready to put out any fires that sprang up. The day before, Mr Macron's favourite brasserie, La Rotonde in Paris had been set alight. Not with him in it, obviously, as he was as far away as possible in China, trying to keep a low profile, but it showed what could happen.

To make things even more miserable, it started to rain really heavily. We felt like drowned rats when we arrived at our apartment where we were greeted by Angele. It took about an hour to recover from the traumatic experience, dry out and find enough energy to go around the corner to the City Carrefour Supermarket.

It wasn't the first time I'd been caught up in the middle of riots. It all kicked off in Athens when I was leading a school trip there to see its classical wonders. As we headed away from the troubles that had suddenly sprung up out of nowhere, I joked with my colleague that I hadn't included riots on the risk assessment, in spite of believing I'd covered every eventuality from bee stings to falling off the pavement!

The riots I had encountered in Ecuador in 2022 were really hardcore. They put huge boulders over all the roads and I mean **ALL** the roads, throughout the country, and they burned tyres that sent noxious clouds of smoke high into the air. It made travel around the country virtually impossible. All I could do was get to Quito, the capital, with great difficulty, but that's another story, and fly out to neighbouring Colombia. They made even their French counterparts look like amateurs!

We had fish and salad and a very large glass of wine for dinner!

A LOAD OF RUBBISH!

We had a lie after all the 'excitement' of the day before and got up at 10:00 AM. We had cereal and headed off for the station at 11:45 AM to get the 12:30 AM to Nantes. It was only a forty-minute journey but, for the first time, when we had our tickets checked, the female ticket inspector asked for ID. We were surprised because there had been numerous days when no one had even asked to see our passes and now she wanted to see not only the passes but also ID. "Do you have your passports?" she asked.

"No", I said. "We don't travel with our passports for security reasons. They're back at our apartment."

"Identity cards?" she asked.

"We don't have identity cards in the UK," I told her. Most of the world, however, do you have I.D. cards. The U.K. is unusual in not having I.D. cards which are normally introduced under an autocratic government in order to control the population. As the U.K. has been a democracy for 400 years, well before I.D. cards were even thought of, they've never become a thing. Several governments have toyed with the idea and a voluntary identity card scheme was set up to test the waters but when only about 10 people, including Mickey Mouse, signed up, it was quietly dropped.

The ticket inspector looked at photos of our passports and moved on. An off-duty SNCF ticket inspector, who had heard the conversation and spoke English, explained photo I.D. was required and that the ticket inspector could have refused to accept our passes. I explained that we left our passports back at our apartment for security reasons. I was still mentally scarred from being held up at gunpoint in Valparaiso in 2020. On that occasion, my passport was back at my apartment but he made off with my phone, money and credit card. Richard and I did, however, have our photo driving licences with us on the Interrail Trip so I decided to travel with those when we were on a day trip from that point on. On the odd occasion we were asked for I.D., these worked a treat!

As we got off the train, the SNCF ticket inspector asked us about our journey. "Your English is good," I told him. "I used to work for Brittany Ferries," he said. "Plus, I've visited England many times; I love England."

After a bit of an unsettled start, the weather clicked on to perfect on the dial and we emerged from the station to blue sky and sunshine! A red sign that spelled out Nantes, so loved by the Instagram generation, stood proudly opposite the station. We walked up to the castle of the Duke of Brittany and around the solid, fortress like structure surrounded by a moat. We then made our way through packs of schoolchildren into the courtyard and around the battlements. The current castle was built in 1466 and it was the home to the Dukes of Brittany until the 16th century and then the Breton home of the French Monarchy. It ceased to be in Brittany as recently as 1956 when a reorganisation in France put it into the Loire-Atlantique Departement de Loire.

Nantes was made of light-coloured tufa stone that shone in sunlight. Sadly, however, the lifting of our mood was dampened by the rubbish strewn streets as we walked up to Place Royale. We and everyone else had to endure the stench of bins that were spilling over. They clearly hadn't been emptied for a significant period of time. The bin men (and women but I never saw a bin woman!) had been on strike for days, if not weeks. In a protest in Paris the day before, rat catchers had thrown dead rats at the town hall. All this rubbish would give them even more dead rats to use as ammunition!

There were some pleasant bistros on the old narrow streets but as you sat on the pavement, you had to look at piles of rubbish which was not very appetising! At least on in the huge square, the rubbish was less obvious so we found a restaurant on Palace Royale, with a view of the emblematic marble fountain which symbolised the Loire River and the maritime vocations of Nantes, a wealthy medieval trading port and formerly the capital of Brittany. Yet again, it hadn't been switched on for the tourist season!

It took a while to get the attention of the very busy waiters but once we'd ordered, the service was very fast. We ordered the Plat de Jour, a meaty piece of Julienne fish fillet (ling in English– a cod like fish). The fish was in a thick tomato sauce but, the vegetables were sadly lacking. Two small, boiled potatoes and a sprig of broccoli. We washed it down with local beer and wine.

After a long lunch, we walked up to the Quartier Graslin, a glitzy area owing to elegant city planning in the 18th and 19th centuries. The public gardens were full of spring flowers and we wandered through Passage Pommeraye, a 19th century shopping arcade packed with high end shops.

Next, we headed for the medieval quarter where history was cheek by jowl with the modern world. As we walked around Saint Peter and Paul Cathedral and through the 13th century St Peter Gate, the only remaining vestige of the town's ancient fortifications, we could hear the excited screams of young people on a hair-raising fairground ride. Just looking up at them poised and ready to plunge down 40 metres made me feel sick and my stomach churned.

Far more sedate was our walk back to the station through the colourful Jardin de Plants whose spring clock was idyllic thanks to the primary colours of daffodils, tulips and primroses, overhung by the soft pink and white of thick, cascading blossom! We had set our return journey for 17:44 PM, not really knowing how long we would want in Nantes. In the end, we were back at the station at 16:15 PM. There was a train on the board back to Angers at 16:17 PM so we decided to run for it. It was on platform 55. As we were running, I had visions of it being twenty minutes away like Ryan Air Gate 55 at Stansted Airport but, luckily, after some platforms with letters, the numbers started at 53. Yes, weird! Don't ask me to explain the logic behind it.

We jumped on the train with 30 seconds to spare. It was a local train with no first class and it stopped everywhere but "c'est la vie" as they say in France! We often jumped on trains with a ticket for the wrong time in France and Scandinavia. We figured that we had a ticket but we just didn't have a ticket for the right time. It wasn't until later that I read horror stories about interrailers being fined horrendous amounts for not having exactly the right ticket, that I realised this may not have been wise. Italy seemed to be the main offender for this unscrupulous practice.

As we were back earlier than expected and the sun was still shining, I decided to go and explore Angers. I take the attitude that 'you have got to get your sunshine where you can'. Richard, on the other hand, takes the opposite attitude believing 'enough is enough' so he headed back to the apartment to put his aching feet up.

I walked down to Angers Chateau which is, like the Ducal Chateau in Nantes, on the fortress end of the scale rather than the fairy tale end. It's perched on a thirty-metre crag above the Maine River. It was built in the 13th century and has stout defensive walls with seventeen round towers that looked like salt and pepper pots!

I walked around it and looked down on the typical French gardens made of small box cut hedges; the gaps filled in with brightly coloured flowers. French gardens are symmetrical in design to bring order to nature. It became popular in the 17th century and spread across Europe to become the dominant style of gardening around the 18th century when it was challenged by the English garden that was totally opposite. The English Garden was designed to be an informal, idealised view of nature. I guess you could say that gardening is a metaphor for the Anglo-French relationship! Two very different styles in competition but, at the end of the day, both wonderful in their own way!

I walked down and along the Maine River. As I looked up at the Chateau and the old town, I thought it reminded me of Edinburgh on its dark rocky pinnacle.

I walked up steps leading to Saint Maurice Cathedral with impressive towers thrusting skywards and some V.I.P. Knights immortalised in stone on the façade. The inside was dark and unimpressive with the exception of an elaborately carved pulpit and ornate canopy.

I had I wander through the old town which was once enclosed by a wall. It housed mainly the clergy in ancient times. The oldest house had been built in 1400! They obviously built them to last back then!

My route back took me past the old Roman city walls. I could smell the pasta Richard was preparing as soon as I entered. With 20,000 steps on the clock, I ached all over but especially in the foot department. I kicked off my boots and poured myself a large glass of wine!

A JEWEL IN THE CROWN!

Not wanting to miss a moment of the glorious weather because you don't know when your next spell of fine dry weather is going to come along, we left at 9:10 AM to walk to the station where we got the train back in an easterly direction to Amboise. With hindsight, we would have stayed in Saumur with its beautiful views of the Loire River and its cheaper price tag. Mind you, the sofa bed that I slept on was more comfortable at the Angers apartment! It was swings and roundabouts!

It was a fifteen-minute walk from the station to the centre of pretty Amboise, my favourite Loire River town. As in Saumur, we crossed the river twice as the river split around an island.

When we crossed the second branch of the river, we could see Amboise stacked up high above the river with the Chateau at its peak. It looked like the tiers of a wedding cake. With the sun behind it, it was impossible to take good photos but I knew that the sun would have moved by the time we returned, back over the bridge so the photoshoot of this diva could wait!

We walked to the historic main square, Michel de Lours and under the arch of the clock tower and down a narrow street full of expensive shops designed to pull in the rich tourists who flocked to the Loire area.

Back at the square, we sat outside a café called Patisserie and Chocolaterie Bigot and surveyed the menu. We decided on an orange hot chocolate with whipped cream. "Good choice," said a short round woman with an attractive face and immaculate grey hair on the table next to us. Louise, who was sixty-four years old, sounded American. She said she'd grown up in California but now lived in Oregon. When she tried to help a couple of women from Chile take a photo, she spoke fluent Spanish and then revealed she had been born in Colombia. Her family was well off and her father, who was an engineer, had got a job in America so the family had moved to escape the drugs cartels.

She said she was travelling on a budget. She was a "Trusted House Sitter" who was looking after a British woman's cat. "I prefer cats," she said because they are more independent and require less looking after. She'd spent some time in Paris, staying with a friend and was returning to Paris after the Loire.

The orange hot chocolate was divine but packed with calories. I hoped the health app on my phone wouldn't find out it was always lecturing me! "You've done less steps this week than last!"

"Correct! That's because I've just got back from spending six months trekking up the Andes! I'm knackered and having a well-earned flop on the sofa. Have you got a problem with that?!"

We wandered south and climbed up to a plateau with Roman ruins. I was expecting at least a triumphal arch but all there was, was a grassy burial mound. The views of the town and the surrounding area, including their River Loire, where stunning and well worth the climb.

We had mussels and chips on the main square. My wine had several small spiders floating in it. I drew the waitress's attention to this. "Oh shit," she exclaimed, loudly. "What the fuck!" I think foreigners often don't realise how offensive swearing in English can be. They hear swearing being used liberally in films and it becomes normalised. She quickly replaced it and blamed the tree above me.

We walked up to the chateau that had more spectacular views and attractive gardens filled with spring flowers and bulbous hedges. Much of the interior had been redecorated to reflect its regal past. Sadly, the chapel with the grave of Leonardo De Vinci was closed for renovation.

As we headed back over the river, I got my desired shots of Amboise!

A NO-TRAIN DAY!

We awoke to more beautiful weather. We decided to have a rare non-train day. Mid-morning, we walked down to Jardin de Plantes and then on from there towards the river. We ended up in a modern development with plenty of walkways and cycle paths. My internal compass was telling me the river, our target destination, was straight on. The trouble was, rivers have a mind of their own and bend, twist and turn. It took a local and Google Maps Offline to get us back on track to the river.

We crossed the river on a modern footbridge and walked past a medieval tower and along the other side of the bank towards the old town. We stopped for a drink at an outdoor cafe overlooking the chateau and old town opposite. When we asked for the menu, the young waiter pointed us to the QR code on the table. "Have you got a paper copy?" I asked.

"No" he said.

"What?" I replied incredulously.

"No, sorry," responded the young waiter, smiling at my exaggerated facial expressions.

"Oh, give the guy a break!" chipped in Richard, unhelpfully.

"They should have at least one paper copy!" I moaned. Now call me old fashioned but I've been using paper copies for sixty years. Okay, perhaps fifty-five years if we take off the time before I could read! I'd only got a smartphone three years earlier. Surely, having a single physical copy for a Neanderthal

O.A.P. like me wasn't too much to ask. I gave up and scanned the QR code. And guess what, it didn't work! The waiter tried. It still didn't work for him either. In the end, he gave us his phone so we could use a saved copy. I rest my case! Technology trials and tribulations over, it was very relaxing sat in the warm April sunshine having a local beer and wine, looking at the medieval times on the opposite bank.

We crossed to the opposite side of the river and went for a wander around the chateau and old town. Richard then retired to the apartment and I went off to witness the apocalypse, a rather wonderful 13th century tapestry about the fight between good and evil. Multi headed monsters fought the noble knights and dukes. A slick film helped me pick out the more subtle features such as mushrooms and birds.

Next stop was the Musee de Beau Arts where there was lots of drama. A very graphic tableau depicted the circumcision of Jesus. Roman soldiers battled with Amazonian women, and the rich wealth of the Roman Empire and Catholic Church were on display.

SERIOUS DELAYS

We got up at 7:00 AM and had breakfast. We left at 8:15 AM for our long journey south to Bergerac in the Dordogne. We had picked trains that didn't require a booking but we were concerned about the Nantes to Bordeaux leg which was on an intercity. As we didn't have a booking, we could be playing musical chairs. Kind people on the Interrail Facebook Groups looked up my journey and advised I could get a booking for €1.50 for certain sections but that the seats in second were fully booked for one section. The picture in first class was unclear but I had visions of us sitting on the train stairs, something I'd often seen people doing since we'd arrived in France. We had a two hour wait in Nantes for the intercity so I'd determined to look at getting seat reservations at a machine or at the ticket office. It had become clear that you couldn't get reservations for French trains online; you had to go to the station so you had to be in the country. It was a steep learning curve!

"I'm not looking forward to this journey," said Richard as we neared the train station. What we didn't know yet was that our journey outlook was about to get a whole lot worse! The departure board revealed our train was delayed by an hour. All other departures then started to show up as delayed by up to two hours. We assumed it was Easter holiday railway works but then an announcement revealed that there had been an 'incident'. Someone had committed suicide at 8:38

AM on the line. Our delay went from an hour to two hours and it became clear that we were probably going to miss our connection in Nantes. We were, however, acutely aware that our inconvenience paled into insignificance compared to the poor family of the deceased who would be getting the worst news imaginable about the same time.

We got chatting to a British man who had lived in France for forty years with his French wife. He said we could get the only train running in the other direction which was going to Saumur. From there we could get a train to Tours and then head south. We went off to platform 2 but when I spoke to a member of SNCF staff, he quashed that idea. "If you go to Saumur, you will just have to come back this way to go to Tours."

It was back to Plan A! We went back to the station concourse which was standing room only by then. I managed to get a seat for Richard by getting a boy to move his suitcase which was blocking access to a seat and then went off to try and make a reservation at the ticket machine. When I got stuck at the "I have an interrail pass" button, I went to see if the ticket office was open. As it was a public holiday, it didn't open until 3:00 PM! The only staff available were cleaners, security guards and women wearing red 'Can I help you?' tabards. Unfortunately, they couldn't help me.

Our delay went up to three hours so there was no chance of us catching our connection to Bordeaux. The station toilets cost a whooping €1 so we went to a cafe bar over the road that had enough people at tables inside and out to use the loo without questions being asked.

Back at the station, our train delay had gone up to three and a half hours. We started to think we wouldn't make it to Bergerac that day where we had prepaid accommodation. We discussed how our inconvenience was nothing compared to the frontline workers who had to deal with the tragedy. "Can you imagine being the doctor or the emergency services called to the scene?" I asked Richard. "It must be horrific for the train driver."

Richard's first job had been with British Rail Property Department. "I heard stories," he told me, "about drivers who didn't know they'd hit someone until the train was back at the depot and..." I stopped him there as the image was too painful to comprehend.

After two and a half hours of delay, all of a sudden, things started to move. The TGV to Strasburg was called and our TER to Nantes came soon after. We departed at 12:30 PM, just over two and a half hours late.

Our only hope was to get the later Intercity to Bordeaux. The Nantes train was very quiet but I dreaded to think what the Inter City would be like with so many people delayed.

When we got to Nantes, however, our journey took a turn for the better. We were met by SNCF staff. A young woman said she would get us seat reservations on the TGV via Paris to Bordeaux. They would be free. "If you just wait there, I'll help these people and then get your reservations and return". I stuck to her like a leech.

She took me to an office and asked me to wait while she got the seat reservations. "It must have been a difficult day for you," I said.

"Yes," she replied, "it was very quiet until the suicide and then very chaotic." She told me that suicides were not unusual. "The driver is immediately relieved of their duty and another driver takes over. They're given psychological help. It is the most distressing when it is a child."

"When did you start work today?" I asked.

"5:00 AM," she said. "I finish a 2:20PM."

"A well-earned rest," I told her.

She left me outside an office with mirror glass. Not wanting to waste time, I did some push ups on the railings. "You're exercising!" she laughed when she returned.

"I hate standing around with nothing to do" I told her. She was clutching our reservations. I thanked her profusely, hardly able to believe our luck.

On reflection, this dreadful tragedy had worked in our favour. It was an uncomfortable thought but not one we could dwell on as we were on the 1:05 PM TGV to Paris and only had 10 minutes to spare.

Two and a half hours later, we were in Paris. It felt strange going back on ourselves. We had a thirty-minute wait in Paris Montparnasse Train Station for the Paris to Bordeaux train which was non-stop and only took two hours.

The TGV sped through fields at speeds of up to 189 mph/311 kilometres per hour. Practically supersonic. High speed HS2 in the U.K. is very controversial because of 'the nimbys', locals who object to the disruption to their rural idyll. There were no 'nimbys' to protest in France because it is a much larger country in area with a similar population. It felt as if the train was going through the middle of nowhere most of the time!

Richard and I were in different carriages which was strange as the train certainly wasn't full. It was a cloudy day. The onboard Wi-Fi and diary writing helped to pass the time, and storks, which could be seen in a wetland just outside Bordeaux, created an interesting diversion.

Once in Bordeaux, we had a one and a quarter hour wait for the Bergerac train. We went and had fresh pizza opposite. Five toppings for €12,90. I had salmon and various famous French cheeses. The French are rightly very proud of their cheese. They have a mammoth four hundred varieties. Mind you, the Anglo-French relationship was seriously strained when it was revealed that Britain produced 700 varieties of cheese at the International Cheese Awards in 2016 so ahead of France by a long chalk! They came very close to declaring the brie and camembert verses the cheddar and stilton wars.

The pizzeria proved to be a pleasant interlude after a stressful day. We would arrive in Bergerac two hours later than expected at 9:30 PM so we didn't want to prepare food at that late hour and it filled the time we had to wait for the train.

The train to Bergerac only offered second class. It was a

bit of a come down after first class TGV. We passed through vineyards as far as the eye could see and the famous St. Emilion Vineyard. We're big fans of St. Emilion wine so it was trilling to see where our bottles of Grand Cru started life.

It was a fifteen-minute walk to our swanky one bed apartment where it took us a while to wind down after a long day. We had, however, make it to Bergerac which was more than we had hoped for earlier in the day!

THE DORDOGNE

I t was ten minutes to the River Dordogne and the old stone bridge from our apartment. House martins flew around the bridge and vultures rode on the thermals higher above. I had a mooch around the old town and then crossed over the river for a view back at the town. "If I'd been asked to describe a view of a typical French town then this would be it," I thought. Shutters guarded the windows of the tall mansions with a mixture slate and terracotta roofs.

When I was waiting at a zebra crossing, I took a quick photo. The next vehicle to approach the zebra crossing was a police car and it drove straight over the crossing, ignoring me. I raised my arms to the heavens. I mean, you don't expect the police to ignore zebra crossings! Mind you, this was France where for years they'd been ignoring zebra crossings!

This caused the police car to go into a sharp reverse. It whizzed back to the crossing. The male officer, who had an audience of a younger female P.C .and an older P.C., said he thought I was taking a photo. How was he supposed to know I was waiting to cross? I let him gabble on in French and then told him I was English. "Oh perfect" he said, with a tone of 'well that explains it all' and off he sped. I would probably have been arrested if he'd heard what I shouted after him!

I returned to the apartment where I found out Richard's ninety-five-year-old dad had been rushed to hospital, and Andrew and Kathryn, two of our children, were going to see him. It wasn't a surprise. We'd spent lots of time with him before our trip when Richard's ninety-three-year-old mum, who lived in the same care home, had died. Life often doesn't coordinate in the way you want it to but our children had been on standby so he wasn't alone. We could have cancelled our three-month trip and found he was still doing the Telegraph Crossword after three-months. He'd lasted an impressive ninety-five years so who was to say he wouldn't last a few more?

After some deep breaths, we walked to the station where I paid for seat reservations for our train to the Pyrenees. It was all fitting into place. Tickets on the interrail app were separate to seat reservations which could only be obtained at the train station in France, preferably from a person rather than an incomprehensible machine. We didn't venture far into Spain but it seemed to be the same there!

We boarded the 1:59 PM train to Sarlat. As the train moved, I observed we were going back the way we'd come the night before. "It must be a branch line," I said.

A few minutes later, Richard, who'd been in charge of finding the platform whilst I got the ticket reservation, looked at the route tic-a-tape in the carriage and announced we were on the wrong train. Unhelpfully, two 1:59 PM trains had departed, one to Bordeaux and one to Salat. It was practically unheard of to have trains departing at exactly the same time. Richard, obviously, had been preoccupied by his dad being taken ill. These things happen!

The kind ticket inspector, a woman in her late 50s, said we could get off at the next station but it would be a one and a half hour wait until the train back to Sarlat. I figured out it would just be the train we would be returning on if we went all the way to Bordeaux. We decided to stay on the train to Bordeaux. After all, it was sunny and a pretty ride through the vineyards.

In Bordeaux we had a thirty-minute wait to return to Bergerac. We got some internet at the train station for an update on Richard's dad and then booked our train. We could have got to Sarlat but it would only have been thirty minutes until the train back, so it wasn't worth it. The train back to Bergerac was crowded and the windows were dirty.

On our return, Richard and I walked to the River Dordogne and then around the old town. We sat in the main square surrounded by hundreds of years of history and had local beer and wine in the sunshine. We were served by a comical young waiter who had a warm disposition but who didn't look entirely comfortable in his role. He brought Manuel in 'Fawlty Towers' to mind. In addition to this, he'd recently had a growth spirt so his trousers were far too short for him.

Richard's dad died in hospital that evening. We were comforted that Andrew and Kathryn were there to say a final farewell for all of us. We didn't sleep well.

SARLAT-LA-CANEDA

Many times, the wrong train took me to the right place
Paulo Coelho

We spent all morning at the apartment and Richard got started on the funeral arrangements for his dad. Helpfully, the apartment had a washing machine. Unhelpfully, it was temperamental. It stayed on '15 minutes to go' rather than tick down to zero for an inordinate amount of time! Richard went ahead to the station and I stayed to hang the washing out as we needed it to start drying. We didn't want to end up with a bag of soggy wet clothes the next day. After a painful wait, the cycle eventually ended but the washing came out boiling hot and dripping wet. I had to use a towel to handle it. Against the clock, I hung it out and put a second load in. I had to run to the station in order to catch the train.

We got the 1:59 PM train in the right direction this time! It was a beautiful journey to Sarlat but the weather gods were not smiling on us. In my book, beautiful scenery is never the same when shrouded in low grey clouds as when it's highlighted by blue sky and sunshine. I could only imagine what its full potential would be as we constantly crossed the meandering Dordogne River and I looked out on the hills that were bursting into life as the spring took hold.

As it was another day and another famous French river, the

slate roofs of the Loire had been replaced by terracotta. Unlike the Loire region, it was our first visit to the Dordogne and I was already hooked and planning our return trip. Think road trip through quaint villages and a gite with views of the river!

At very small Sarlat Station, it said "Centre Ville 1km". It should have said "edge of centre ville 1km." When we got to the so-called centre ville we realised, much to our chagrin, that it was still a kilometre to the old town!

Sarlat definitely had superstar qualities. Born in the 14th century, it reminded me of a French Oxfordshire. It was full of sturdy mustard and honey coloured stone buildings. The trouble was, the continuing damp and drab weather was not showing it off at its best! We decided to go for a hot chocolate to warm up and get some Wi-Fi. We found a cafe opposite the cathedral and clock tower.

When the waitress came over, I asked, "Avez vous, internet?"

"Speak French," she snapped.

I thought I was. I tried again. "Avez vous Wi-Fi?"

"Non," she snapped.

"We'll go elsewhere," I snapped back.

"You won't find Wi-Fi anywhere in Sarlat," she countered.

"Yer, right" was my parting shot and guess what, up the road, on the main square, we found a very pleasant waiter and very pleasant Wi-Fi!

We whiled away a bit of time and then, all of a sudden, as if it was a gift from God, sunlight bathed the square. I raced out to soak it in and take some photos. It wasn't a perfect dome of blue sky but it was a big improvement. I left Richard in the cafe and wandered back around town for a sunlight encore! In one small square, there was a bronze statue of some geese in a nod to the area's fondness for foie gras. French law states that foie gras belongs to the protected cultural and gastronomical heritage of France." It is not, however, without its controversies as it involves force feeding birds to fatten them up, a technique that goes back as far as 2,500 BC when it was practised by the Ancient Egyptians. France is by far the largest producer in modern times and it is clear that you mess with this tradition at your peril in these parts.

After our experience in Nantes when we had ended up jumping on an earlier train with no ticket downloaded using the app, I had taken to downloading two return options onto our day ticket and the app seemed to accept this so long as there was no overlap in times. We got the later train back to Bergerac where we had fish and salad, far less controversial than foie gras!

BACK ON THE PICKET LINE!

I t was another strike day. The train we had intended to catch was cancelled so we got the 1:00 PM and checked with the apartment that it was okay to check out late. "Yes, that's fine," he said, clearly sympathetic to our predicament with the trains.

The train was met in Bordeaux by SNCF security heavies. They had more fire power than a British Bobby! Some passengers were detained, probably for fair dodging. I'm pretty certain one had been hiding in the toilets and smoking! A double crime!

It was inclement weather on the way to Bordeaux with heavy bursts of rain. It was, after all April, a month famous for showers! We hoped, however, that our fifty-minute walk to the apartment, on the other side of the city and our longest yet, would be dry but fat chance!

Most of the walk was along the wide bend in the River Garonne, a cousin of the River Dordogne. As we neared the centre we could hear the sound of chanting, music, drumbeats and firecrackers. We assumed it was a protest and it was. We watched them pass as it was certainly a spectacle: part demonstration and part carnival! At the front were sinister looking young men with black hoodies and masks; then came a bit of colour with banners and flags waved to the sound of drums, music and chanting. Red flares shot up into the sky. After a loud bang they descended slowly. It wasn't as tense and frenetic as the Angers protests and there was no sign of counter attacks by the police but one had to remain vigilant as these things can turn on a sixpence.

It started to rain and by the time we cut in and made our way up to the apartment on St Herbert Street, we were like a pair of drowned rats, yet again!

It was a studio apartment, unlike the other apartments which were one bed apartment so I could sleep in the lounge to avoid Richard's snoring (although he claimed he slept in the bedroom to avoid my snoring!). We shopped around the corner and had egg fried rice for dinner. By the time we got home, we wouldn't want to see pasta or rice for a long time but it is an easy option when you are travelling and staying in apartments of all different shapes and sizes. You never know how effective the hob and oven will be, or the extent of the kitchen utensils. Some didn't even have a sharp knife!

A DAMP DAY IN BORDEAUX!

I t was a wet and miserable morning. We had mushroom and cheese omelettes for brunch and hoped the weather would improve. The weather forecast promised more of the same but with the possibility of a bit of sunshine between the showers.

We went out about 2:30 PM and headed for the Jardin Public. There was a significant uptick in weather, with the first blue sky of the day, and it led an immediate uptick in my mood. The trouble was, within a few minutes the blue sky had been chased off by chunky slate grey clouds that glowered ominously at us! It turned out this would be the order of the day from that point on!

We admired the Monument aux Girondins on Palace des Quinconces, a place of execution. Four republicans were beheaded there in 1792 by the infamous guillotine. At its base is a fountain whose statues represent city of Bordeaux, the Garonne River and the Dordogne River. The bronze fountains symbolise the Triumph of the Concorde and the Republic, whose chariots are pulled by seahorses. The French love a bit of symbolism in their architecture almost as much as their over-the-top baroque.

We walked past the nearby ornate neoclassical theatre and

JAYNE DEAR

then down Saint Catherine Street, the longest pedestrian street in Europe and great for shopaholics! When it started to pour with rain, we dived into a cafe and had white hot chocolate and Wi-Fi.

After about an hour we walked up to the cathedral. The organ was playing when we ventured inside. Particularly interesting was the town hall opposite the cathedral whose huge wooden doors into its courtyard had been badly burned during recent riots. I remember seeing angry protesters setting things alight on the news in the build-up to our planned month in France and thinking, "and we chose to go a country in chaos because.......?" I tried to comfort myself with the fact that the media often make the situation look far worse that it really is in reality but we'd already encountered two protests in two weeks so on this basis, it seemed more like reality than exaggeration!

We passed Grosse Cloche (big clock) and headed for Saint Michael Basilique pursued by yet another shower. We walked along the Garonne River past Pont de Pierre, the most famous bridge; Porte Cailhau and Place la Bourse, all famous landmarks in the centre of regal Bordeaux, and returned to the apartment with very wet clothes. Thank goodness for the heated towel rail on which to dry clothes!

84

THE CHICKEN FACTORY!

We left mid-morning and walked to St Seurin Basilica, yet another pilgrimage stop on the Camino to Santiago de Compostela. They get everywhere! The weather was much brighter and more settled so we passed by the sights of the day before to get better photos and added some Roman Ruins. The Roman Palais Gallian is a 3rd century CE amphitheatre where lions used to roar back in the French Roman Empire known as Gaul.

We cut it fine to get the 12:28 PM to Perigueux. Richard had struggled to run since having knee replacements. It ended up with me running down the platform, waving my arms frantically at the train that was still sitting on the platform but with only seconds to go! The train driver was leaning out of the cab, chatting to ticket collectors. As Richard swung on to the platform, thirty seconds behind me and with me with one leg on the train, the driver kindly beckoned to Richard that he could slow down.

We boarded the crowded train whose final destination was Limoges and sat next to two men. The train went ten minutes late after all that so our mad dash had been in vain but you just don't know that!

I didn't look too closely at the two men in the seats next to us. In conversation, I asked if they were brothers. This proved to be wide of the mark and when I looked more closely, I could see they were father and son. Ayoub, the son, was fourteen years old and spoke good English. His father, Faruk, was thirty-seven years old and didn't speak much English. They were speaking Spanish to each other, so I reverted to speaking in Spanish to Faruk as my Spanish is better than my French. Fourteen-year-old Ayoub translated when we got stuck. They were from the Mediterranean coast of Spain but Faruk was originally from Morocco. Ayoub's mother was Spanish. Ayoub had a two-year-old brother. Faruk proudly showed me a photo of him sat in a shopping trolley.

Faruk was working in a chicken processing factory in Limoges. "We process 60,000 chickens in seven hours," he told us. "It's all done by machine." He mimed the chickens being hung up, plucked, cut up and packaged by machine.

"What do you do?" I asked.

"I hang up the chickens by their legs," he said.

"Are they alive?" I asked. I had visions of distressed and squawking chickens running through my head.

"No" he replied, "they're gassed in the lorries."

I was wide eyed and open mouthed during most of his account. I know, of course, that abattoirs aren't pleasant places but I never thought the process through in quite such graphic detail. In addition, it was making me rethink my decision to eat meat again after thirty years of being a pescatarian. I'd given up eating meat in my late twenties because of factory farming but over three years of continuous travel in countries such as Argentina where not enjoying their meat feast known as asado was practically a crime, punishable by being given a lettuce leaf and frozen veg, I started to eat some meat.

Perigueux was along the Dordogne and then hang a right along the L'Isle River. Once in Perigueux we had a fifteen-minute walk to the centre. We wandered through the old town and up to the enormous domed cathedral. The walkway along the river afforded the best views of the cathedral and old town.

We had a hot chocolate overlooking the cathedral. The friendly owner apologised for his English accent and bought us pastries to go with our hot chocolate. The weather was much drier and more settled but not perfect.

The train on the return journey was much quieter. Once in Bordeaux, we walked along the river. As it was a Saturday, it felt as if the whole of Bordeaux had turned out. The wide pedestrian promenade along the bend in the river was frenetic with people out and about, and eager to enjoy some spring warmth at last. It had certainly been a chilly spring to date!

We walked up through Palace des Quinconces before we passed yet another Joan of Arc statue and crossed through the Jardin Public to get back to the apartment.

I went to get supplies at the Carrefour City and then, as the weather had, at long last, improved dramatically, I walked down to the St. Louis de Chartrons Church where a service was just finishing so I slipped into hear the organ and see the colourful flowers that now adorned the church post lent. A woman went on to the steps leading to the alter to take a photo and was told off by a woman in authority (or at least she thought she was!). The woman taking the photo put her straight. "Oh, I'm sorry I thought you were a tourist," said the officious woman. She didn't notice me slipping in behind the photographer to get a few photos!

The sky was a deep blue all over and the setting sun lit up the ancient buildings. I continued on towards the river, passing the covered market where hundreds of young people encircled it, drinking and chatting. When I reached the waterfront, I turned around and returned to the apartment where we had fish, salad and an early night in preparation for an early start!

UP AT SILLY O'CLOCK!

I love travel. It's my passion and my life blood. There is, however, one thing I absolutely hate about travel and that is getting up early! The alarm went off at 5:00 AM after the usual fitful night of sleep. As night owls, we cannot just go to bed early.

We had everything ready to grab and go! It was still dark as we emerged onto the deserted streets of Bordeaux but they were well lit. A young man sat in a white Mercedes that had its lights on, just up the street. It was hard to work out what he was up to at that time in the morning. Was he hot wiring it? As we turned left and headed down to the riverbank, I looked behind me several times to check we weren't being followed.

We walked along the river which, unlike the evening before, when it was thronging with people, was generally deserted. A few young men passed us on their way home from a Saturday night out but otherwise, we had the place to ourselves. Huge colourful lantern style lights lit our way and made me feel as if I was in oriental Shanghai or Saigon rather than French Bordeaux!

Near the station, disco music boomed out from a building where a nightclub was still in full swing. It was 5:45 AM, for goodness sake!

Our Inter City train left at 6:27 AM. It was still dark but it wasn't long before the sun came up and flood light the green French countryside as we raced towards Narbonne on the

Mediterranean coast.

First class was practically deserted and we got a block of seats to ourselves but the ticket inspector still wanted to see our seat reservations that cost €10 each. It's one of the reasons France is not popular with interrailers. I felt cold on the train and ended up with two hoods up. I dozed off but I revived myself with the pain au chocolat and pain au raison we'd bought the day before to have for breakfast.

We had just over an hour until our train to Perpignan. We walked up a street at right angles in search of a much needed shot of caffeine but ended up back at the station cafe which was perfectly respectable but expensive.

We caught our train to Perpignan at 11:05 PM. By now the double expresso was coursing through my veins so I had renewed energy to enjoy the lagoon we passed by. At one point, the train passed along a slither of a causeway. The deep blue of the Mediterranean was in the distance and the lagoon was home to flamingos, a rare sight in Europe. When we spotted a huge flock that was a haze of pink, I just got my eyes focused on them when a goods train flashed noisily past and obscured my view. They were disappearing into the distance by the time we were clear of the clanking goods train.

Low wooded hills had been replaced by craggy orange and brown limestone mountains covered in olive green scrub.

We'd been sending messages to our daughter, Kathryn, who was on a flight from Stanstead to Perpignan as she was joining us for the next two weeks. We'd hoped we could meet up with her in the short time we had at Perpignan Station before the 12:11 PM train to Villefranche de Confluent. It was, therefore, a relief to see her smiling face as we came down the steps from the platform.

VILLEFRANCHE DE CONFLUENT

T he train to Villefranche de Confluent passed through orchards and fields of artichokes. As the train slowly climbed into the Pyrenees, we passed through towns perched on rocky crags with fortresses, ready at a moment's notice to repel invaders.

After forty minutes, the mountains started to close around us and we were completely swallowed up by a deep gorge by the time we reached Villefranche de Confluent, a spectacular medieval fortified town on a confluence in a river, hence its name.

From the station, we followed the mountain river where meltwater danced around huge boulders, to the French Gate, a gate in the imposing medieval fortress walls with watch towers at regular intervals. Inside, I felt as if we should find an army garrison but it was a street of handsome three Storey townhouses with colourful shutters. It positively glowed in the rays of sun that hit the facade of the buildings. No longer were the high walls protecting the inhabitants from invasion. This UNESCO World Heritage town now welcomed the invasion of tourists to its quaint gift shops.

We dropped our bags at friend, Nicky Oakin's holiday home which we'd rented for two weeks and which was full of character. It had a courtyard in the shadow of the high medieval town walls. An elegant white staircase snaked its way up the historic town house to the first floor where there was a lounge, kitchen, bedroom and bathroom. It continued on up to another three bedrooms and another bathroom.

It was one of the few houses that had a balcony. When we sat on it, we were entertained by house martins swooping through the air and diving into nest under the eaves opposite. Higher up, encircling the Liberia Fort, were Egyptian vultures.

We walked up to a small square where we had paninis, a half-litre carafe of white wine for a very reasonable €5.50 and beer. It was definitely a place to watch the world go by. An elderly man with long grey hair, beads and rugged leathery skin, sat on a bench and chatted to other locals. The dogs added local colour. One scruffy white dog chased after some bikers it took a dislike to and another huge white dog looked like a wolf.

The towers of the town hall and the church were offset by a bright blue sky which contrasted well with the local pink marble of the paving stones and ornate church doorway. As we had a wandered around the ancient streets, we realised that nothing was open to stock up on essentials as it was a Sunday. This was very common in Catholic countries. We knew this but we were still invariably caught out! We ended up having pasta and tomato cuppa soup!

A SHOPPING EXPEDITION!

Richard and I had coffee, bread and cheese on the balcony and then set off to the train station to get the 11:43 AM train to Parades, two stops down the line. At the station, which was deserted, there were two members of staff. It turned out that the famous Little Yellow Train was partly replaced by a bus service until the end of April because of rocks on the line until Fort Liberia, roughly halfway, where you could still do the second part of the journey.

When the train in the opposite direction to Parades didn't arrive at 11:43 AM, I went to check where it was. "Oh, it's a bus service," said one of the two members of staff with nothing to do. She looked out of the window to the forecourt in front. "It's gone."

"Didn't you think to mention it?" I asked. What did she think we were doing, sat in the train station waiting room?

We returned to the house as we had another one and a half hours until the next replacement bus. To drown our sorrows, we went and had lunch and a drink at the cafe on the square with Kathryn.

We returned in good time for the 1:43 PM bus to Parades and it left on time from the front of the station. Once in Parades we went to check the time of the return bus. "It's outside", said the woman behind the counter, "you need to go now!"

"No, I'm asking for later," I told her, but at least she made the effort to make passengers aware it was a bus rather than a train.

We walked down the Main Street to the Super U Supermarket where we shopped and put our groceries into our large backpacks. I suggested we put the backpacks into the trolley and push it to the station. I could then return with the trolley. Richard wasn't happy about this idea but I said we should give it a go.

We set off up the road like a pair of rogue teenagers. The trolley was wonky but we were distracted by the fact that Richard had left his walking pole behind when we had loaded the shopping into his backpack. He returned, but within five minutes it had disappeared! I returned to enquire in French but no luck. I did, however, learn that the humble shopping trolley in English is called, rather splendidly, le chariot in French. I returned to Richard who was angrily pushing le chariot towards the station.

We were confused about which bus to get back. In the end, we got a local bus rather than the SNCF bus by mistake but this came with the advantage of a drop off right by the French Gate rather than down at the station with a ten minute walk.

We went for sangria on the square so we could decompress after our difficult shopping trip and later, Kathryn prepared potatoes aux Gratin for dinner and we played a card game, just to emphasise that we were on a family holiday.

DAY TRIP TO NARBONNE

We got the rail replacement bus at 11:43 AM and changed to a train halfway down the line. In Perpignan, Kathryn got the TGV and we got the local TER so we didn't have to pay extra. We were due to arrive a mere ten minutes after she arrived at the station in Narbonne. As we approached Narbonne, the cathedral rose up out of the flat coastal plain. Narbonne had been a port in medieval times but it had silted over and was now fifteen kilometres from the Mediterranean.

Narbonne is not the greatest of French cities and it is overshadowed by the stars of Provence, just up the coast but it is worth a day trip.

It took us fifteen minutes to walk to the Robine Canal with its medieval bridge of merchants. It wasn't quite Florence but it was pleasant enough.

The main square was dominated by the ancient Archbishop's Palace and Town Hall which now house a number of museums. We enjoyed the sunshine over lunch at a restaurant on the square. I had sea bream, salad and chips for €15. Kathryn had a vegetarian salad and Richard had a 'house' burger which was probably a 'horse' burger as we were in France!

In the centre of the square is a Roman road, the Via Domita. It was the first Roman road built in Gaul and linked Italy and Spain. Small children jumped around on the huge black shiny stones on which the deep cuts of Roman cart tracks were still clearly visible!

We had ice cream at a parlour on the main square. I was tempted by the unusual lavender and honey flavour but was unsure because of its lilac colour. A young French woman told me it was her favourite. "It's delicious," she said and, as if to prove a point, it was loaded onto her two-scoop cone. "I always have lavender and honey."

"Are you a local?" I asked her.

"I live in Montpellier but I visit here very often as my parents live here."

She was right, lavender and honey ice cream was delicious. She sat near us, just outside the ice cream parlour so I could thank her for a good recommendation.

Richard and Kathryn headed for the supermarket near the station. You had to think through your food and drink options when you were staying in a place with no food shops beyond a bakery and when you were reliant on public transport, neither scenario being something we were used to.

It was, strangely, a train all the way back to Villefranche de Confluent. Perhaps they were working on the line earlier but had gone home for their tea.

BUS TRIP!

Richard and I were up early at 8:00 AM. We have breakfast on the balcony and then caught the bus heading in a westerly direction towards Porte Puymorens. The weather was sparkling and the scenery was spectacular. It was hard to find enough superlatives to describe it. Densely wooded mountains rose up from above the steep sided gorge that the road snaked through. High above we were treated to views of high peaks decorated by the last remnants of snow from the previous winter.

The road followed a similar route to that of the hibernating Little Yellow Train. Workmen were abseiling down the rocky cliffs, fixing wire mesh to prevent rock falling onto the tracks. From the road, we had a good view of the impressive viaducts along which the Little Yellow Train operated. The only blot on the landscape was a young man on the bus who slouched back on his seat, engrossed in his phone. He had long greasy hair and bad body odour. I guessed that he was too addicted to his screen to look after himself properly. A very modern affliction!

We were due to get off at Fort Romeu, which I soon discovered was an area, not a town. I consulted the female bus driver. A passenger added advice and the driver said "après" so I returned to my seat. At one stop, she came back to speak to me, clearly as confused as I was. "Does anyone speak English?" she asked in French. An elderly man tried to help. None of the teenagers just behind him who had probably been sat in an

English lesson that morning, volunteered to help.

In the end, she dropped us at the end of the road leading to the train station. It didn't appear to be an official bus stop. We made our way to the Little Yellow Train Station. Here, a young man spoke good English. He confirmed the times for the Little Yellow Train. What he couldn't confirm was any details for the local bus back to Villefranche-de-Confluent. "There's a bus from here at 5:50 PM," he told me.

"So, the train gets in at 5:50 PM and connects with the bus?" I asked. He had a crisis of confidence at this point and said he'd ring a colleague. When he came back to me, it wasn't good news. Not only did the bus not meet the train, but it also didn't even stop outside the station. We'd have to wait nearly two hours and it was a fifty-minute walk up to the village above where the bus stop was outside the post office.

Talk about no joined-up thinking! As SNCF had cancelled half the Little Yellow Train line, it would have made sense to offer a bus or at least have an agreement with the local bus company to drop off and pick up without too long to wait. It appeared the train and bus company didn't get on and refused to communicate.

The Little Yellow Train rolled into the station right on time. It should actually have been called the Little Yellow Graffiti Train as it was covered in graffiti down one side. For a scenic tourist train, this was very disappointing. They'd cleared the graffiti off one side but that left most of the windows down the other side covered in the thickly painted tags of the graffiti morons. It made the carriages dark and when the train went down a hillside with the unobscured windows facing the hillside, you missed the landscape stretching beyond the graffiti. Personally, I would have placed 24/7 security with big vicious dogs on the sidings where the Little Yellow Trains lived. When caught, I would have made the graffiti morons lick the paint off with the vicious Alsatians growling near their testicles! That would soon have put a stop to it!

After I'd taken a few photos and done a quick recce, Richard and I boarded and sat in the only carriage with clear windows on both sides. The train wasn't very full but everyone else had to endure the graffiti. The Little Yellow Train left with a toot of its horn and wound its way across the grassy Alpine meadow. This section of the journey wasn't the most awe inspiring but at least we got the experience of travelling on this narrow-gauge wonder. It took us one hour and fifteen minutes to get to the Latour De Carol Enveity, the end of the line. Here, one of the Little Yellow Trains was fitted with a bright yellow snow plough. It looked as if it should have been one of Thomas the Tank Engine's friends! It is one of the few places in the world where 3 gauges meet – the Little Yellow Train narrow gauge, and the French and Spanish gauges.

The man at the station back at the start of the Little Yellow Train route had said no buses ran back to Villefranche-de-Confluent until 4:30 PM. On that basis, it was better to return on the Little Yellow Train and get the bus from there. We didn't, however, feel the need to have another Little Yellow Train experience so we consulted the timetable at the bus stop outside the train station, just to check that what he had told us was correct.

It appeared that there was a bus going at 1:30 PM. Some women were waiting for it. I went to check at the train station. The woman there said she thought that there was a bus but wasn't sure as it was a different company. There was a bus sitting at the stop but it was to Foix, in the opposite direction. A kind woman said the Foix bus went at seven minutes past so I could ask the driver but when the driver of the bus to Foix turned up, he just shrugged his shoulders and raised his palms to the heavens.

A local man confirmed that the bus was on its way but when a taxi stopped in front of the waiting women, I panicked. Did they know something we didn't? Thankfully, only two got in, leaving one still waiting for our bus.

Much to our relief, and only a few minutes late, the bus drew up and we climbed aboard. We had intended to get lunch before returning but gave up on that option, reluctant to hang around for several hours further down the line.

It took two hours to get back to Villefranche-de-Confluent where we had a wander around the town with Kathryn and returned for very French fondue for dinner in the courtyard under the high medieval town walls. Late in the afternoon, sun started to flood in for a short period of time, making it a very pleasant experience.

UP WITH THE EAGLES!

I went to the bakery, just up the road to get fresh croissants, pain au chocolat and pain au raisin and then we had our very French petit dejeuner in the courtyard. One has to make the most of being able to step out of one's front door and walk a few steps to a French bakery.

Midday, at the time when only 'mad dogs and Englishmen go out in the mid-day sun', we climbed up the steep rocky hillside and through pine and Mediterranean oak forests to the Liberian Fort. It said it would be twenty minutes from the train station. Ten minutes on, it still said it would be twenty minutes! Thirty minutes later we got there. The views down three valleys, thanks to the confluence, were spectacular.

We walked around the ramparts and gazed out from the arrow slits and turrets. There were prisons and a bakery but the various mannequins on display in them were rather tacky. It would have been better to have left the past to the imagination of the visitors, in my view.

Many tunnels wound their way around beneath the ground, like a rabbit warren. When a noisy school group who came past, most said 'bonjour' to us, then the tunnel became thick with dust kicked up by their feet. They certainly had a wealth of history to take back to their classroom with them.

From the front of the fort there were impressive views of the fortified town of Villefranche-de-Confluent. I had to look hard to pick out the main features amid the sea of roof tops but eventually, I found our holiday home with the balcony where we sat and had breakfast.

A tunnel with 734 steps went right down to the way town far below. They warned over fifties to be careful. Bloody cheek! At sixty, I felt I was quite a bit fitter than many forty-year-olds! Mind you, if I'd had to flee up to the safety of the fort with the marauding hoards in hot pursuit during medieval times, I may have struggled.

Sadly, the bridge over the railway and river with access to an ancient gate was being renovated so we had to go the long way around! Once back in the village, we made our way to the square to treat ourselves to a drink. The young woman serving refused to get us a menu and pointed to a distant board. "What about wine?" I asked as it was not on the board. "Can we have a menu?" I repeated. Another waiter had tried to get us to use the QR code last time we'd visited but it didn't work without internet so he'd reluctantly got us menus which were being willingly offered on our first day. She gabbled something about wine by the glass but we wanted the carafe we'd had on previous visits.

We left and enjoyed our own wine and cider in our own courtyard. We resolved not to return to the restaurant/ bar on the square, a decision confirmed as wise by its very low score on Trip Adviser. I added my 5 pennies worth!!

DIPPING OUR TOES INTO SPAIN!

Richard and I had cereal on the balcony which had now become our favourite spot. The elderly woman opposite would hang out of the window at all times of the day and watch the world go by. She was probably lonely and bored so this flow of people up and down the narrow pedestrianised street must have been a source of entertainment.

After coffee with Kathryn in the courtyard, we got the 11:43 AM bus and train to Perpignan train station which is the centre of the universe. I'm not kidding! Salvador Dali, the famous surrealist painter, came to this conclusion during his lifetime. He was seen pacing the platforms taking measurements and in 1965 he painted 'Le Mystique de la Gare de Perpignan'. I like some of Dali's artwork, particularly the famous 'The Persistence of Memory' with the limp clocks draped around a desolate landscape but you have to admit that he was a bit mad!

We had two hours until our train south to Portbou, just over the border into Spain, so we walked towards the centre of Perpignan. We had a hot chocolate beside the river where it was sunny but there was a chilly wind. I walked down to Le Castillet, formally a medieval city gate and entrance to the old town, to capture it in the sunshine.

We walked back up the river to the station and went to the other side of the station where there was a Lidl. It was much cheaper than City Carrefour so we did a big shop. We had taken our large backpacks to fill with shopping but before we could begin packing, they were checked inside at the checkout. It felt a bit invasive but we weren't singled out because they checked everyone's bags, including the old dear in front of us who had a trolley on wheels. I couldn't imagine a less likely shoplifter but I guessed it would be a good cover! They clearly had a problem with people shoplifting! When we emerged from the store, I noticed some drunken down and outs swigging back the strong stuff. Did they stuff that up their jumpers?

We caught the train to Portbou at 2:06 PM. Once clear of the flat plain that encircled Perpignan, we wound our way through the eastern side of the Pyrenees that plunged down towards a rocky coastline which was dotted with orange roofed towns. The dramatic train line often skirted right along the edge of the coast where it was sandwiched between the Pyrenees and the Mediterranean. Vineyards spread across the steep terraced slopes.

Close to the border with Spain, a huge area had burnt to a crisp only a week before. This was concerning as it was only April and the temperatures had barely hit twenty degrees celsius, let alone the thirty five degrees celsius that were regularly recorded during summers in the area these days. In addition, it was going to be quite a few bottles of Merlot that didn't get filled! A great shame!

The train stopped in Cerbere, the last stop in France, and police got off. We got the impression they were monitoring the trains for illegal migrants coming north from Spain. Mind you, as Spain and France are both part of the Schengen, it couldn't be hard for migrants to cross the border at points where it can't be policed.

Eventually the train set off again to Spain. We soon entered a long tunnel. "When we emerge from this tunnel, I guess we'll be in Spain," I told Richard. Sure enough, as we emerged from the tunnel, the daylight was Spanish and we were soon pulling into Portbou in Spain.

As Spain uses a different gauge to France, I guessed our train would just turn around and go back to France. I told Richard to stay put and went to check my theory. An elderly French woman getting on the train said it was going to Perpignan. The Spanish departures board said the train was going to Cerbere. Not helpful but at least it was back in the right direction!

In the meantime, Richard, against my advice and rather stupidly, had got off the train, dragging both huge backpacks laden with shopping. "Get back on," I told him. "It's going to Perpignan." A man in jeans who boarded shortly afterwards, confirmed it was going to Perpignan and he should have known as it turned out he was the train driver!

The ticket inspector hadn't checked our tickets on the way down but he did clearly clock us because the fact we were still on the train confused him. He was at pains to let us know that the train was going back in the same direction. We assured him that this was fine. He just looked at us as if we were mad!

Back over the border in France, a police officer boarded the train and shouted "passports". He seemed to ignore most people on the train. This was a good thing as we didn't have our passports on the basis we were staying in Schengen!

It was a short change of trains in Perpignan and then on to Villefranche-de-Confluent train. The train was crowded. I sat diagonally opposite an elderly lady but had to do battle with her suitcase which was taking up my foot space. She wasn't happy and muttered to herself. At the other end of the age spectrum, there were some very noisy toddlers sat near us.

Gradually the train emptied as we rose up the valley, stopping at every town clustered on the hillside and dominated by a fortified church. At every stop, I willed the muttering elderly woman and the noisy toddlers to get off but they only departed the train just a few stops before Villefranche-de-Confluent, leaving just a handful of passengers to alight at the end of the line.

It felt like a long trek back to the house with our shopping laden backpacks. Kathryn's friend, Heather, had arrived earlier and we sat in the courtyard to have pizza and red wine from the new wine box in order to celebrate her joining us for a week.

A PROPER TRIP
TO PERPIGNAN!

I went to the bakery and got croissants and pain au chocolat. If you got there too late, you found they had sold out of various items you had on your list. It was clearly first come, first served!

We caught the 11:10 AM train to Perpignan. We had a wander past the Le Castillet where we went through its huge arch and on to the old town and the cathedral. The medieval Loge de Mer with its ornate windows, doorways and carvings, and the grand Plaza de la Republica were not to be missed.

It was then a long way to the Palais des Rois de Majorqedue. It seemed a bit strange that the Dukes of Majorca, a Spanish island, had a palace in France but, like all border regions, possession had been a game of ping pong over the years. It was currently French but for many years it was in Spanish hands.

We got back to the café-restaurant by the river just as they stopped serving at 2:00 PM! Richard was not happy! He was looking forward to his Plat du Jour! By way of compensation, we got pizza slices from the bakery at Lidl and ate them on the train.

SALSES FORTRESS

Richard and I got the bus and train to Salses Fortress. It was a short walk through the deserted town of Sales-le-Chateau to the fortress. It was very common in France for towns to appear as if they had been hit by the apocalypse and all the residents had been wiped out.

Once under the railway line, we headed for Salses Fortress, a great hulk of a building. Its thick, solid walls looked as if they could easily repel the fiercest of armies. If you got past the first wall, you still had the moat and a far higher wall to clear.

It was originally built by the Spanish to police the border with France which was further north in 1497. It cost a whooping one fifth of the Spanish crown's annual budget but was worth every penny because in 1503, the Spanish had to resist a siege even before the fortress was fully completed.

A few decades later, there was a bit of hockey cokey. In 1639 it was captured by the French and then recaptured by the Spanish in 1640. Following the Catalan Rebellion against Spanish Crown, the French army surrounded Perpignan and a besieged Salses surrendered in 1642. With the Treaty of the Pyrenees in 1659 the French-Spanish border was pushed back to the Pyrenees, leaving the fortress in French hands, where it has been ever since. Once it lost its strategic importance, Louis XIV turned it into a prison and there was even talk of pulling it down. Luckily, that option was too costly, so it was still standing when Richard and I arrived for a wander around on a sunny afternoon in 2023.

We were not the first illustrious guests. Charles V, who at one point ruled half of Europe, also visited in the 16th century whilst the castle was in excellent condition. By 2023, the few internal areas were in ruins but you could still inspect the large ovens in the bakery which were big enough to produce bread for a garrison of 1,500 men. That's a lot of loaves! Also of interest was the dairy and cowshed where a few cows produced milk for the soldiers.

We got the train back into Perpignan with the intention of shopping in the Lidl but as it was a Sunday, it was closed. That meant we had to hang around at the station for an hour. "Do you speak French?" asked a dodgy looking man who sat next to Richard.

"I think we need to check our train platform," I said to Richard so we could make a quick exit.

Once on the train, a young man was tapping a card loudly on the table. I ignored this, in spite of it being very annoying but when he put techno music on his phone, I asked him to use headphones. He ignored me! I put some rival noise on my phone in the form of a political podcast I listen to and turned the volume up full. Richard, who had been listening to something using his headphones, offered them to me, probably worried I was about to be stabbed to death! I told him it wasn't the point but, luckily, the youth got off at the next station!

Going interrailing in 2023 had prompted me to read the diaries from my Interrailing Trips four decades earlier when I was in my late teens and early twenties. It was fascinating to see how I'd changed over that time. Okay, there was obviously the small matter of a few extra wrinkles and some grey hair but what was most striking was how I was less likely to challenge what I saw as intolerable behaviour in the eighties. It was a fascinating insight into my younger self. I guess we grow in confidence as we get older which may also be seen as growing into a grumpy old woman! When we're younger, we tend to be more self-conscious about what other people may think or how they may react but as we get older, we just don't give a stuff and this is where I'd arrived.

In 1986, I recorded that on the train to Harwich to catch the overnight ferry, there had been some unruly young men who were drinking and smoking in what was a non-smoking carriage. My immediate reaction to my twenty-four-year-old self was, "Why didn't you say anything?" but at the time, I would have been a similar age to them rather than the age of their mother as I was now. In addition, I'd had thirty-five years of experience of dealing with unruly little gits as a secondary school teacher. Anyway, I was pleased to read they got their just deserts because they weren't allowed to board the boat!

After pizza and alcohol in the courtyard when we got back, Kathryn and Heather watched a Rom Com! Well, that is how it was described. I love both a 'rom' and a 'com' but this was sadly lacking in both departments if you ask me so I gave up and went to bed!

MONTPELLIER

Richard and I got up early to catch the 7:50 AM train to Montpellier. It was a bright sunny morning. From the balcony we watched the sunlight creep down the mountain side as the sun rose ever higher in the sky. From the train we could see a fresh dusting of snow on the Pyrenees, a sight to gladden the heart and make getting up early worthwhile! It showed that winter hadn't quite released its grip.

We had to change in Perpignan and Narbonne. At Beziers Station, a woman was taken ill. The train couldn't move until an ambulance had attended. Like in the UK, the ambulance failed to turn up within minutes! The ticket inspector came into the carriage to explain the reason for the delay. As this was all in French, I wanted to clarify the situation. A middle-aged woman told me the woman had had a seizure. "They're still waiting for an ambulance to turn up," she said. About twenty minutes had already passed so this was concerning.

"They're taking their time," I commented. "It is like this in the UK these days. It can take hours!"

"Yes. I'm here because my father was taken ill," she told me. "My mother rang for an ambulance but one never came. Five days later she had to take him to the hospital herself when he continued to decline!"

The train driver came out of his cab and was chatting to passengers. "What can you do?" he said and went off for a cigarette. The train got going again after about a thirty minute delay. The middle-aged woman and forty-two other passengers had by that stage, missed connections to Paris, but as the middle-aged woman and I mused, it was a minor inconvenience compared to the poor woman who had eventually been carted off in an ambulance!

When we arrived in Montpelier, we walked up to Place de la Comedie, surrounded by elegant and typically French domed buildings that looked as if they should have been in Paris.

We sat at the Theatre Cafe on the square and had a two-course set meal. I had gazpacho and Richard had mozzarella salad to start. Far more newsworthy were the horse burgers we had for our main course. When ordering, the waitress asked, "and do you want the fish for main?" She probably assumed that as we were British, we wouldn't order horse burgers! I still remembered the uproar when people realised the burgers they'd bought at the supermarket contained horse meat rather than beef. In fact, the horse burgers we were eating now probably started out as one of those cute New Forest ponies. Yep! They're all owned by a horse breeder, and some get loaded on to trucks and sent off to France to be made into burgers! Next time you're in the New Forest, don't look at them and think, pet ponies! No, think horse burger!

We wandered up to the Arc de Triomphe, built to glorify the Sun King, Louis XIV. The great man himself was immortalised by an equestrian statue but he looked suspiciously like a Roman centurion in order to add a little extra grandeur. Little did he know that his great, great, great grandson, Louis XVI would meet an untimely end when he had his head severed from his neck by the guillotine, alongside Marie Antoinette, his wife of "let them eat cake!" fame. How times changed!

From the promenade, one could see the surrounding countryside and the Cervennes Mountain Range. A fascinating feature was the Chateau d'Eau, a neo classical water tower that connected to an aqueduct that supplied the city with water. Both were built in the eighteenth century. The tower's classical columns and the aqueduct's arches were quite a spectacle!

We had a wander through the old town known as L'Eausson, chock full of narrow alley ways, bustling squares and medieval mansions. In spite of the very narrow, pedestrianised status of some of the alleyways, one man still insisted on riding his moped through them, weaving in and out of the pedestrians. Where were the police when you need them?

It was quite breezy and Richard and I were both coughing and sneezing. I'd never knowingly suffered from hay fever but this felt suspiciously like hay fever. It felt as if there was something in the air!

We made our way down steep roads to Saint Peter's Cathedral, a honey-coloured building with two towers and an imposing portal whose twin pillars look like modern day space rockets. We had a quick look inside and then, as it had clouded over, we decided to try and get an earlier train.

We did a mad dash to the train station where we managed to get on unreliable Wi-Fi and change our train ticket. Richard dashed to the supermarket next to the station and got a few essentials like beer and wine, while I did the tickets and we were on an earlier train by 4:51 PM.

On the way up to Montpellier, despite the delay for a medical emergency, it had been calm and peaceful with deserted or half empty carriages. On the way back, it was totally opposite. Half of France had turned out to catch the train and they all had medium to large suitcases in tow! It was mayhem and stressful! I sat opposite Richard but when another seat became available, he pointed it out to me so I moved there, only to have a man the size of the incredible Hulk occupy the seat I had vacated to give him more leg room!

We had twenty-nine minutes in Perpignan so I did a trolley dash to Lidl! Once on the train to Villefranche-de-Confluent, we managed to get seats with no one opposite us but I had to move because I realised the window was covered in graffiti! It was like being in a prison van. Not that I've ever been in a prison van, obviously, but I can imagine that this is what it would be like! Some woman about my age was chastising a group of boys for vaping. My French is not good enough to fully understand back chat but I'm pretty certain this is what it was. They did, however, desist and when they got off a polite "au revoir" was exchanged with the woman. Young or old, the French are very polite when it comes to the pleasantries of life!

A DAY OFF!

Having the pass made me feel as if I should be using it while it was valid. Every time we went on to it, it told us how many days we had left. A forecast of cloudy weather, however, gave us an excuse for a train free day.

Mid-morning, I wandered up to the bakery and I mean wander. I needed a break from rushing for trains! Richard and I did lots of recharging of batteries during the day a.k.a. sod all! In the afternoon, Kathryn and Heather walked up to the cave, a famous walk locally, with fabulous views. Richard and I did the far less strenuous walk around the outside of the Villefranche-de-Confluent walls and then back through the Spanish Gate.

THE VENICE OF FRANCE!

Having slobbed around the day before, Richard and I were up at 7:00 AM and left at 7:50 AM to get the 8:09 AM train. There was a beautiful mirror image of the mountain in the lake but we travelled past it far too fast to photograph it.

We changed trains in Perpignan and worked our way north to Sete on the coast. When travelling along the lagoon, the train disturbed a flock of about five flamingos and they took off beside the train, their long wings propelling their long necks and legs into the air. They soon turned away from the train, no doubt intent or looping around and returning to their rich feeding ground. They were still there on our way back so it must have been a lucrative spot to feed!

Sete was made-up of canals leading down to the Mediterranean Sea. Although it wasn't quite Venice, I felt sure like it must have been compared to Venice on more occasions than I'd had hot dinners! We crossed a large grey bridge, the sort you see in the Netherlands where canals are more numerous than roads, and wandered down the main canal, lined by elegant mansions and crossed by flower strewn bridges. There was the ubiquitous tourist train and many people eating lunch outside restaurants. As our train had been twenty minutes delayed, reducing our time in Sete to only two hours, we didn't have time to order lunch.

When we ordered a hot chocolate at a cafe bar, I left Richard and went down to where the town met the Mediterranean Sea, passing a huge harbour full of yachts, watched over by a large lighthouse. The immense blue Mediterranean spread for as far as the eye could see on the outside of a huge seawall. A fortress guarded the coast on a hill to the south.

Back at the restaurant, they'd had a change of heart and refused to serve hot chocolate on the grounds that they were only serving lunch. Feeling rather disgruntled, we started to make our way back to the train station but we did manage to fit in a quick hot chocolate further up, sat overlooking one of the busy bridges.

Our train was, of course, delayed on our return to Perpignan so we were concerned we wouldn't get our train connection to Villefranche-de-Confluent but in the end, we made it with minutes to spare.

We were back at Villefranche-de-Confluent at 4:30 PM where there'd been a display of merens horses, a hardy Pyrenean Mountain breed. All that was left was piles of their manure but Kathryn had taken some photos.

A ROAD TRIP!

R ichard and I got the 9:43 AM bus and train combo to Perpignan and then we went one stop north to Rivesaltes. From here, we walked for an hour and ten minutes through vineyards with distant mountains to the airport to pick up a hire car. It was warm and sunny and felt as if summer was starting to put out its tentacles. After one slight detour that had led us to backtrack so we could cross a main road, we reached the airport perimeter fence. The trouble was that we were on the opposite side to where we needed to be so we had to follow the fence right round to the other side to access the terminal.

At one point a Hercules military plane, propellers whirring, flew low over our heads. It was very dramatic and, yet again, far too fleeting to take a photo.

When we arrived at the airport, we were bang on time to pick up our hire car at 12:30 PM. Unfortunately, no one had told the SIXT Car Hire desk which was deserted. A sign announced we could ring a number to get service. As I didn't have a French sim card, I didn't want to pay a fortune to do this. I went over to the "Information Desk" where three women were having a natter. This teeny tiny airport was deserted so this seemed like overkill. I interrupted their gossiping and asked if they could contact the SIXT representative for me. It was a firm "non!".

Luckily, there was a woman from another car hire company

nearby and she rang for me. The rep would be at the desk in five minutes, she told me. I thanked her, grateful for her help. "Thanks for nothing, ladies!" I called out to the information desk women as I walked back to the car hire desk. "You can go back to chitchatting now! Oh, pardon me, you never stopped!"

A very nice man arrived to serve at the desk. A French man who lived in Hanoi and had a Vietnamese wife, slipped in front of us while I went to the toilet. We then had a problem with the card machine turning euros to GB pounds. We couldn't work out how to solve it, and as it was adding a 3.5% conversion fee, I wasn't best pleased. The rep didn't understand why I was so upset at the conversion until it was there in black and white on the rental contract. "Oh, I see why you're angry," he said. As it was a block, rather than a charge, we just had to hope it never came to pass.

This trick by credit card companies to make more money out of you is a perennial problem. I'd lost count of the times I'd had to fight to get the charge put into the local currency. The poor people on the ground have no idea what the devious card company is trying to do but I refuse to pay this 'conversion fee' which is quite frankly criminal! I have painful memories of the shenanigans it's caused when paying in foreign petrol stations and supermarkets etc. I may not be good at maths, but when it comes to finances, I'm a genius. I know all the ways there are to avoid foreign currency transactions! Martin Lewis and I are best friends!

We drove into the centre of Perpignan with the intention of parking near the Palais de Majorca for free. It took a while but, eventually, we managed it. The advantage of having an Interrail Pass is you can arrive smack bang into the centre of town and you don't have to pay for parking or worry about the meter running low when you are sightseeing, eating or shopping. Okay, you don't get the flexibility afforded by a car but generally it felt very liberating. With low emission charges and fines being imposed across Europe as we speak, an interrail pass will become an even more valuable commodity.

Richard headed to the cafe by the river where he met Kathryn and Heather and had coffee, beer, wine and salad. I went around the rather bare Palais de Majorca so I could see it in sunshine. The best bit was the commanding views of the Pyrenees in the distance which you could see for free without even paying to get in so it was rather a pointless exercise but I'm a tick a box addict! There, I said it!

The one bonus of having a car for a few days was we could get off the beaten track to places the train didn't reach. On the way back to Villefranche-de-Confluent, we stopped in Eus, a stunning mountain village with stone houses spilling down over the steep mountain side. It was crowned by a huge, fortified church that dominated the skyline. In medieval times, resources were scarce so churches doubled up as fortresses. They were ten a penny in this region.

As we wandered up through the village to the church, we enjoyed spectacular views of the valley and mountains opposite. A rare swallow-tailed butterfly landed on buddleia bushes. We lingered to watch it press its long proboscis into the nectar rich flowers. After some steep climbing, we treated ourselves to drinks on a terrace perched on the edge of the mountainside in order to further soak in the fabulous vistas of the valley.

Our holiday home had Cluedo which was a blast from the past going right back to my childhood. It had been a while since I had declared that murder had been committed by Colonel Mustard using the dagger in the library!

ANDORRA

fter breakfast, we drove west towards Andorra on twisting and turning roads that were not good for Kathryn's travel sickness. We retraced the route we'd taken on the bus, through the steep side V-shaped valley and then across the high plateau. It had only been just over a week since we had last travelled this route but already there were more flashes of bright green across the hillside as spring took hold.

As we approached the border with Andorra, the valley closed its jaws around us again. Spring had come late to this land of little light. For most of the year, by the time the sun rose up over the steep mountains, it was soon descending over the other side. Even though it was nearly May, the valley was still decorated all over with splashes of white spring blossom.

We rose up over a steep pass and were soon at the border with Andorra. I'd learnt from a woman on our bus, whilst heading for a ski resort in Andorra earlier in the year, that Andorra is an independent island in a sea of Schengen. In addition, it had a very lax and porous border. I was the only person on our coach to get my passport stamped on the way in and out of Andorra for that trip. Having arrived in Toulouse, this meant I didn't have the full 8 days of my 90/180 used up. When planning our interrail trip, I had wrongly assumed that Norway and/or Switzerland, who were not in the EU, were also not in Schengen. Most of Europe was now in Schengen and new entrants to the E.U. like Croatia, were being consumed at a fast rate! This was not good news for British passport holders who were now subject to restrictions.

We parked just into Andorra. We could have entered with no questions asked as I got the impression that Andorra didn't police its borders. Just for the hell of it, Richard and I went into the customs and immigration building and found the French immigration office. We approached the window and were not noticed by the immigration officer who was sat on the computer with his back to us. Was he liaising with Interpol about the next international drug smuggler who might try and sneak across the border? Hell no! He was browsing YouTube. This had to be the best gig in the French Immigration Service! Richard and I smiled at each other. It took a few moments for him to realise we were there. He jumped up out of his seat and stumbled towards the window, clearly surprised that he had customers. I explained that we wanted to be stamped out of France. "You're going to Andorra?" he asked.

"Yes," I told him. I just failed to mention we weren't going far into Andorra. He fumbled around in a drawer for a key that opened the safe. He opened the safe and took out the stamp that recorded in our passports that we had left France on 25/4/23. Job done! We did a scenic drive into Andorra and then turned the car around and drove back into France, not bothering with to get our passports stamped. No one batted an eyelid. Did that make us illegal immigrants?

We retraced our steps and stopped at Mount Louis, a medieval fort, perched very strategically on the top of the pass. It was, in fact, still in military hands. We passed through the gateway above which fluttered with the flags of the France, Catalan and the E.U. I have always assumed Catalan was entirely in Spain but had recently realised that the region also straddled France, owing to border movements back in the day. In modern times, I don't think that French Catalan gives France the kind of hassle that Spanish Catalan gives Spain with its vigorous and sometimes violent demands for independence.

We crossed the moat and went through a second gateway. If the enemy got through the first gateway and over the moat, they had little chance of penetrating this solid beast. Inside was what Kathryn described as "a rather run downtown." We walked around the ramparts with views down the valley to the east, perfect for spotting any enemy armies approaching and then walked towards the bastion that was under military control.

Here we were met by a very serious notice that stated, in no uncertain terms, that access was restricted. There was a walkway around the outside of the walls but you had to stick to it or you'd be shot. Well, it didn't actually say you'd be shot, obviously, but it gave that impression. Having finished reading the notice, we were expecting a barbed wire corridor with watchtowers and spotlights. In reality, what we got was poor signage which meant that, unbeknownst to us, we were soon straying from the prescribed route. We passed through cowgate, opened up to keep cows out of the town and then turned left on the outside of the huge fortress wall. I started to lag behind after a stop to apply sun cream, so Richard, Kathryn and Heather turned another corner, well ahead of me.

When I turned the corner, I saw Richard retreating towards me. This section looked like a moat. A three arched bridge crossed it and on the bridge was a soldier in uniform and armed with a famous French assault rifle (according to my military advisor a.k.a. Richard). With him was an older man in civies. "They told me to turn around," said Richard.

"Where's Kathryn and Heather?" I asked.

"They got through unnoticed." he replied. This gave me hope.

"If they can do it then I can!" I thought. I proceeded along the moat. There seemed little chance they wouldn't spot me as they were looking in my direction.

"You can't come this way," they called down.

I later told Richard that I'd shouted back, "What you

going to do? Shoot me?". What I actually did was engage them in conversation whilst continuing to move forward. "My daughter's gone through that way," I called up, using my hand to give them the impression she was seven years old when in reality she was 25 years old and 5 foot 9 inches tall. They now spotted Kathryn and Heather who by then had passed under the bridge and gone up the steep steps in order to go through the gate that guarded the entrance to the castle.

By now, I was under the bridge where one of the archways was protecting a military tractor. "Your daughters are up here," said the man in chivies who turned out to be a security guard. Not sure why the army needed a security guard! He pointed at a set of steps up onto the bridge, and once up the steps, I found Kathryn and Heather. The soldier directed us out through the gateway above. He said we could go to the tourist office and pay €7 to access the fort.

We decided against this and returned to the car. From there we drove to Bains de Saint Thomas. This took us off the main road and through a very narrow and steep sided gorge. We ended up in Saint Thomas which was a tiny village and didn't seem worthy of the recommendation my friend, Nicky, had given it. It had two streets, each of which took about ten seconds to walk down. I walked down one of the streets to the far end of the village where a bubbling stream raced down the hillside. Here there was the remains of an old water mill. Some of the locals stood around chatting and a dog ran up to me, barking excitedly and bouncing around me. I returned to the car via the other ten second street and we drove further up the winding mountain road to add De Bains to the name of the place.

Bains de Saint Thomas looked more promising. There was a car park that was very busy. A sign promised a three hundred metre walk to the thermal baths. The route was along the side of a steep wooded valley, the same valley along which the stream I'd just encountered raced along far below. The thermal bathhouse was from a bygone era. Very hot water came out from a pipe and ran down the mountainside and people bathed in various sized and shaped pools. Kathryn and Heather decided to return to the spa baths the next day.

We returned to the house and after a snack, I decided to do the locally famous cave walk. Kathryn and Heather had done it a few days before in reasonable weather but I decided to wait for perfect weather and that was what was now on offer so I couldn't resist. Kathryn walked with me through the town and through the Spanish gate at the far end and then on to the start of the walk. Here, I continued on my own, up a narrow path that wound its way back and forth across the mountain side. The views were breath taking, both along the valley in which Villefranche-de-Confluent sat and down a valley opposite, running at right angles.

Huge metal avalanche nets ran across the hill. After about forty-five minutes, I reached a small stone Chapel. Kathryn and Heather had said the climb from there to the cave entrance was only five minutes further on but it was steep and over bare rock. "There were plenty of people round. If you run into any difficulty, you should be fine!" said Kathryn. Unfortunately, when I did the walk, there was no one around to rescue me if I got into difficulty!

I proceeded up what I thought was the rocky path. I could see the gaping hole in the rock that was the entrance to the cave, high above me. I rounded a rocky spur and then came to a steep drop in the path. I lowered myself down it, falling the final section.

Once down, I started to panic I wouldn't be able to pull myself back up. I had visions of Kathryn and a Mountain Rescue Team coming up the mountain to rescue me with torches and calling my name in order to locate me.

At least they knew I was up there. When I get into difficulty on my solo trips, I worry there will be no one to come and rescue me with a torch. Back in the U.K. it would take a day or so before they realised that I hadn't been in touch. They would know my general location but not exact whereabouts. By the time the authorities came looking, I would probably have been eaten by wolves.

As I mulled this over in my mind, I realised that the two-metre drop in the path was the least of my worries. I was in front of the cave, but the entrance was about 6 metres above me. There was no more path, it was just a sheer vertical rock. There was a small pile of rocks there so I tried standing on them but that didn't even dent the task I faced. I looked for some hand or footholds and tried to get some grip but it was impossible and looking up at the cave entrance way above, I was concerned that even if I did get up there, getting back down would be even more dangerous. It was definitely a "risk of serious death or injury!" scenario. I had seen some photos of Kathryn and Heather inside the cave, including one of those posy Instagram photos of their feet in a shot looking out of the cave which acted as a frame for stunning scenery, so I knew they'd made it inside.

It looked, however, as if I wasn't going to get my Instagram shot. I felt very frustrated. I really hate admitting defeat but even I couldn't see a way ahead. The pile of rocks suggested other people had been there, pondering the same dilemma. I was confused as to why Kathryn would let me go up there alone if it was practically impossible.

I made the decision to retrace my steps. Regret was mixed with relief when I managed to haul myself up the two-metre rock face with some difficulty but successfully. Something, however, still didn't feel right. Kathryn and Heather are in their mid-twenties, and they had each other to help them get up the rock face but all being told, I didn't think they could have managed that six metre rock face. I replayed our conversation. "Dad couldn't do it with his bionic knees but you'll be fine. Kids were doing it. It was over sheer rock but there are chains to pull you up". It started to dawn on me that there must be another way up to the cave that I'd missed. Kathryn said it was easy to find but they had the benefit all the other hikers on the trail who they probably saw coming in the other direction from the cave.

A short way back, I saw chains in three loops going up the side of the cliff. This had to be the right track. Five minutes later, I was in the cave snapping away to achieve the perfect Instagram photo, before making my way back to the town, with the final rays of sun rising up over the mountains opposite.

On my return, I had a wander around Villefranche-de-Confluent which took on a different face when all the day trippers had departed. It was eerily quiet, and I could imagine it was haunted by the ghosts of medieval merchants and craftsmen. The medieval bridge over the river which had been closed for repair had just opened so I was the first person to cross!

DOWN WITH
THE LOCALS!

Mid-morning, we drove to Prades where they hold a market in the medieval town square every Tuesday and Saturday. Under plane trees that had been heavily pruned but were just starting to sprout bright green leaves, stalls full of local produce were set out. Cheese, wine, bread, meat and crafts were being sold.

As an added bonus, there was a Catalan festival. Locals dressed in traditional costume were dancing, singing and playing instruments. One dance to music involved adults forming a circular human platform on which a child was hoisted up to do a victory pose. It reminded me of similar spectacles in Mexico.

Catalan was being spoken on stage and a huge vat of drumsticks was being prepared over a fire in a marquee. Richard took Kathryn and Heather to buy swimming costumes for their spa experience but I stayed on to watch more of the festival. It also gave me an opportunity to go to the church dedicated to Saint Peter, the first Pope. A huge statue of him took pride of place in the middle of the baroque altar. He was a portly man and not at all what I imagined this disciple of Jesus Christ to look like. He held his hand up in what looked like a victory pose, making him look more like Winston Churchill than Saint Peter!

We drove south past vineyards and orchards then over mountains. The route was full of twists and turns. Cork trees spread over the slopes and Kathryn started to go green at the gills, owing to travel sickness, so we had to stop for a break.

Once in Ceret, we soon found the object of our visit, a medieval stone bridge. Kathryn, Heather and I crossed the modern bridge but Richard went straight onto the medieval bridge. Just as he walked on to the bridge, he witnessed a car crash. The medieval bridge, designed for carts, was cut off to modern day cars, but there was a sharp bend to take cars away from it and around to the modern bridge. One young man in a small red car was going far too fast and lost control. He destroyed a bollard and did serious damage to his car but with people around, including Richard, walking onto the bridge, it doesn't bear thinking about what may have happened. We walked down to the other side of the bridge for a view but it was largely blocked by gardens.

We had a quick look around the town which was lively with diners in pavement café-restaurants. It used to be popular with artists a century ago but its sparkle had long since faded.

We returned via the anti-travel sickness route which meant going down to Perpignan and then back up the valley. It wasn't so scenic but it was a much less stomach churning option for Kathryn.

After a quick snack back at the house, Kathryn and Heather went to the luxuriate at the Hot Springs and Spa in Bains de St Thomas. Richard acted as their chauffeur and I spent three hours cleaning the house. I think we know who got the better deal!

MIGRANTS!

We left the house at 8:00AM and drove to Rivesalates where we filled up with petrol. Richard dropped me at the train station with all the luggage and I said goodbye to Kathryn and Heather. He headed it off to drop them and the car at the airport and then walk back to the train station.

I had an hour and a half to kill on my own in the train station waiting room before Richard would return and three hours before our train to Beziers. It was cold and windy. Two station waiting room doors leading in and then out to the platform didn't closed so the wind whipped right through. Two other doors that were closed because they were no longer used, had big gaps at the bottom, causing draughts.

Although no trains were due for about 40 minutes, I wasn't alone in the waiting room. Four young men who spoke Arabic, slouched on seats either side of the waiting room. Otherwise, the place was deserted. As I had all our valuables, I have to confess that I felt a little uneasy. I knew that this wasn't logical and that they were probably migrants, in France to get a job and escape poverty in North Africa, not to rob me at knifepoint, but it didn't stop me feeling nervous. They were all small in height and stature. The tallest was about my height but the others were shorter. I judged them to be about twenty years old.

As other passengers started to arrive for the 9:40 AM train

to Portbou, one of the young men got a middle-aged French cyclist to help him buy a ticket. When he said "thank you" in English, I asked him where they were from. "From Morocco," said Bashir who said he was twenty-one years old. He was travelling with Samir 21, Fahim 23 and Abdollah 20. "We are illegal," he said. Bashir explained he had left his passport in Turkey with a friend. I asked how they got to France. "We flew to Turkey," he said and then walked through Turkey, Bulgaria, Macedonia and Montenegro, before slipping over the boarder to Italy. It had taken three months to get this far.

They weren't, however, staying in France, they were going south to Spain where Bashir's older brother lived. "He's got papers," he said. "He drives lorries. He came illegally over the Mediterranean in a boat three years ago."
"There's no work in Morocco" they told me. "When we get work, we will send money back to our families."

They had got tickets to Banyuls-sur-Mer, the penultimate stop before the Spanish border. They had obviously been advised not to try to cross the border by train.

"There are police at Cebere station checking passports," I warned them. "It's best to stay away from there!"

"How far is it to walk to Spain?" they asked me.
"Probably not too long," I assured them. "It's ten minutes by train."

They showed me short videos of them walking through a snow-covered forest in Bulgaria and on a bus in Italy. We exchanged Instagram details. When their train arrived, they offered to help me with my bags on to the train. They only had small daypacks for their three-month journey! "Oh, no thanks, I'm waiting for my husband," I explained. "Good luck finding work in Spain." These young men had gone from potential robbers to sweet young men whose tenacity I really admired. It can't be easy leaving home and travelling through a different continent to get work. As the train drew out of the station, I wondered what the future had in store for them.

When Richard returned, he complained about walking in

the windy conditions. It was a stark contrast to the warm and sunny weather of the walk to the airport. We still had an hour and a half to our train to Beziers. I added more layers as I became colder and colder, and there was no station toilet so I had to find a quiet siding to spend a penny.

We were so close to the airport, we were able to watch Kathryn and Heather's Ryanair plane take off.

BEZIERS

F inally, at 12:16 PM, our train to Beziers arrived and in one hour and ten minutes, we were in Beziers. The city is in a dramatic location. We'd passed by several times in the week before. The train crosses the wide river and perched high above the river with its new and old stone bridges, is Beziers Cathedral.

The good news was that the apartment was only seven minute's walk from the station, through an attractive park with a huge and dramatic war memorial at its entrance, complete with a winged angel, soldiers and eight French tricolour flags. The bad news was that it was up a very steep slope.

More bad news had come at the station. I'd agreed with the owner of the apartment that she would meet us at the apartment at 12:30 PM. When I logged on to the station Wi-Fi, I had a message saying her friend would meet me there instead and she gave me her number. It wasn't clear if I had to ring her friend or whether she would just be there at the agreed time.

I'd already explained that I didn't have a French SIM card so couldn't call from the apartment. When we got to the address, it turned out that number two was, in actual fact, about six apartments. There was an array of bells and buzzers to press. The owner admitted that she was new to renting out an apartment and it showed. The best hosts provided a key safe and detailed written instructions/photos of how to access the property. This approach made for much lower levels of blood pressure at check-in. I rang every button beside the main outside door and someone buzzed me in. The hallway and steep stairs were dark, dingy and dirty. I left Richard with the bags and proceeded up the three flights of stairs, knocking on every door in a vain attempt to find "the friend". No one answered.

In the end, I had to go up the road and beg for Wi-Fi at a café-bar so I could ring the host. "My friend is there," she insisted.

"She is not," I insisted. I returned to the property and took a photo of Richard in the doorway to prove that we were there, and her friend was not. Back at the café, I sent her the photo.

"My friend is with your husband," she messaged. I returned to the property by which time the friend had turned up, let Richard in and gone. The one bed apartment was very pleasant and in spite of all the check-in hassle, it was good value for money. It had a balcony and seating looking out over a tree lined pedestrian boulevard.

As the sun had come out and the wind had dropped, I decided to go out to explore Beziers' historic centre. I left Richard relaxing at the apartment and wandered along the pedestrianised boulevard, through quaint squares and along narrow medieval streets painted in pastel colours. The cafes and restaurants were doing a roaring trade.

When I reached the cathedral terrace, I enjoyed the views of Orb River below and the flat plain that stretched as far as the mountains in the distance. As I've mentioned, the views of the cathedral from below were spectacular but I entered it with a sense of weariness. I'd been in more Catholic cathedrals in the last five weeks than I'd had hot dinners. One can get too much of a good thing. The ornate altars, cherubs, grand columns, intricately carved pulpits and choir stalls had started to merge into one. The Cathedral of St Nazaire, however, immediately endeared itself to me. It had a quirky information leaflet that was written in the first person. For half an hour, it took me on an enchanting tour. "My reconstruction began in 1215," said

JAYNE DEAR

Saint Naziaire Cathedral. "In silence, listen to my stones, they are telling you something about the story of my life, they are speaking to you," it continued. "The small windows, sunken into the deep stonework recalled that I was a dark church. Every morning I would welcome the dawn light by an opening in the axis choir as a symbol of the resurrection." At the end of the tour, Cathedral Naz, as I had come to know my new friend, ended by thanking me for my visit.

Opposite the cathedral was a Victorian prison being converted into an upmarket hotel. It seemed to be a strange juxtaposition of institutions. I wondered what my mate Cathedral Naz would have thought. Mind you, Jesus Christ was all about forgiveness! Sadly, however, it wasn't yet open so I couldn't sneak in for a look as I had in Oxford where there was a similar prison transformed into a posh and unique hotel.

There was a series of lifts to get down to the river where I walked over the old medieval bridge and then back over the new bridge for some classic views of Beziers and its old bridge.

Once back up the hill, I followed the signs to the Roman ruins. As I went around in circles trying to find them, I hoped they would be worth it. They weren't. It was a hole in the ground with a few old brick walls.

THE LONG WAY ROUND TO SWITZERLAND!

We left the apartment at 8:50 AM to get our 9:21 AM train for a 4-train journey to Vevey on Lake Geneva in Switzerland. Thankfully, what goes up, must come down so our return to the station was downhill all the way.

Our first train to Avignon was busy but we managed to get seats and space for our luggage. We'd failed to get TGV reservations, even though we had tried to purchase them at a train station a week before we wanted to travel. Interrail had a set quota and once they were gone, they were gone. "It's a popular route for interrailers," the man at the station told me. I think issues related to seat reservations had got worse since my early days of interrailing but even in 1988, I'd noted in my diary that we'd had to spend the entire journey in the restaurant car on a Spanish train because the train was full and we didn't have a reservation. It was in the days of 'smoking' and 'non-smoking' compartments so the restaurant car was thick with smoke. Banning smoking on trains by 2023 was certainly one big improvement, if you ask me!

As we zipped along the Mediterranean coast into Provence,

we were treated to scenes of bright red fields full of poppies. In Avignon, we had forty-three minutes until our next train so I left Richard with the luggage and raced up the road to try and find a supermarket that was open to get some supplies in France and before we entered Switzerland. I wanted to shop somewhere we didn't need to take out a second mortgage to buy a basket of groceries! Switzerland, where we were headed, was going to be a whole new ball game. Someone on Facebook said, "If you want to make Sweden seem like a cheap destination, organise a trip to Switzerland and then change your plans and go to Sweden instead!" Never a truer word said. I'd already been open mouthed at the cost of accommodation in Switzerland. Many on Facebook advocated going to Eastern Europe with the Interrail Pass. I respectfully disagreed. If you want to get value for money, you need to use the eye wateringly expensive Swiss trains. I travelled halfway across Bulgaria (a very big country that is many times bigger than Switzerland) for fifteen quid in 2021. In Switzerland, you can barely go ten minutes up the line to the next town for that! Hence, we had planned six days of train travel in Switzerland.

As it was a public holiday, the first supermarket was closed. The second, a City Carrefour, opened until 1:00 PM so I did a trolley dash, aware that the time was ticking away. I ended up with green tea instead of mint tea and fruit flavoured black tea instead of simple fruit tea in my rush to get everything so it may have been a false economy.

In the street there was a May Day protest taking place. In the spring sunshine, it felt more like a parade than a protest. There were brightly coloured costumes that included pink, orange and blue; flags of all the colours of the rainbow represented the many different causes; and there was singing, dancing and music, alongside the obliquitous megaphones. As time ticked away, I had to dodge in and out of the crowds as I went against the tide of people that filled the street, to return to the station.

Our train from Avignon to Valence had been displayed as "fully booked" on the SNCF website. This was strange as it was a TER and, therefore, not a train you could book. It was a public holiday so I knew that the trains would be crowded, plus we faced an eight-hour train journey in four parts. This in itself had made me feel nervous, so this was all I needed. I took to Facebook to get advice.

"That's ridiculous!" said one fellow interrailer. "You can't reserve a TER!"

"You seem to have found the only unbookable train that is fully booked!" joked another.

One of the "experts" said, "SNCF stop selling tickets online on busy days but no one can stop you getting on as you don't need a reservation and besides, you can still buy a ticket at the station."

This put my mind at rest to a certain extent but I was still apprehensive. In the end, the train was only half full. Perhaps SNCF's actions had put people off! I wasn't complaining. Another bonus was that we could travel in first class again! After several weeks of slumming it with 'the peasants' in second class in southwest France where there was no first class, we were surprised and delighted to see first class carriages were back again. What's the point of paying for a first class Interrail Pass when there's no first class?!

We followed the Rhone Valley north with many glimpses of its famous river weaving its way through a landscape of steep craggy cliffs either side. We changed trains in Valence and headed up the Haute Rhone to Geneva. The blue sky and sunshine of the South Coast of France was then replaced by heavy clouds and then, as we rapidly approached Switzerland, the train was enveloped by heavy rain that made it was impossible to see much beyond the train windows, let alone the beautiful scenery of the Haute Alps Region.

The rain did abate as we passed along some lakes but it remained cloudy. My heart sank. The one thing we needed in beautiful Switzerland was good weather but you are totally at the mercy of the weather gods. It's no use blaming The Pope, Donald Trump or Vladimir Putin. No one can influence the weather! You get what you get. You just have to pray and that's exactly what I did.

As we approached Geneva, we got up to prepare to get off the train as we had a very tight nine minutes until our next train. On drawing into the station, the train lurched violently to the left and then back to the right. Richard nearly fell over and had to quickly grab a handrail. "I think the train driver thinks he's a rally driver" observed Richard.

"Yes!" I replied. "It's like a Ryanair landing!"

We leapt off the train and looked for the signs to get us to the right platform. There were none. We followed everyone else down a ramp. A sign said 'French Customs' and that was it. We went around and back up another ramp but just found ourselves back on the same platform.

Starting to panic, we descended the ramp again. We now had only five minutes to our train to Vevey. We, therefore, took the only other option which was open to us other than going around in circles for the rest of our lives and that was to follow the signs to French customs. Switzerland had been in Schengen since 2008 so there were no customs but they had clearly not bothered to take the signs down. It was a great way to confuse travellers like us who didn't know their way around this huge station.

We raced down a very narrow corridor that had been customs back in the day but was now deserted and, eventually, we emerged into a station tunnel with platforms leading off it. We only had three minutes to go so we frantically searched for an electric board to find the right platform. We had got used to how it was done in France but this was a whole new country and way of doing things so we felt rather out of sorts.

With one minute to spare, we found our platform number and sped towards the ramp leading to it with thirty seconds to go. We've all heard of the saying, "You can set your watch by the trains in Switzerland." I was a painfully aware of this as we flew onto the platform and clambered, very unceremoniously, onto the train. It was off within a few seconds!

AU REVOIR FRANCE!

I'd enjoyed our five weeks on French trains. I'd always thought of the French as a bit standoffish and aloof but on this trip they couldn't have been friendlier. My negative attitude towards the French stemmed back to when a French woman laughed at my attempts to speak French many years earlier; and, of course, the Anglo-French relationship has always been one of love hate.

On our 2023 trip, I got the impression that more French people were learning English owing to the English language dominated world in which we now live. This was breaking down barriers. For years, the French had tried to protect the French language and make it a force to be reckoned within the world but they seem to have realised that they were fighting a losing battle with the advent of the internet and increasing globalisation. I always used to chuckle when the French were the only country to speak in their native language at the Eurovision Song Contest when everyone else used English. When the U.K. left the E.U. they suggested, probably rather tongue in cheek, that English should no longer be the language of the E.U. I'm not sure what the Irish thought about that! "People want to watch online films in the native language," one Frenchman told me, "and that's normally English." Don't get me wrong, I always try to speak the local language and I think the French and other countries should protect their languages against the rising domination of English thanks to globalisation. We certainly don't want the whole world speaking English with a Californian accent, now do we.

"I'm going to miss the bing, bang, bong!" said Richard.

"The what?" I asked, a bit concerned about what he'd been up to.

"You know," he said, "at the start of all the train announcements!"

FIRST CLASS
SWISS STYLE!

Mind you, as we settled down into Swiss first class, all ideas of missing France were quickly washed away. It was state-of-the-art! We could look forward to six days of luxury. From our plush wide seats, we enjoyed the views as we coasted towards Vevey, a small town on the eastern side of Lake Geneva.

As it's a small country and we only intended to spend time on the western side, we had been advised on Facebook to base ourselves in one place. Interlaken and Montreux were both suggested. I'd looked at accommodation in those places and been left coughing and spluttering at the high cost of accommodation compared to France.

A hotel offering studio apartments in Vevey had caught my eye because it was half the cost of everywhere else. It had a 5.7/10 review rating which is low in my book. I went through reviews in detail, trying to gauge whether it was going to be a hell hole or not. It was cheap, well by Swiss standards - it was still €100 per night and, therefore, more expensive than anything in France. With three months of travel, we wanted to keep accommodation costs down. We could afford the more expensive accommodation and weren't on a student grant anymore but I wanted value for money!

Some previous guests said it smelt and was very rundown. Others said the staff were often absent. On the other side of the coin, some reviews said it was good value for money and in a great location. Some simply gave it 9/10 or even 10/10.

When dates in May started to sell out because other travellers had recognised that this was much cheaper than elsewhere, I decided to take the plunge and book five nights. Oh, and how glad I was! I gave it an 8/10. It was a bit hot in the room which wasn't serviced every day but it was spacious and far from rundown. Its location in pretty Vevey was very central and it was close to the train station. The fact that it was only a few seconds walk to the lake with its breath-taking views of the Alps was a big bonus.

From our room, we had views of the town hall and the mountains behind. Of course, if you're in Switzerland, there's always going to be a mountain in the view! The room was clean and light. I had no complaints about the decor. My "genius" status on booking.com had meant we'd been upgraded to a three-person studio so we had a double and a single bed.

The kitchenette was essential as around the corner at a cheap and cheerful pizzeria a Margarita pizza would set you back €30. I kid you not! I always find a Margarita pizza is a good gauge of restaurant prices. We call it the 'Margarita Pizza Test'. In Italy, not that long ago, we were getting them for €4. With inflation, they'd gone up to about €12 in the U.K. but that was still a long way from €30. As one woman said on Facebook, "It's not that I can't afford the restaurant prices in Switzerland, it's just that I refuse to pay those silly prices!"

GENEVA

T he weather to the east, into the Alps, was forecast to be dodgy for the next day so we went west to Geneva. It was blue sky all the way along Lake Geneva as we wound our way along the edge of the lake.

If a country's train network can be judged by its train toilets, then Switzerland's train network was by far superior to France's train network. The toilet on this train was huge and circular. It smelt very fragrant and had a colourful mural of a hydrangea plant, giving it the feel of the ladies' powder room in Harrods rather than a train toilet. Every Swiss train had cleaners patrolling up and down, constantly cleaning and disinfecting handles etc. I never once saw a French train being cleaned which probably meant they were only cleaned properly every couple of months when they ended up in a siding. In addition, they often lacked the basics such as water and toilet paper. Mind you, the Swiss toilets were so sophisticated that they had an array of confusing buttons. At one point, I made a request for the train to stop at the next stop (on the mountain routes, stops were often "on request") when I actually intended to open the toilet door!

In addition to great train toilets, Swiss trains had great communication systems. They told you exactly where to stand to get onto 1st class so there were no stressful scenes where we watched as first class went whizzing past, leading to us to legging it down the platform, as in most countries. There were live arrivals and departure boards on the trains so you could look up the platform for your next train even before you got to the station.

Once in Geneva, we attempted to get Wi-Fi at the station. It was bad enough in France where you had to fill in a form every time with your e-mail address but in Switzerland they insisted on sending a text with a code to your mobile. The reason we wanted station Wi-Fi was because we didn't have Wi-Fi on our phones to receive messages. I went to the information desk. "You've got 'aeroplane mode' on" he told me.

"I know" I replied, "that's why I want station Wi-Fi."

In the end, he got a code sent to his mobile so Richard and I could get on the station Wi-Fi. Once he got us on then he said, "You've got Wi-Fi for ten minutes."

"That's not a lot of good!" I told him. He shrugged. As it turned out, we did only have Wi-Fi for ten minutes but we didn't need a code from then on to log onto station Wi-Fi so that was something. This was particularly useful in order to access live timetables and look for platforms when changing trains.

We headed into the centre of Geneva for a re-run of a visit we'd made on our 1988 Interrail Trip. The city looked very majestic in the sunshine. The large and sturdy buildings along the waterfront reflected in the river which was fringed by colourful pots full spring flowers. Equally colourful were the ducks and other waterfowl such as grebes with bright red, brown and deep green feathers on display.

Geneva oozed wealth. The names of luxury brands were ever present! Sadly, the iconic lake fountain wasn't working so we had to satisfy ourselves with the flower clock in the English gardens. As we walked up to the old town cathedral, we stopped at Starbucks for Internet. We just sat in a quiet corner and didn't buy a drink as we would normally, owing to astronomical prices. It's okay for the Swiss who earned double the annual wage of someone in the U.K. but foreign visitors struggled with the prices.

We wandered through the Place du Bourg-de-Four where the Swiss were having slap up meals in the warm sunshine. Tourists were distinctly absent at the restaurants. Streets leading to the cathedral were hung with huge colourful Swiss and Canton flags.

The simple and austere Protestant Cathedral of Saint Pierre where Calvin preached for many years was a contrast to the over the top Baroque cathedrals of France. Richard sat in the 15th century beautiful Macchabees Chapel while I went up to the towers to see the views of Geneva and the lake.

Finally, we walked past the historic cannons once used to defend Geneva against its enemies and on to the impressive Reformation Wall, which included Oliver Cromwell in the frieze.

It was a twenty minute walk back to the station. Here we popped into the mini market to get some lunch. When I came to pay with notes I had left over from a trip to Switzerland seven years earlier, I was told the notes were no longer legal tender. I had the equivalent of £130 which was a significant amount. The hotel had taken £18 worth to pay for the city tax so they hadn't had a problem with them! "I think you can exchange them at the bank," she told me. "There is one opposite."

I went over to the bank where there was a queue moving at a glacial speed. I pushed to the front of the queue to check I could change my notes there before getting into the queue. "No" he said. "You have to go to the National Bank."

"Where's that?" I asked. He gave me an address verbally. "Can you write it down?" I asked.

"You need to join the queue" he replied.

"What? Join a queue for something you can't action?" He wrote the address on a post-it note.

Richard and I looked up the address at the nearby Starbucks. It was, annoyingly, just up the road from our last destination, The Reformation Wall. Richard stayed at the cafe and I walked for twenty minutes to the Swiss National Bank. When I got to the address there was no sign of what I imagined the Swiss National Bank to look like. The English National Bank is a grand neoclassical building in London. I was concerned that the bank clerk had sent me on a wild goose chase to piss me off because I'd pushed in.

I went into a money exchange office, on the basis that they were in the same business and they directed me over the road to a modern building, which couldn't have looked more different to The Bank of England! I joined the queue there but was then told to take a ticket at the machine. It was all very frustrating! I was, however, relieved to see one of the ticket buttons to press was "old notes".

After a fifteen-minute wait, I was served by a young man who was the spitting image of Jack Whitehall, the comedian. He handed me my new notes, which looked remarkably like the old notes and said they were changed two years previously.

I returned to the train station where Richard was running the gauntlet of thieves and beggars. It had all the ingredients - rich country; busy hub; travellers carrying cash, cards and mobiles. As I neared the station, I witnessed some dodgy looking characters acting suspiciously. A man looked around fervently and then handed something to a woman who had a pram but no baby. I may have been totally wrong but I suspected they were part of one of the gangs that the posters at the station warned travellers about.

We got a train to Lausanne an hour later than planned. From Lausanne Station, we climbed up a steep hill to the old town. It wasn't a Swiss classic. It had the typical fountain with a brightly coloured medieval figure and a few historic buildings but that was about it.

We treated ourselves to a hot chocolate in the square. It was nearly €5 but it didn't even come made-up for that! You had to pour the powder from a packet into hot milk yourself!!!

We walked up another steep hill, past old merchant houses to the cathedral where there were some more old streets and great views over the city but, overall, it didn't engender a wow factor and never really endeared itself to us.

A homeless man was washing himself in the fountain as we returned to the station. It must be tough being a down and out in expensive Switzerland!

We returned to the hotel, cutting out the Montreux stop after the bank note debacle. Richard returned to the apartment and I went down to the lake to enjoy sunset. It was a sunset that had been enjoyed by Charlie Chaplin who'd lived in the area. His statue stood beside the lake. A large metal fork art insulation stuck into the lake captured the final rays of sun, as did the distant mountains. It was heart-warming after a difficult end to the day.

THE GOLDEN PASS

I like trains. I like their rhythm, and I like the
freedom of being suspended between two places,
all anxieties of purpose taken care of.
Anna Funder

W e awoke to perfect weather for the Golden Pass
train journey, billed as one of the best in the world.
We felt very lucky. Travellers on Facebook had
done if the week before and, to be quite honest, the weather
was dreadful. The weather in this part of the world is very
hit and miss so you take your chances. In my opinion, it's not
worth doing the Alps in bad weather. If the mountains are
enveloped by low, grey clouds then what is the point?

Luckily, we had no such problem and headed off to the
station in the early morning with a spring in our step.
We'd been advised by the Facebook groups to take the Belle
Epoque Train from Montreux rather than the more expensive,
crowded panoramic train that followed the same route (and
required a hefty supplement). It was a short hop up the line to
Montreux where the sage advice proved to be spot on.

The panoramic service left at 9:30 AM. A temporary check-
in desk had been set up on the platform and it was being
operated by two men from the Golden Pass Panoramic Express.

For ten minutes there was a very entertaining scene of total
chaos when two large but very distinctive tour groups turned

up. One group was from the Far East and the other group was from India. They had tour group leaders with them who weren't doing a very good job of guiding them to the correct seats in the correct carriages. They milled around, chatting and taking photos as the time to departure ticked away.

Eventually, the Far Eastern group filtered onto the train with minutes to spare but the Indian group was still on the platform. The time ticked down until there were just seconds to go. "You need to board the train!" shouted their tour leader, the panic in his voice palpable. Suddenly it was like a scene from Mumbai Train Station. There was a stampede with people pushing and shoving each other in a bid to board the train. For the poor tour group leaders, it was like herding cats!

Richard and I smiled, entertained by the disorderly spectacle. Waiting for a train can be boring so any distractions are welcome. As the last person boarded, the train drew out of the station, and we were left in peace. Unusually for Switzerland, it was a few minutes late!

Shortly after its departure, our 9:50 AM Belle Epoque train drew into the same platform. Boarding was a whole different affair. When Richard and I boarded the first class carriage, we had it to ourselves for about ten minutes. As the time of departure approached, more people boarded but it was never crowded, to the extent that we got a double and quadruple set of seats to ourselves. This meant we can move around and get good views on both sides.

The equivocally named Belle Epoque train first went into service in 1871 and had much in common with its famous cousin, the Orient Express. It was probably the closest I was ever going to get to the Orient Express whose prices are off the scale. The Belle Epoque, on the other hand, was just part of the pass! What a bargain!

We wound our way up the steep northern slope of Lake Geneva. The mountains on the southern slope reflected in the lake, creating a scene that was reminiscent of a scene from an impressionist painting. Once on the high Alpine plain with mountains rising majestically in all directions, it was like going back in time. Ancient alpine villages dotted the landscape. The dark wood of the large houses and barns had aged like a fine wine over centuries. In the past, I imagined that life would have been very tough up there in the winter but global warming had probably changed all that.

They were already preparing for winter which was long at these altitudes. The hay meadows were being cut and the hay was being bundled up, ready to feed hungry cows who would spend the long winter in hot and steamy barns to protect them from the elements. As it was spring, they would have recently been released from their winter confinement and could be seen contentedly chewing the cud on the lush pastures.

I was glued to the idyllic landscape. Bright green alpine meadows were interspersed with splashes of yellow spring flowers; carpets of dandelions, buttercups and cowslips. Shiny white peaks fringed the scene, high above in the distance. Some people slept and others talked incessantly on their phone. I just didn't get it myself. Why would you want to miss out on a second of this magical landscape?

One young couple really got into the spirit of things and ordered a bottle of champagne; a meat and cheese platter; and posh Kambly Callier biscuits. All this came to a whopping 114.80 Swiss francs (similar in euros). Having splashed out so much, I expected him to get down on one knee and propose but I'm afraid I'd been reading too many Jane Austen novels and the journey ended in Zweisimmen without even a clink of champagne flutes. Very disappointing!

In Zweisimmen we transferred to a panoramic style train for more fabulous Alpine views on the way to Spiez, where there was a rail replacement bus service to Interlaken Ost. The Interrail Pass App, unhelpfully, said the rail replacement bus wasn't included in the pass. I begged to differ. The clue was in the title, "rail replacement bus." Unusually, no one could give me any definitive answers on Facebook about this dilemma. I added it manually and hoped for the best; but I still felt nervous about the section, all the same, so when the inspector came round, I decided to ask her for the lowdown on the rail replacement bus, particularly from where it departed.

The ticket inspector was a woman in her late fifties. She didn't wait for my ticket to load and moved on down the carriage before I could ask any questions. Once the ticket had loaded, I was worried she wouldn't return to check it and would just move on to the next carriage. "Do you speak English?" I asked, not wanting to assume she did but certain she probably did speak English.

"Yes," she replied.

"Can I ask a question about the bus?" I asked her.

"Wait one moment, Madam. I'm helping other clients," she commanded.

"She's very brusque," I said to Richard, sarcastically.

"Try and stay calm," he said, seeing me going red with anger. She did return to answer my question and for Richard's sake, I didn't tell her what I was thinking.

The exchange had been witnessed by a fellow passenger who apologised for the ticket inspector's his rudeness. "I'm Swiss German," she told me. "But I lived in the U.K. for fourteen years, so I understand that the Swiss Germans can come across as being rude. They are very direct."

I have a dear Swiss German friend who is the nicest and kindest person you could wish to meet but she is both brusque and direct. It's just her way.

"It's particularly common among older Swiss Germans," said our fellow passenger.

"I did check she could speak English," I added.

"She would probably have been rude to me if we'd been speaking in German," she concluded.

Our fellow passenger kindly advised us on the best way to get to the bus and told us that we should sit on the left-hand side for the best views of Lake Thun.

In the end, we found the bus easily! In fact, we found a whole fleet of them. "This one is the first class bus and this one is the second class bus," said the bus driver when I went to check which bus to get on. "No, only joking!" she laughed. It was a refreshingly jovial exchange after my ticket inspector experience!

We found seats on the left-hand side before the bus became very crowded. As there were eighteen minutes until departure, I was able to enjoy the views of the lake from Spiez, perched high above the lake. Once we set off on the bus, the views of the lake, as the bus skirted along the edge of its shore, were equally wonderful.

Once in Interlaken, we had an hour until the next train on to Luzern, the end of the Golden Pass route.

We went for a walk so we could admire the superstar peaks that formed the backdrop of Interlaken. The Eiger, Jugenfrau and Monch Mountains are big hitters and world famous. On a family holiday in 1977 with my mum, dad and brother, Paul, we'd gone up the Jungfrau, through ice caves, to see the famous glacier. It was an unforgettable experience.

Having described how we'd spent two fabulous weeks at a Euro Camp Site in Interlaken to Richard, he responded with, "lucky you, I never went further than Wales as a child."

We stopped for a picnic lunch near the station and caught the train to Luzern to complete the Golden Pass. I did some ducking and diving in order to be first into the first class carriage and to bag some prime seats. Little good it did us, however, as once the carriage had started to fill up, we realised that small panels above the seats indicated the seats were reserved. We moved to single seats opposite.

One minute before the train left, an elderly couple came racing down the platform and jumped on to our first class carriage. I assumed they had reservations but it soon became clear they didn't. As the train was about to leave, however, they sat in the reserved seats, on the basis that no one was likely to turn up and claim them at that stage. They were right and the train moved off, leaving me seething that they were in "my seats". I might not have reserved them but I had a moral right to them. I only just stopped short of tipping the "old dears" out of 'my' seats. After all, it wouldn't have been a good look, and it wasn't their fault they had stolen 'my' seats. It was the fault of the inefficiency of the train company at the end of the day for showing seats as 'reserved' when they weren't reserved.

The situation was compounded by the fact that it wasn't long before I realised, I was on the wrong side of the train! For Richard, it was all about legroom but for me it was all about "the view". He was always telling me to make up my mind as I switched sides and moved so I didn't have the sun shining in my eyes or could get better views. In fact, I'd probably go so far as to say, I'd kill for a decent view!

In this instance, we are on the wrong side for the glorious views of the lake. I had to, therefore, take action. There was a spare seat next to a small child in a four-seat combo on the other side. He had a window seat but he was so small that I could see over him. His American parents, who were opposite, looked a bit shocked when I plonked myself down but they recovered themselves and asked if I was enjoying my trip to Switzerland. They were with their parents, their child's grandparents, who were in their sixties and sat on the other side of the aisle. They were travelling around Switzerland on a Swiss Rail Pass for 10 days. As the Americans only get two weeks annual leave plus public holidays, they were returning to work shortly after landing back in the U.S.A. The parents were exhausted by it all and slept for much of the idyllic journey.

The train took us along the edge of the north shore of Lake Brienz. Particularly impressive were the dramatic waterfalls crashing down the mountainside opposite. They gave me something to talk about with the little five-year-old Ronan. One tumbled down the mountain and divided into two ribbons that then joined forces for the final descent. I described the path the water would take in the water cycle to him. "Which age group did you teach?" asked his mother.

"11-18," I replied, "much older than Ronan."

They told me they did the trip with Ronan in mind because he loved trains. "He will have lots to tell his friends when he goes back to school," I said.

"He's home-schooled," his mum told me.

"Oh, that's interesting," I observed, trying to stay neutral on the subject.

"We were both home-schooled," she told me.

Once at the end of the lake, we double backed and went up and over a pass, heading for Luzern.

In Luzern, we took the shortcut back. Luzern to Lausanne loops north of the Alps through rolling hills but during the two and quarter hour journey, the white peaks of the Alps were ever present off to the South.

Near Lausanne, we descended through the world-famous UNESCO World Heritage Lavaux Vineyards which clung to the steep slopes, aided and abetted by ancient stone terraces. There is evidence that there were vineyards here in Roman times but the current vineyards date back to the 11th century when Benedictine and Cistercian monasteries controlled the area.

From Lausanne, it was a short hop back to Vevey where Richard and I walked from the station down to the lake so we could enjoy the sunset with the giant fork!

THE MIGHTY MATTERHORN!

Luckily for us, the weather got stuck on blue sky and sunshine so we were up early and on the 9:05 AM train to Zermatt. Richard wasn't quite signed up to the programme but, as I said to him, "We need to make the most of this good weather in photogenic Switzerland".

We changed trains in the rather wonderfully named Visp and boarded a bright red Matterhorn Gotthard Bahn Train that climbed a very steep gradient. The snow-covered mountains towered over us and waterfalls gushed with melt water. A typically light blue river raced down the mountain beside us. Some slopes were full of scree, poised dangerously on steep slopes, threatening the tracks. Earlier landslides that had delivered the scree could be seen above. Then, as we neared Zermatt, continually gaining altitude, fingers of snow reached for the tracks.

Zermatt, thanks to its famous backdrop, was very crowded. Without the Mighty Matterhorn, Zermatt would just be one of those thousands of pretty Alpine villages. Of course, Toblerone Chocolate had done a great marketing job over the years!

Richard and I visited Zermatt and the Matterhorn on our interrail trip in 1988 when we travelled there via Geneva! It had left a lasting impression that I had now been able to feast on for 36 years! We could have used the money to buy a sofa but it wouldn't still be around after 36 years, now would it? In 1988, visitors were mainly Europeans but now it was very popular with travellers from the Far East and around the world.

I had read online that you could get good views of the Matterhorn after a seven-minute walk from the train station. In addition, two minutes on from there was a view from a bridge over the river. We had precisely forty-six minutes in Zermatt before our train back to Visp. On paper, that should have been perfectly adequate. Unfortunately, when it comes to Google Maps and us, that is rarely the case!

We walked at a brisk pace up to the terrace outside the Town Hall. Here we had our photo taken with the town and Matterhorn behind us. We teamed up with a group of friends from Bern, who were on a day trip, and took each other's photos.

A local pointed us in the direction of the river. It was a bit of an up and down route and I was aware that the clock was ticking. Eventually, after what was about ten minutes and certainly not two minutes, we reached the river with a very enticing view of the Matterhorn.

The Matterhorn has to be the most recognisable mountain in the world. It even beats the mother of all mountains, Everest, in that category. In surveys, nine out of ten people could recognise the Matterhorn but only one in ten could recognise Everest. I made that up, obviously, but you get the picture!

The Matterhorn here, rose up like a huge white witch's hat! I felt very tempted to dwell and soak up the wonderful views but the time was ticking down fast. Richard started to walk back and I dwelt five minutes longer and took a few more photos. I stretched it so far that I had to sprint to get back to the train station in time. Our friends from Bern, coming in the opposite direction, greeted me with some surprise as I sped past them, puffing and panting so much that I could only wave at them! I caught up with Richard near the station and we caught the train back to Visp with only a few minutes to spare.

As I'd pushed myself to the very limit (I constantly forgot how old I was!), I'd really irritated my chest. Once I got my breath back on the train, I started to cough. A man on the opposite side of the aisle got his mask out of his backpack and put it on!

Once back in Visp, which really should be a town in a fantasy novel, we continued on to Andermatt, following the famous Glacier Express train route. One tunnel went on for about twenty minutes, equivalent to the Channel Tunnel. I realised later from a post on the Interrail Facebook Page that I'd made a copy of that I could have avoided this tunnel by adding via Frutigen station to the Interrail Pass. "You don't see anything going through the tunnel" said the helpful Facebook group member. She was stating the bleeding obvious but I was more annoyed with myself for not having actioned this excellent suggestion! Mind you, there is lots to take on board when organising a complex three-month interrail trip so I tried not to be too hard on myself!

Once out of the tunnel, it wasn't hard to see how the route had got its name. The snow had long since melted in the valley, if there ever was much in these days of global warming, but solid and unstoppable bright white glaciers inhabited the mountain tops and would do all summer. I'd read a report that all snow in the Alps had melted for the first time in the summer of 2022. The glaciers were certainly in retreat and I wondered which summer the report would come that there were no more glaciers in the Alps. Sad but probably inevitable in the current trajectory! Even in my lifetime, I can remember thick snow in the valleys at lower elevations in the Alps in winter but that was a thing of the past.

After travelling for two hours, we approached the high mountains of the pass, a sea of white. This is where, even in May, the train passes through a snowy white landscape, according to my American friends from the previous day who had done this route a few days earlier. The glacier route goes all the way to the eastern side of Switzerland and I'd travelled much of this route with my Swiss friend in February which was spectacular. The lake in St Moritz had still been frozen! Sadly, we didn't have the time to carry on. Even with a three-month interrail pass, hard choices had to be made.

The two female ticket inspectors had been a bit brusque when checking our tickets but, when I asked if it was the same train returning back down the valley, they said it was and that we could stay on the train. As we had fifteen minutes before the train departed, I went off to the station supermarket to buy some drinks and left Richard on the train.

When I returned to the platform, the two female ticket inspectors and a male ticket inspector wouldn't let me on the train. "But my husband's on there," I told them indignantly. When the train doors closed and the train moved off, indignation turned to panic. "Where are you taking my husband?" I cried. I now became a source of entertainment for other passengers on the platform who were also waiting for the Visp train but, unlike me, were not in the unfortunate position of having lost a loved one.

"That wasn't the Visp train," the male inspector assured me.

"So where is my husband? He was on the train on this platform and now it's gone". An engine came through and shortly after that, a train drew into the station. The male ticket inspector, who'd gone further up the platform, came down to report that he thought he'd spotted Richard on the train.

I found Richard who had had his own drama. Whilst sitting on the train alone, it had started to move. He was worried that he was being taken off to the other side of Switzerland or, at the very least, to a siding and went and banged on the train driver's door. Richard normally shies away from communication in foreign speaking countries, preferring to let me take the lead as I can get by in most western European languages or I learn a few phrases, plus I'm less worried about communicating when there are language barriers, a.k.a. making a fool of yourself! In this instance, however, he had no choice.

Luckily, Switzerland is a very bilingual country with four different official languages. I heard train staff switch with ease between French and German. Most of the Swiss Germans speak good English. On this trip, I'd been surprised at how many French speakers spoke reasonably good English now so I was sure the French speaking Swiss, who were less precious about the language than their neighbours, had no problems speaking English.

The driver assured Richard in very good English that there was no need to worry. "I'm just moving the train so another train can use the platform. We will go back! This is the train to Visp."

Once on the train, I found a seat diagonally opposite to Richard for the best views. When the male ticket inspector, who turned out to be quite jolly, came through the carriage, he joked that even though I had been worried about where my husband was earlier, I now didn't want to sit next to him! "Yeah!" I said, smiling at him. "I don't know why I didn't just let you just take him off to a siding so I can have a quiet life."

On our journey from Brig, where we had to change trains to continue on to Vevey, we witnessed some suspicious behaviour. Some unlikely looking characters came through first class and went into the toilet at the end of our carriage which showed an engaged sign for about thirty minutes. Helpfully, red and green WC signs are shown in the carriage to indicate whether the toilet is free or not, so you don't have to make a wasted journey. "That's a very long time to spend a penny," I joked.

"Yeah" said Richard, "especially as I want to go to the toilet."

We assumed they were fare dodgers. In Montreux, the train was delayed for ten minutes and, unusually, we had no announcements as to why the train was delayed. They normally say, "We are waiting for an express train to come past," which in France I suspected usually meant, "The driver has nipped off for a quick fag!" Trains in Switzerland are rarely delayed. If they are, then it probably means that they started life in Italy and arrived late in Switzerland.

As we eventually moved out of the station, Richard noticed that four heavily armed police had a suspect pinned to the ground on the platform. "Wow, that's a heavy-handed way of dealing with fare dodgers!" I joked, but we suspected that there may have been more to it than that.

We were treated to a beautiful sunset over Lake Geneva to end the day. We walked directly from the station down through the old town of Vevey to the Lake so Richard could admire the view. I think he would have preferred to "admire the view" from his bed in the apartment but he thanked me for it, once there, because it was truly awe inspiring!

SURFING IN LAND LOCKED SWITZERLAND!

T he weather wasn't the stellar perfect weather we'd had for two days but it was still very good. We took a train to Thun on the northwest tip of the lake of the same name, changing in that well known hub, Visp, a place whose station we knew well by then.

On the second leg of the journey, we boarded a first class carriage that was huge and practically empty. We realised it was a "quiet zone", as there was a small sticker telling you this. "Oh, that's good," I said. "Some peace and quiet."

We sat down, at least five rows from everyone else. Several minutes later, we started to discuss our travel plans for the next day when we were travelling back to France. At this point, a man who was probably in his thirties and in a suit, approached us. "You have to be quiet!" He told us very assertively.

"I wasn't aware we weren't being quiet," I replied, feeling rather affronted.

"You can't talk. You must be silent," he said.

"It says quiet," I replied, pointing to the sign. That's not the same as silent."

"You must be silent," he repeated and walked off, leaving me feeling flabbergasted. It wasn't as if we were having a rave. We weren't singing, laughing or dancing in the aisles, for the goodness sake!

The sign itself had much to answer for. In French and Italian it said "silent" but in English it said "quiet" NOT "silent". Ironically, in German, it used the word for quiet and our officious friend was Swiss German. "Well, we will have to whisper," I said to Richard, but he refused to even do that.

Thirty minutes later, two women got on at the other end of the carriage and chatted away to each other. We waited for Mr Officious to tell them off but he didn't. I resisted the temptation to give Mr Officious a piece of my mind about his selective policing of the carriage on our way out but, as we got off, Richard redeemed himself. "There are two women talking up there! You need to go and speak to them," he said sarcastically.

Thun is not in the Premier League of Swiss towns but it's pleasant enough. It was a short walk to the river and the medieval centre. Flowers lined the river and large colourful flags hung down the medieval streets.

We crossed the wooden covered bridge where someone was surfing in the fast-flowing river. I kid you not! I never expected to see surfing in landlocked Switzerland. The surfer was in a full wet suit! I could see why! The meltwater must have been freezing. He'd tied a rope to the railing beside the river and was using that to keep himself from being swept down the fast-flowing river. In Hawaii they ride the waves into the shore but here they were going against the flow. It looked thrilling and he made it look easy but I suspected it was far from easy.

The Germans have a word for the river wave, "flusswelle." The rapid force of water gushing down from Lake Thun and through the bridge, created waves on the river Aare. The Obere Schleuse, an 18th century wooden covered bridge was one of two wooden covered bridges where you could watch surfing. The second covered bridge, Muhleschleuse, was even more of a spectacle with four people surfing in rotation because you could stand in the shallows at the side of the river and then launch yourself into the fast-flowing centre of the river. The only woman surfing was very impressive. In my opinion, she was better than the men! I'm just saying!

We bought a picnic lunch and went off to have it on a bench in the park beside the river. Blossom floated off the trees like snow and landed in the river to be carried away by the current.

The theme of "one of those days" continued with the return journey. The train from Thun was delayed by an "incident" in Italy so we had to scramble around to change our train passes so we didn't miss our connections in Bern and Lausanne. First class was on the top deck for enhanced views. Richard and I sat on opposite sides of the aisles in the huge and far from crowded train carriage. As Richard and I chatted, having checked it wasn't a "quiet carriage", I noticed an elderly woman staring angrily at me. At first, I thought I was imagining it and that she just had a 'resting bitch face' that just happened to be looking in my direction.

About five minutes later, however, she got up and grabbed her coat. She muttered angrily at us. "I don't know what your problem is!" I told her, "This isn't a quiet carriage!"

"You should sit together!" she spat at me with positive venom.

"We can sit where we like," I spat back with equal venom as she stomped off to the other end of the carriage, still muttering angrily as she went.

Ironically, when we got off in Bern, she was up at the other end of the carriage talking on her mobile phone! Talk about double standards!

We got the train to Montreux where we had a wander along the lakeside, lined with huge late 19th century and early 20th century hotels, originally frequented by European aristocrats.

There was a craft market along the lakeside promenade that was thronging with people. One of the stalls sold "English food and drink". They had Marmite and Yorkshire Tea, of course! It suggested there must have been plenty of expats in the area.

We passed the Freddie Mercury statue, a reminder he lived in the area, and watched the lake steamer come into port. We could have used the lake steamers as part of our pass but there just wasn't the time on this trip. We went far enough to see Chillion Castle, romantically poised on the edge of the lake before turning round.

On our way back to Vevey, a woman came through the first class carriage begging. I joked with Richard that she couldn't have paid for a ticket as it would have taken a month of begging just to pay the fare! In two days of travelling on Swiss trains, we'd paid for our three months first class passes! A man at the end of the carriage gave her some money and she went off looking happy.

We bought ice cream at the coop and went down to the lakeside to eat them, happy that we'd chosen little known Vevey, a beautiful hidden gem, to stay rather than expensive and overcrowded Montreux.

We got back to the apartment at the early hour of 6:30 PM, absolutely exhausted from our travel around western Switzerland over the previous four days. We'd made the most of the good weather but we were paying for it now!

BACK TO FRANCE!

We had the luxury of a lie-in. After a cheese and mushroom omelette for breakfast, I went off for a wander around Vevey and then we headed for the train station mid-morning. Here, we caught a train to Geneva where we had to go back through the defunct customs corridor from a bygone era, in order to access the French trains.

Even though we got a first class carriage on our French train to Chambery Challes les Eaux, it was like going from first class on Singapore Airlines to up the back of near the toilets on Ryan air! When I used the toilets, I pressed hard on the old-fashioned foot operated button, circa 1980s, to flush the toilet and the separate foot pump for water to wash my hands but no water was forthcoming and the smell suggested it had been like that for a while!

As we progressed westward, past lakes and through the craggy Hautes Alps, the weather deteriorated and more clouds piled in. We arrived in Chambery Challes les Eaux one hour and nineteen minutes later. At twenty-two letters long, the name of the town was second only to the length of Villefranche-de-Confluent, where we had stayed earlier in our trip. I felt for the locals who had to fill out any official forms in triplicate! A jolly train inspector said "bonjour" as he came through the carriage.

"Bonjour" I replied with gusto that equalled his. He gabbled something at us in French. "What did he say?" asked Richard. I think he said, "It is nice to have someone who's cheerful;

they're a miserable bunch back there!"

At the train station, I managed to get TGV reservations from Lyon to Lille. This was a relief because I had been looking at all sorts of combinations to travel north so we were in Lille and ready to return to Blighty on the Eurostar in a few days.

It took us twenty minutes to get to our apartment hotel. As we walked along the pedestrianised boulevard, we were struck by the noise of squawking birds. Looking up into the trees, it became clear that there was a large rookery, the length of the street.

Further on, we passed the unusual elephant fountain with large life-like elephants protruding out on all four sides and spraying water from their trunks. They carry a column with a statue of General de Boigne on top and tributes to the great man who earned his fortune in the East Indies, around the base. The statue was erected posthumously in 1838 to recognise that he had passed on some of his considerable wealth to the town. Amusingly, the elephants are known locally as the rear-less four!

Once at the hotel, we managed to get a free upgrade to a larger room. It's always worth asking, especially if the hotel is unlikely to be full. As the sun came out, the view from the balcony of the mountains was splendid.

Mid-afternoon, we went for a wander around the medieval centre of Chambery which in the past had been the capital of Savoy, an Italian Kingdom. The Italian influence was mentioned in the on-line information about the town but it felt very Swiss to me.

In the warm sunshine, the pastel-coloured medieval mansions positively glowed. The centre was buzzing and thronging with people so we sat and had a few drinks in the middle of the wide pedestrianised centre. It was a great place for people watching and admiring the stately buildings, until the bloody tourist train pulled up and blocked our view!

LYON

We paid €84.82 for the hotel apartment but it included breakfast which would have been €13.80 per person according to a plaque on the back of the door. That made the room €57.22. Mind you, we didn't go down until 10:00 AM as check out wasn't until 12:00 PM so it became brunch. It was a big buffet spread with hot and cold food on offer as well as freshly squeezed juices and freshly brewed coffee. By the time we'd finished, they were practically paying us to stay in the room!

I had a wander to the impressive castle of the Dukes of Savoy. Sadly, most of the castle was closed to the public and the small exhibition area was mainly in French with a few token English boards.

On my way back, I popped into the church where, as it was a Sunday there was a service taking place. It was packed. As I gazed up at the ceiling, I was impressed by the stonework but something didn't seem quite right. On closer inspection, it turned out to be a painting of carved stonework, rather than the real thing.

The train to Lyon was only one and a half hours and it was a thirty minute walk to our apartment down one of the longest streets in the world. We turned onto it at #155 and it took twenty minutes to get to #322, our apartment. It would have felt like a long trudge down the road even without our heavy loads. And I'm not just talking about our heavy backpacks, our big brunch was weighing us down too!

When we eventually got there, we found it was a very pleasant apartment in an old-fashioned building with stone stairs full of fossils. Its biggest plus point was that it had a washing machine so we could wash our clothes.

The next day, we had a lazy morning, still exhausted from our long days out and about in Switzerland. The weather forecast was full of bright weather but not until the afternoon so we set off in the early afternoon to explore Lyon. We'd been to Lyon on two previous occasions but only in passing for half a day each time. We'd never actually stayed in Lyon.

I had decided, in my wisdom, that it would be nice to go somewhere that we hadn't been before. I settled upon the Basilica of Notre Dame de Fourviere. Google Maps said it was a one hour and nine minute walk but I'd learned not to trust Google Maps. Lyon is France's third largest city so that should have rung alarm bells. The basilica was on the other side of the city so it was like going from one side of Manchester to the other. I've never walked from one side of Manchester to the other side but I'm pretty sure it would take me more than an hour and nine minutes. The trouble with Google Maps is it caters for all ages and abilities in one estimated time. You should really be able to enter a bit of data to help it make a more accurate assessment of how long it's going to take. Mountain goat or tired old sheep? We all know which end of the spectrum I'd be!

Not only was it on the other side of the city, but it was also up a very steep hill. They never tell you that on good old Google Maps! It could be seen from all over the city, just to prove that point.

We set off down the longest street in the world. Halfway down it, near the station, the police were out in full force. About ten police vans were lined up in the street and the tram line had been blocked off. It was yet another public holiday for Victory in Europe Day, so they were clearly expecting trouble and, as a consequence, were on high alert. It took us nearly an hour just to reach the first river. We still had to cross the second river and get to the Old Town. An online guide said it was "almost an island". As, I said to Richard "it's either an island or it's not". It isn't an island but two rivers, the Saone and the Rhone that meet a bit further downstream. At best the area between the two rivers could be called a peninsula.

Shortly after crossing the second river, we found steps leading up to the basilica. It was steep and, therefore, a hard slog up to the halfway point where we crossed the road to a park and a path that wound its way up in a series of switchbacks. It was hard going and whilst I didn't time it, it felt like a few hours to reach the basilica from the apartment, not one hour nine minutes. More like two hours and nine minutes! We collapsed on to a bench at the top. "We're definitely not spring chickens anymore!" I said to Richard.

The spectacular views of Lyon from the terrace next the basilica helped to ease our aching limbs. The weather was improving so there was plenty of blue sky on display! The basilica was built between 1872 and 1884, after the French Russian War. The people of Lyon vowed to build it if they were victorious. It is affectionately known as the upside-down elephant owing to its four identical towers and an additional 5th tower in a different style. It is a mixture of gothic and byzantine styles with a richly decorated interior. Some might say it's over the top; full of elaborate mosaics and paintings. One image, of course, featured Joan of Arc. It was over 600 years, since the demise of Joan when this cathedral was built but they were still obsessed by the peasant woman who took on the 'evil' English! In keeping with the over-the-top theme, the crypt below was nearly as big as the main church.

We returned to the old town and had a wander, with the intention of finding somewhere to get a well-deserved drink. We found a seat outside a cafe on a pleasant square. There were just two problems. Nearby were two of the world's worst buskers. A singer and guitarist duo were performing a song with only had one word, "tango". It was catchy for about five seconds and then intensely irritating. The second problem was that the cafe only sold alcohol free drinks. The people on the next table had some colourful cocktails but they were 'sans alcohol'. A café bar with no wine list in France! That's was a new one on me! I thought wine was a religion in France!

We moved down to the next square where they sold alcohol aplenty. As it was a public holiday, the old town was thronging with people. We watched some small children jumping from short stubby concrete bollard to short stubby concrete bollard with a mixture of amusement and concern. "It's going to end in tears," I said, my heart in my mouth as a two year old tried to copy a four year old who had managed the feat.

"Yes," agreed Richard. "I fear some teeth may be knocked out." There was no sign of the parents.

Owing to our aching limbs, it was a long slog to get back. We got lost at one stage and ran into the aftermath of a serious protest. The windows of a bank were completely smashed in. They had shattered into thousands of pieces that littered the pavement. The bank was totally open to the elements. You could have just walked in through the windows and sat at a desk. There was no sign of either protesters or police so I could only assume it had only just happened. The protesters had scarpered and the police had yet to respond.

By the time we got back on track and trudged up the longest street in the world, we were beyond exhausted. We didn't have to carry our backpacks, but I felt as if I was carrying a Mini Cooper! At one point, I started to feel that we would never reach #322! Once on the sofa, I looked up the number of steps I'd done! 20,599! It felt more like 40,599. Of course, the simple number of steps didn't account for the element that fell under the category of "mountain climbing"!

ONWARDS AND UPWARDS!

L uckily, our train wasn't until 11 AM so we could let our aching limbs recover with a lie in. We had a mushroom and cheese omelette and set off along the longest road in the world to the station at 10:10 AM.

It was pleasant weather in Lyon but as we travelled further north on the TGV to Lille, the weather deteriorated and it became wet and miserable. This was a shame as it was attractive, arcadian like scenery. Richard and I each had a single window seat so we could enjoy the rolling hills, dotted with medieval villages and farms but good weather would have been preferable.

I think we'd been spoiled on previous TGV journeys. On this trip, the Wi-Fi didn't work and the toilet door wouldn't lock. It looked like a first-generation TGV to me but three hours and twenty-six minutes passed quickly in my wide and comfy seat with a table. I was still surprised at how quickly long train journeys went! I'm in my element watching the world go by so I guess that helped.

As we reached the northeast region of France, the scenery became flat and boring. We skirted Paris and stopped at Charles de Gaulle Airport. Not having to cross Paris on the metro was the big advantage of getting the Eurostar from Lille rather than Paris.

Once in Lille, it was a twenty-five-minute walk to the People's Hostel, Lille. It was the same chain as we'd stayed in in Paris for our first two nights so we hoped it would be as good. I'd booked a twin room but I'd received a message to say they couldn't guarantee my bed choice. This was after I paid for the "non-refundable" room, of course! I felt rather irritated by this and sent a message in reply saying I would be very upset if I didn't get my bed choice.

On arrival, the first thing I said was, "I hope I've got my bed choice - two singles. We are checking in very early, so I see no reason why they aren't available."

"I don't know," said the young, female Spanish receptionist, "I will need to check what the cleaning lady has allocated you." "The cleaning lady allocates rooms?" I commented, rather surprised but I decided to stay calm until she checked to see if we had our single beds. She disappeared off and returned several minutes later with good news.

Lille is spitting distance from the Belgium border and it is more Flemish than French. Our room in the attic of a medieval townhouse had a sloping roof that had Richard swearing and cursing more than once when he hit his head on it. The beauty of having single beds was we could move them around to avoid the sloping roofs.

We prepared dinner in the communal kitchen. Not Richard's natural habitat. There were two others cooking so it felt crowded. We got chatting to a couple who had moved around Europe for three years. He worked digitally and was from Norway. She was from Afghanistan so we chatted about her experiences growing up there. That is what I love about staying in a hostel. You meet all sorts for people from different places and different backgrounds that you wouldn't normally meet.

When the weather improved in the middle of the evening and the sun came out, we walked to the Grand Place (also known as Palace du General de Gaulle in honour of the great man who was born in Lille). We sat and had a drink in the middle of the square, a good place for people watching. Some people came and went with a purpose, crossing the square to get home or meet up with a friend for a meal. Other people begged for money, and some sat and chatted at the base of the monument in the middle of the square. A group of migrants from Sub Sahara Africa gathered in the square with their bikes and takeaway food containers, waiting to go and pick up and deliver their next food order.

By the time we headed back to the hotel, darkness had descended and the square had been lit to create a colourful montage of stately buildings. The streets on the way back were buzzing with young people drinking at the bars, leading us to conclude that, as it was a Tuesday night, they must be university students who didn't need to get up to go to work the next day.

HOMEWARD BOUND!

I made tea and coffee in the communal kitchen and we had cereal in our room. We had to check out at 11:00 AM but stretched it to 11:30 AM as the weather was rather inclement. We put our bags in the bag storage and as I handed in the key, I tried to disarm the Spanish receptionist with, "Many thanks, great stay as ever." It didn't work. "

"You were supposed to check out at eleven," she said, po-faced.

"I'm a booking.com genius," I added, "it gives us late checkout." She gave up.

We walked to the centre to see the sights and headed for the Grand Palais, assuming it was historic. As we walked out of the historic centre, I started to doubt whether the Grand Palais really was grand, in spite of it being signposted alongside all the historic sights. "It's probably that 1960s monstrosity," I said to Richard, pointing at a tower block. It wasn't but it was a modern monstrosity and turned out to be a concert venue.

We returned to the cathedral where there was a service going on and then walked up to the Belle Arts Museum. Richard sat in the "relaxation area" and I went around it. It wasn't until the end that I got to the stars of the show – the masters.

We collected our bags and headed for the station over cobbles that were becoming the bane of our lives with our heavy backpacks and aching limbs. The Lille Eurostar

Terminal was much calmer than St Pancreas International. I managed to get my passport stamp buried on a busy page of stamps and the waiting room was reasonably quiet. Boarding wasn't the chaotic bun fight we'd experienced at London St Pancreas so we boarded feeling calm and relaxed.

The Interrail app said the 16:35 PM departure would take twenty two minutes to reach London! That would be supersonic but, in reality, it was an hour and twenty two minutes, owing to the time difference.

On board, passengers who had come from Brussels were already tucking into their meals. We had the chicken salad and wine. As on our outbound, it was a snack dressed up as a meal. Coffee, which was unavailable on the way over to France, was slow in coming but the good news was that the weather had become much brighter in order to enjoy the flat Pas de Calais countryside, as we raced towards the Channel Tunnel. The bad news was that the windows were so dirty that it was hard to appreciate what was on the other side of them!

Once on the other side of the channel, it was business as usual with low grey cloud! "Welcome to Britain!"

When we arrived in London, we had a few hours before our direct Hull Trains service to Beverley at 18:48 PM, a three-hour journey. Richard went off to get a few supplies as the cupboards would be bare when we got home.

I sat and watched the queues to get a photo taken at Platform Nine and Three Quarters, complete with a trolley and suitcase halfway through the wall as if disappearing off to Hogwarts by magic. It was free to get a photo but the station had its own security and photographer, theme park style, to take photos of participants. They handed out scarves and held them up so the official photographer could get the perfect shot of them about to disappear through the brick wall. I went over to take a photo of the scene but soon realised I was in the wrong place because everyone asked me to take a photo for them so they didn't have to pay for the expensive official photo. After taking photos of three groups, I decided to resign as the Unofficial Platform Nine and Three Quarters Photographer and moved.

The huge Harry Potter shop next to Platform Nine and Three Quarters was selling the official photos and doing a roaring trade in selling Harry Potter tat!

Once on our 18:48 PM train to Beverly, the friendly ticket inspector came around to check the tickets but said he couldn't read our big QR codes with his reader. He didn't seem bothered and went off to check other tickets. Some seats were marked as 'reserved' but no one ever got on to occupy them.

The great thing about first class in Britain is that you get food included in your ticket. The drinks trolley came around and I got a coke. "I'll give you two," said the young man, "as they are so small. Do you want biscuits?"

"I never say no to biscuits," I replied. He rattled off the choices. "Oh, decisions, decisions," I joked.

"I'd go for the white chocolate chip cookies," said the friendly ticket inspector. They were, indeed, delicious and when I mentioned this to the ticket inspector he said, "when he comes around again, he'll give you some more!"

The "main course" was a pack of sandwiches and a bag of crisps with mineral water!

Once in Beverly at 9:50 PM, we had to move up two carriages to get off as the train was too long for the platform. The ticket office was all shut up so I couldn't greet my nemesis, Snotty Sue, from our outward journey and see what she thought about my complaint! She was obviously at home on the loo!

The powers that be had got back to me. They'd apologised for her behaviour and said it wasn't what they expected of their staff. They said they would have 'a chat' with her!

As we walked home, across Beverley, I jokingly asked, "how many minutes?" as normally we had Google Maps on to give a countdown. Four military jets roared across the sky, as if to mark our return.

At 11:00 PM, back at the house, we decided that the snack on the Eurostar and snack on Hull Trains didn't quite hack it so we shared a pizza!

When we planned the Interrail trip, the idea was to have a few days at home to rest and pick up our camping gear for Scandinavia. Unfortunately, this didn't account for the deaths of Richard's elderly parents. In many ways it was a blessed relief as they were ready to go but in our few days back home, we had to finalise arrangements for their joint funeral which was two days into our 'break' back home. Our children joined us so that was pleasant and we took the attitude that life is never simple.

PART TWO

Trains are beautiful. They take people to places they've never been, faster than they could ever go themselves. Everyone who works on trains knows they have personalities, they're like people. They have their own mysteries.

Sam Starbuck

THE NORTH SEA

F ive days later, we started Part Two of our inter railing trip at 5:30 PM. Well 5:35 PM to be precise once we'd all squeezed into the car that was loaded with too much luggage and Richard had unlocked the house, huffing and puffing as he went, to get my mobile phone that I had left on the table in the lounge. You can't get very far these days without your smartphone, especially when you've got your Interrail Pass loaded onto it!

We would have left a few hours earlier, or even a few days earlier, if Andrew had had his way; owing to our house in Beverley being a Wi-Fi desert!

We went the long way around through the flat agricultural landscape of the Holderness Plain, rather than tackle the centre of Hull and at the boat terminal, we waved Kathryn and Andrew off and headed for check in. As a veteran of the Dover to Calais route at the height of the school holidays, it seemed remarkably quiet and calm. We'd travelled by car through Dover on so many occasions that I struggled to remember the last time we had been foot passengers on a ferry.

We were given our boarding passes and told we could board. At security, a late middle-aged woman who was short, dumpy and had bottle blonde hair, asked, "Do you have any sharp objects or alcohol?"

I paused whilst I thought, "Do I declare my small nail scissors? Technically they're sharp but I'm pretty certain I can't hold the boat up with them." Then there was the whisky we'd decanted into two plastic bottles for use in Scandinavia where you needed to be a multi-millionaire to afford any kind of alcoholic drink. I was surprised at the question. It wasn't as if this was a Caribbean Cruise! "No," I replied, as convincingly as possible but aware that I would never pass a lie detector test. They let us proceed.

I was wrong about the cruise. Okay, the North Sea may not have much in common with the Caribbean, but many of our fellow passengers were on a mini cruise to either Rotterdam or Amsterdam! I know, who would have thought. I raised my eyes and made a face when relaying this to Richard, being the travel snob that I am but, fair play, it's better than nothing!

From what I could gather, the itinerary for the two night mini cruise was board, get pissed, have dinner, get pissed, watch the live entertainment in the bar (which included an Abba Tribute Act), get pissed, sleep, eat a full English, disembark, board a coach to Amsterdam or Rotterdam (I know which I'd prefer) spend seven to eight hours seeing the sights, get pissed, return by coach to the boat, repeat the overnight crossing, disembark the next morning with a trolley load of duty free!

Post Brexit, the booze cruise was back and even I had to admit to doing a few of those with the car via Dover and without the Abba Tribute Band!

On boarding, we were greeted by two cheerful Filipino crew. Suddenly, something clicked in my brain and I remembered all the hoo-ha a few years before in the media when nice Mr P&O had sacked all the U.K. crew and replaced them with crew from the Philippines who could be paid peanuts rather than the national minimum wage as the job was carried out at sea. I'd vowed never to travel with P&O again but, of course, this had never crossed my mind when I'd booked this only option to continental Europe. It's like all those people who complain about Ryan Air but when it comes to it, they're as cheap as chips so no one can resist their bargain basement fares! And they know it!

"You've got a bunk bed," one of the Filipino crew told me. "You want to upgrade to two singles for £20? I sensed he'd learnt his bargaining skills at the street markets of Manila.

"No thank you," I replied. "We'll survive!" We needed to save our pennies and our pounds for very expensive Scandinavia. "Please can you direct us to our cabin?"

"Along there and up two floors to level 10. You can take the lift." We took the lift and after a significant walk, found our cabin. It was a huge ship. The Pride of Rotterdam had hundreds of shoebox cabins but my guess was that only a fraction were occupied.

We deposited our bags and headed off to find the sun deck. I think there was more than a dollop of hyperbole used in the naming of this deck. There was, indeed, some mid evening Hull sunshine to enjoy but it wasn't exactly the Mediterranean. To prove the point, I had to return to the cabin to get my coat. I got a bit disorientated on my return and went down the wrong corridor. It was like a maze. I went up, down and around until I eventually found cabin 10161, feeling as if I'd just completed a marathon. We were at the front of the boat. Do they call that the bow? If you looked down the long straight corridor, the perspective gave the impression that anyone at the other end was from Lilliput and in a really small frame. It reminded me of one of those optical illusions where mirrors are used to give the impression that there are hundreds of projected images back a long and never-ending corridor.

Back on the sun deck, our fellow passengers on the next table were on their third pint and we hadn't even set sail! The boat was due to leave at 8:30 PM but set sail at 8:00 PM. I wasn't sure how that worked. I imagined cars racing up to the gangplank as it was raised and footpath passengers legging it along the boarding bridge only to see the boats sailing off into the sunset. As check-in closed 90 minutes before departure and that had expired, they could get away with it, I supposed.

Sailing down the River Humber was a dramatic experience.

The skies over Hull darkened and heavy rain showers could be seen descending from the huge grey clouds. Luckily, we kept the blue skies as we sailed past power stations with huge flames shooting up from a thin chimney, green grain silos and gas storage plants. Colourful ships lined the docks and jetties, having coal or liquified natural gas off loaded or waiting to take on board containers or grain.

When the huge spherical orange sun descended below the low grey clouds it was behind a curtain of rain, creating an unusual out of focus image. I'd seen many spectacular sunsets in my time but none quite like this one.

There was a school group on board. They were, of course, very excited about setting off on an adventure. They congregated on the decks and chatted like starlings. The girls in their shorts and crop tops made me feel positively cold. I hoped that their cabins were nowhere near ours. I had experienced many wonderful school trips and was a great advocate of them but I had enough knowledge to know not much sleep was had on the first night. A group of girls told me they were third years from Glasgow and were going to Paris. "You'll love Paris," I told them, "but be careful of your phones and money on the metro."

Having swung from the north bank to the south bank with the curve of the river, we started to manoeuvre back to the north shore. You could still see Hull in the distance and the Humber bridge poking up over a small rise created by a bend in the river. A bright orange band of light lit up the city, the bridge and the docks but the dark menacing clouds continued to bore down. We passed Grimsby with its famous Sienna inspired tower. Grimsby is well named as it is a truly grim place so the tower is the only hint of Italy!

Richard threw in the towel and retired to the cabin. I tried to stay until the bitter end and our grand entry into the dark expanse of the North Sea. The Lincolnshire Wolds bubbled up in the failing light to the south, a telecommunications tower clearly visible on one of the hills, lit by red lights, and to the north we passed very close to the tip of Spurn Point, a very long sand spit. I know it's very long because we walked down it the year before and it seemed to be never ending. There was still a hint of land to the South but even I was ready for bed so I returned to our cabin.

We couldn't pull down my bunk bed. We read the instructions on the wall that said, "release the safety catch". We pushed every protrusion and pulled on every catch but in the absence of an obvious safety catch, I went to reception for help. On my way there, I passed the mini cruise passengers who were by then on their sixth pint and singing along to the ABBA Tribute Band.

The Spanish purser said he would come and help us. As we walked back to the cabin, I asked him about the Filipino crew. "Most of what they said on the news was lies!" he said emphatically. "Some reports said they earn £3.00 an hour and that's just not true!"

"But it's still not the national minimum wage and many Brits lost their jobs!"

"Yes, but many Brits were happy to go. They got a payoff and it's an awful job!" He pulled the bunk bed down as if he was a Strong Man World Champion; either that or we were pathetically feeble.

The windowless cabin was a bit like a prison cell and unnervingly dark but it did the job for one night. We had the advantage of a calm crossing with some gentle rocking to lull us to sleep. I'm sure it's very unpleasant on a stormy night, especially if you suffer from motion sickness.

BACK ON THE CONTINENT

We awoke as we approached the Dutch coast after a good night's sleep. We hadn't heard a murmur from the Scottish school group which probably meant they were on the other side of the boat. The 8:30 AM arrival into Rotterdam had seemed very civilised until it dawned on me that 8:30 AM was the new 7:30 AM because we'd lost an hour!

On disembarking, there was a bit of a bottleneck at the bottom of the escalators. Richard and I got separated because I took the stairs to get past the hold-up but Richard didn't get the memo! Dutch border control was a strange mixture of friendly and officious. "Hello," said the border guard, greeting me with a smile. "What is the purpose of your visit?" I was very tempted to say red hot sex for a week in Amsterdam but it was too early in the morning for jokes in response to a stupid question. I don't function well until I've had at least one cup of coffee coursing through my veins so I chickened out and just said 'leisure'.

Another consideration was getting my stamp squeezed onto a page with no space. He was very obliging in this department. If I'd made a flippant comment, he may have slapped it in the middle of one of the few pages I had left for full page visas. When I got a new passport, nine years earlier, I wasn't thinking about becoming a full-time traveller and I certainly never predicted huge Schengen Area stamps every time I set foot in Europe!

The bus from the port to Rotterdam Central Station had to be booked online with P&O. It was an outrageous £10 per person but seemed to be the only option according to the good people of the Interrail Facebook pages. The bus was the team bus for Feyenoord Rotterdam, who were top of the Dutch Football Premiership. I liked the idea of this posh premiership bus that normally chauffeured footballing premiership prima donnas, transporting ferry passengers during the week; it made sense in this cost-of-living crisis!

I had booked the 10:35 AM train from Rotterdam as I wasn't exactly sure what time we'd arrive in Rotterdam. When we got to the platform there was a 10:05 PM to Gouda ready and waiting to depart. I asked a gaggle of ticket inspectors if we could take the earlier train. "Yes," they replied cheerily so we hopped on, congratulating ourselves that we had managed to get ahead of the game. We had, of course, spoken too soon! There was a long day of train travel to go and frequent changes so plenty of scope for things to go wrong.

We travelled through some classic Dutch scenery with polders and a few windmills but there was no sign of the famous Tulip fields. As it was late spring, we'd probably just missed this spectacle. We were only on the train to Gouda for twenty minutes. The next leg to Amersfoort Central was also a short hop of only thirty six minutes. In Amersfoort, there was a wonderful little platform cafe so we managed to get two cups of decent coffee.

After sixteen minutes and a much-needed shot of caffeine, we were on our way again. So far, so good. What could possibly go wrong? An announcement on the train that said it was only going as far as the Dutch border, that's what! I hunted down the ticket inspector to ask her what was going on. "The train is cancelled because of the strike in Germany," she told me. Now let's get this straight, this was the strike that never happened! Yep! What a crazy world we live in! When I'd been planning the start of our Interrail Trip Part 2, a few days earlier, I'd got some weird messages on the rail planner. It said, 'There are no services on this section of the journey.' This was the start of a number of vague messages that would plague Part 2. It could have meant any number of things like 'You can't get ham, egg, chips and a cup of tea' or 'Don't expect loo paper in the toilet', who knows! One of the fabulous 'rail experts' on Facebook said that it would be as a result of the five-day strike in Germany that had been cancelled. Five-day strike? I didn't even know there had ever been plans for a five-day strike in Germany! This was good for my blood pressure but what wasn't good for my blood pressure was all the repercussions caused by a threatened five-day strike that was cancelled at the 11th hour, such as staff and trains in the wrong places! The general consensus on Facebook was that by Tuesday, our day of travel, things should have calmed down. Sadly, that proved to be wishful thinking and there we were being unceremoniously tipped off the train on the Dutch-German border.

I joined a long queue at the information desk to get an answer to the question, 'How the hell do we get to Osnabruck so we can get the connexion to Hamburg?' Richard stayed in a very crowded station cafe with the luggage until I got the answer to the question which was, 'Take the train one hour later towards Osnabruck.' We were now back to square one. So much for being ahead of the game! Luckily, the journey to Hamburg was trouble free after the one-hour delay.

The scenery was flat and agricultural and after weeks of vineyards there was not a vineyard in sight, and it was mainly boring wheat fields but we could relax in first class which was quiet and peaceful.

Our hotel in Hamburg was a fifteen-minute walk from the station. As with many of our Part 2 Northern European hotels, it was an old office block converted into cheap hotel rooms. Well, I say cheap, it was €180 a night! The young Argentinian receptionist had obviously fallen asleep during the Customer Service Training! "Hello, Jayne Dear, booking.com," I said with a smile.

"Fill in a form," she told me with a flick of her head to indicate they were on the nearby table. There was no hint of a smile.

We were on the 7th floor which required us to go up in the old, rickety circa 1960s lift. Richard and I, plus our two huge backpacks could barely fit in. Our twin room was small and dark but it did have an ensuite. I warned Richard to enjoy a last night of an ensuite because in the land of the midnight sun, ensuites in our price range would be rare!

As there was early evening sun, I left Richard slobbing on his bed and headed out to see the old 19th century warehouse district, Speicherstadt. The very tall buildings that lined the waterways stored tobacco, coffee, dried fruit and spices back in the day. I started
with the famous view of the Water Castle, a solid looking building that was an island in the canal. The sun was hiding behind one of the many clouds but when the cloud eventually shifted out of the way, the sun bathed one side of the warehouses, leaving the other side dark and moody.

I zigzagged across the area using the many metal span bridges and booked a table for 8:00 PM at the Fleetschlossen Restaurant, a red brick architectural jewel that was built in 1885 and had started life as a customs house. From grand beginnings, it had slipped to being a fire watch house and later a public toilet block. In 2004, it had re-gained its self-respect when it was restored and turned into a cosy little restaurant.

As I returned to the hotel, it started to rain. Back at the hotel, I went in search of the kettle in the communal kitchen. The Argentinian receptionist had told me not to bother with the kettle in the kitchen as it was dirty. When I went to check its condition myself, I found it didn't even exist! My only option, therefore, was to get reception to give me two paper cups of water. As they were being filled, I chatted with the

Argentinian receptionist and her male Argentinian colleague about my wonderful experiences travelling around Argentina.

I made tea in the room and then Richard and I set off for the restaurant. We started with spicy fish soup and then Richard had curry wurst, that famous German dish, and I had back fish. Richard washed his down with a pint of the local brew; probably the last beer of decent strength he'd see for a while.

After a long night on a boat heading south and a long day on a train heading north, we were still south of our starting point, Beverley in Yorkshire.

SCANDINAVIA, HERE WE COME!

I was excited about the prospect of spending six weeks in Scandinavia. I feel as if it's a spiritual home! Ever since I discovered I was 32% Scandinavian, I've been promoting my credentials as the descendent of a Viking princess. It got me loads of street cred when I was a teacher. "Mess with me and I'll give you a blood eagle," I'd tell them, jokingly, of course! "And you don't want to meet my Uncle Viking Blood Axe!" How can I be so precise? My daughter bought me DNA testing kit for Christmas. All it took was £97 and a quick spit in a test tube and, hey presto, I knew all about where I'd come from. I was more Scandinavian than anything else, in actual fact. It wasn't a surprise. My fair hair and blue eyes are a bit of a give-away! If it had come back as Nigerian with a hint of Ghanaian then I think we'd all know they'd been chucking the test tubes in the bin!

At 7:30 AM, I went down to the reception to get hot water for tea and we left at 8:15 AM for the short walk to the station to catch our 8:56 AM train. After our trials and tribulations of the day before, we were hoping for a much calmer and trouble free journey but no such luck! I was dying for a coffee but all the queues for coffee at the station were a mile long so we proceeded to our platform. Here we realised our train was going to be very crowded. Even first class was packed! No sooner than we had sat down than we were turfed out of our seats by a young Canadian couple who said they had reserved the seats we were in. It transpired that all the seats in first class had signs that said 'may be reserved'! "How unhelpful is that?" I moaned to the Canadians. "Mind you, you don't have a great railway system in Canada!"

"No," they agreed, "just one line in the entire country!"

Richard and I moved to the other end of the carriage and sat on single seats opposite each other. When the ticket inspector came round, I complained about the vague reservation signs. "In the U.K., the signs give specific details about the sections that are reserved."

"I agree," he replied, unexpectedly, "That's what we do in Germany but this is a Danish train. He practically spat out the words 'Danish train'. Blaming the other country is a pattern on cross border trains! Well, why wouldn't you? He was probably thinking, "That shut her up!"

At the border, the police boarded and checked passports. "Isn't Denmark in Schengen?" I asked, knowing full well it was.

"Yes, it is," said the officer. "So why are passports checked?" I asked.

"They must be checked on borders," he told me. This was hardly the point of Schengen. No one had checked our passport between France and Switzerland or Holland and Germany, all in the Schengen. I suspected that, like on the French-Spanish border, the Danish police were checking for illegal migrants and would turn them around and send them back to Germany if they found any. Denmark had experienced a huge influx of migrants in recent years but, in reality, checking passports on trains wasn't going to stop migrants entering Denmark because they could just walk across the border. I'd met many migrants on my recent travels who had employed this tactic.

At the Danish border, the German crew was swapped for a Danish crew. The female ticket inspector tried to move my bag to the next carriage. When I protested, she said she needed to move my bag so she could use the shelves it was leaning against for tea, coffee and snacks. "Fair enough," I said, the words coffee, tea and snacks being music to my ears. A man helped me move my backpack up onto a luggage rack, not a feat I could have performed alone. Unfortunately, the tea was black and green and the coffee was instant but as Richard and I hadn't had our first coffee of the day, we tried a cappuccino instant coffee. As a coffee snob, I wouldn't normally touch instant coffee with a barge pole but I'd recently started eating meat again so I figured I could give an instant coffee a go. To say it was revolting was an understatement but it did wake me up. "What do you think?" I asked Richard.

"Not as good as yesterday's station cappuccino," he moaned. On a more positive note, there were packets of dark chocolate and the female ticket inspector brought around snacks. I had porridge and Richard had a rye bread sandwich. I popped a few sachets of long-life milk into my bag for when I could use my travel coffee maker to make the real deal. As we crossed the flat agricultural landscape of Jutland, I got to talking to our German neighbours, a family of three. They were going to Copenhagen for a long weekend as it was a public holiday the next day for Ascension. We'd been plagued by public holidays since the start of our trip. I know that sounds a bit rich coming from someone who used to enjoy thirteen weeks school holiday a year but they led to crowded trains. It was much easier when they were all in school and work!

We crossed a long bridge and causeway on to Funen Island. As we approached Copenhagen, Danish trains really didn't cover themselves in glory. They announced the train would be nine minutes late. As we only had sixteen minutes to catch our connexion, this was concerning. They said the Stockholm train would wait and announced the platform. They said there would be train staff to meet the train to direct passengers. The Gothenburg train wasn't mentioned so I asked the female ticket inspector about it. "There'll be an announcement closer to Copenhagen," she told me. There was an announcement that gave the platform. "At least we'll be able to ask all those helpful train staff waiting on the platform," I thought.

We were ready and waiting to get off the train as soon as it drew into the station. We flew onto the platform looking for signs to get to platform 5. There were none, diddly squad! And all those helpful train staff? Nowhere to be seen! As we headed towards the station building, I looked behind us and saw an overhead walkway to other platforms. "I think we need to go up the steps," I shouted urgently at Richard. We turned around, climbed the steps and then flew down the stairs to platform 5. Three young backpackers just ahead of us were also heading for the Gothenburg train. "It's not this platform, it's platform 7," said a member of train staff. We all turned around and raced back up the steps. We ran, in a blind panic, along the walkway, desperately searching for platform 7, aware that one false move and we would miss our train. We rushed down the steps onto the train with seconds to go. Recovery time? About thirty minutes before we could even speak without gasping for breath!

We crossed the famous Oresund Bridge into Sweden. At eight kilometres, it's the longest road and rail bridge in Europe. And then it was good riddance to our brief encounter with the Danish train system!

Once in Sweden, we got chatting to some Swedish commuters. They asked if we were heading to Norway for their Independence Day. "It's crazy!" they said. "The whole country goes mad!"

"No, we're staying in Gotenburg overnight," I replied. Commuters in Sweden were heading home for Ascension Day, the next day, like the Germans. "The weather is going to be good," they told me. We got talking about the pandemic. I told them how I'd admired Sweden for being a total outlier in the world by refusing to shut everything down.

"We got a lot of stick from the rest of the world but it was the right thing to do," said one commuter. "I had to tape over my car number plate when I went abroad because there was so much negative feeling towards us!"

We joked about not being able to cough in public anymore without getting funny looks or people moving away from you. Peter, one of the commuters, said he had been eating peanuts during the pandemic when one got stuck in his throat and made him cough. "I had to hold up the packet and wave it vigorously to let people know that was why I was coughing and not because I had the dreaded lurgy."

The conductor announced that you couldn't drink your own alcohol onboard. When I looked quizzically at this, one of our new train buddies explained, "They introduced that rule for the Norwegians and Finns who come over the border to Sweden for the cheap alcohol."

"I guess it's all relative," I joked. "I haven't come to Sweden for cheap alcohol!"

As we approached Malmo, our smooth run up the West Coast of Sweden to Gothenburg became our not so smooth run up the West Coast of Sweden to Gothenburg. It was announced that there had been an 'accident' on the line, north of Malmo. The destination changed from Gothenburg to Malmo. Our new train buddies helped to translate for us what was going on. They said we would have to get a bus to Lund and then catch the train from there up to Gothenburg.

We couldn't believe it! After all our hassles in Germany and Denmark, it was a case of, here we go again! The train gods clearly weren't smiling on us. Luckily, Peter, one of our new train friends, took us under his wing. "Just follow me," he said. We found our way up to the main concourse along with many other confused passengers. Here we were greeted by hundreds of helpful station staff all directing us onto conveniently placed buses.....No, only joking, in reality there wasn't a member of the station staff to be seen. We followed Peter along the length of the station to find the bus. I remember thinking, "I wouldn't have a clue where to go if we didn't have Peter to follow!" Outside, there were various coloured buses. We ignored the green buses which were presumably city buses and headed for the yellow buses. Once at the yellow buses, we were directed over to the other side of the canal. As we crossed to the other side of the bridge, lots of people seemed to be heading back to the station. Peter, our guardian angel, spoke to a man who said the trains were running again.

Back inside the station, it was still chaos but at least the train staff had got off their backsides, put the Internet shopping on hold, grabbed their high vis jackets and got themselves onto the concourse to answer questions. "You sit there," said Peter, "and I'll find out what time the train goes and from which platform."

I asked one of the station staff in high vis what sort of 'accident' had taken place. I was hoping it wasn't another suicide. They will never use the word suicide, preferring something more neutral but word soon gets around, as it did in Angers. "A lorry drove into a bridge," he told me. "They had to stop the trains until a structural engineer had inspected the bridge."

"Bloody hell!" I thought. "All this chaos because some bloke couldn't drive properly. "He was probably just looking at his playlist!" Perhaps it wasn't a sacking offence, but I really hoped that he was being hauled into the office and given a severe reprimand as we sat waiting to get on the move again!

Peter returned to say that the train would leave at 4:08 PM from platform 4 but it was probably best to wait a while before proceeding to the platform as they could change the platform. It meant an hour's delay. Peter lived one hour and twenty minutes further up the line in a place called Angelholm which he told me meant Angel Island. "You should be sat in your garden having a beer at the start of your long weekend," I told him.

"Yes," he sighed, wistfully, "you never know what's going to happen!" He'd worked in management at IKEA for 30 years but in the last eight years he'd worked for a partner company, the Ikano Bank, run by the sons of Ingvar Kamprad, the founder of IKEA.

"Did you meet the great man?" I asked.

"Oh, yes, many times," he replied.

The platform was worryingly chock-a-block with passengers because passengers from the 3:08 PM were now being combined with passengers from the 4:08 PM. When the train arrived, we pushed our way onto the first class carriage and managed to get the last three seats. "All the seats on this side say, 'may be reserved'," said Peter. We'd heard that one before! "They're not reserved on the other side." Peter had to ask a young woman to move her bag off the only seat left in the carriage so he could sit down. I didn't understand the Swedish exchange but it was fairly obvious that she felt that her bag had a right to the seat. His reply was uncompromising and he was soon sitting in her bag's seat!

Sure enough, at the next stop a woman got on with a reservation for my seat. Peter, being the sweetheart that he clearly was, gave up his seat instead and stood in the aisle with many other people and chatted. "We get to know each other on the commute," he said. I'm reliably informed by Richard that this never happened on the C2C commute from Essex to London a.k.a. the Misery Line. When Angelholm was announced I said, "Ah, your stop Peter. I now know two more words of Swedish! Before I met you I knew the Swedish for 'yes' and 'hello' but now I know the words for 'Angel' and 'island'.

"You also know the word for 'cancellation'" he said, laughing.

"And 'delay," joked the woman he'd been chatting with.

"That's sadly true," I replied. "Thank you for all your help! Enjoy your well-deserved beer in the garden!" We felt great very grateful to this stranger for helping us out during what will forever be known as 'The Malmo fiasco'!

When I travel, the kindness of strangers never ceases to amaze me. On my first interrail trip in 1982, my friend and I were buying an ice cream from a street ice cream machine when a man came out of nowhere, paid for the ice creams for us and then off he went, not wanting any thanks.

On our next interrail trip, Jessica and I met some Welsh

electronics students at a bar in Lagos in Portugal when they noticed the Welsh dragon badges on Jessica's bag. We enjoyed an evening of laughter and jokes before Jessica and I headed back to our accommodation. It wasn't long before we realised we were being followed by a shifty looking man so we walked back up to the busier main street, hoping to shake him off. Concerningly, however, he continued to follow us. Just as we were starting to panic, we bumped into the four boys from the land of dragons and they offered to walk us home! Mr Shifty must have got the shock of his life when we produced four heavies to scare him off and we never saw him again!

As I like to couch surf and hitchhike on my travels, I am very reliant on the kindness of strangers. It never ceases to amaze me how kind my couch surf hosts are, putting themselves out to give me a bed, a meal and even a guided tour; and when I took up hitchhiking in later life, I got a myriad of lifts throughout Albania, Argentina and southeast Asia and met some lovely and interesting people. Top lift? A ride in an ambulance!

It is very easy to get paranoid about threats from people who want to do you harm but it is best to keep it in perspective. Don't get me wrong, I was held up at gunpoint and robbed in 2020 in Valparaiso in Chile so I know all about the scumbags of this world! At the end of the day, however, 99.99% of people mean you no harm and are kind, helpful and supportive when you're out of your comfort zone and in their jungle!

GOTHENBURG

We arrived in sun kissed Gothenburg at 7:20 PM. I hate to go on about it but we were an hour later than scheduled! We walked across the huge square in front of the station and then over both the canal and the river and through the botanical gardens.

Fifteen minutes later, we were at our hotel. It was two floors of an office block and our twin bedroom was an end room with lots of light. I was glad we didn't have a smaller, windowless room on the other side of the corridor. What we didn't have, however, as we were now in Scandinavia, was an ensuite bathroom. There were shared toilets and showers opposite. Luckily, we'd come prepared with our travel toilets; perfect for a quick wee in the middle of the night! My own little ensuite! Who wants to emerge into a corridor at 4 AM? Certainly not me!

As it was already 8:00 PM, we set off to find historic Haja District and a restaurant. Reception had shown me where it was on a paper map so I took that rather than put it into Google Maps. Big mistake! I was soon totally disorientated. I'll never moan about Google Maps again! Richard was grumbling loudly under his breath about having been on the train all day and that he just wanted to eat, not sightsee. My plan to parachute in and see a specific area of a city I'd been to twice before had been seriously compromised by the hour's delay.

I asked two young men for directions. "We've only been

here for five hours but we know it's down this way. You can come with us because we're going that way." One of them spoke English with a public schoolboy accent. For a moment, I thought he was English but he'd just lived there for three years. I always contend that the Scandinavians speak better English than the English! "We're from Norway," they told me. "We have come for the weekend to escape Norway's National Day. It's crazy!"

"We've heard about it," I replied.

"It's mainly for children. We loved it when we were kids but not anymore." They turned off but told us to continue on.

Once in the old town, we had a wander and a meal at Hemma Hos Restaurant in the heart of the old town. The restaurant was full of young couples gazing into each other's eyes over a candle lit table. As we'd been married for nearly thirty four years, Richard and I were more interested in our Swedish meatballs with mashed potato and lingon berries in a rich sauce. Richard had a pint of weak local beer and we worked out that we were level with Aberdeen.

ONWARDS AND UPWARDS TO NORWAY!

S o, it was going to be third time lucky, right? Surely our third day of train travel in rich and efficient northern Europe would be trouble free? We knew it wouldn't be even before we went to bed. I'd downloaded my journey a few days before. The train departed for Oslo via Trollhattan at 9:50 AM, a very respectable time.

When Richard, however, went to upload the identical journey to 'my trip' on the Rail Planner app, he couldn't find a 9:50 AM, there was only a 9:30 AM. It transpired that the Gothenburg to Trollhattan section had morphed into a bus. The Trollhattan to Oslo leg was still a train but it said 'conditions apply'. I didn't have a clue what that meant and nor did the 'rail experts' on Facebook know. We decided to delay our start and give ourselves more time by going on the next departure at 1:30 PM.

Our room was very reasonable £49. This was an absolute bargain as it included breakfast. The spread included bread, meat, cheese, cereal, yoghurt and fruit. They even had filtered coffee.

After breakfast, while Richard relaxed in the room, I walked back to the Haga District to see it with some sunlight as the sun had set by the time we got there the day before. It had a Scandinavian vibe with many wooden houses.

I got back to the hotel just before check out at 11:00 AM. Richard said they'd already been banging on the door to check we knew checkout was 11:00 AM. Reception had been closed before I'd left so I hadn't been able to ask for late checkout. I found the cleaning woman who was rapidly heading in our direction. "Do you speak English?" I asked. She didn't but conveyed she was from Kosovo. I pressed on in English but she clearly didn't understand. She replied in Kosovan which I obviously didn't understand. Having reached an impasse and concluded we were getting nowhere, I returned to the room. Her colleague popped up at 11:20 AM and gave us 10 more minutes. He said we could sit in the breakfast room so we headed up there and whiled away the time with a cup of tea. Here we met a woman who was also in Sweden to escape the dreaded Independence Day. Escape from Norway on Independence Day was clearly a thing.

We retraced our steps to the station where I left Richard with the luggage and set out to find the elusive bus. It said bus on the station board but that was it, no signs or, heaven forbid, people to guide us in the right direction. I found a young woman in a high viz jacket who, as it turned out, wasn't a member of station staff but she agreed to try and help me anyway. Once I'd explained my conundrum, she said the bus went from the bus station. "So, it doesn't even go from the train station?" I asked, incredulously.

"No, you need to go out of here, turn left, through the square, ignore the two bus stops, keep going past the big building and then go right about five minutes later."

Unbelievable! It felt as if they sold you a ticket and then went, 'Make your own way there!'

Before we left the station, I went down some steps to the station toilets. Unlike on a train where there's a toilet that's much beloved by my weak bladder, there are no toilet on many buses. I was directed to a posh hotel reception style desk where there was a charge of one pound to have a wee! I don't pay much more for a bed for the night in South America or South East Asia!

We headed for the bus station where I had to ask around to find the right bus but I did, at long last, find two helpful train staff. And there was me thinking they'd become extinct! We got the bus to Trollhattan where we caught the train to Oslo.

ACROSS THE BORDER TO NORWAY!

We crossed the border into Norway at 3:42 PM. It was a country we planned to explore from top to bottom and inside out on this trip. It was my fourth visit. I'd originally visited whilst interrailing in 1986. It was Richard's first time. He didn't seem as excited as me at the prospect of adding a new country to the list! When I was crossing a border from Cambodia to Vietnam the year before, a young man in the queue to get our passports stamped proudly announced it would be his thirtieth country. "It's my ninety second," I told him.

"Wow!" he said. "Ninety-two? That's way more than me!" He sounded very deflated. I hadn't meant to take the wind out of his sails.

"I've still got one hundred and five to go! You're much younger than me," I told him. "You've got plenty of time to catch up!"

On the journey north, I saw my first moose and several deer. One of my most vivid memories from my 1986 Interrail trip across Swedish Lapland was a huge bull moose with the classic horns crossing the train tracks. It was a magnificent beast and luckily, it avoided the train and lived to fight another day.

Oslo Central was like the United Nations. People of all colours and creeds were milling around this large station. We found a seated area as we had an hour and a half to wait for our train to Sandefjord and I got talking to some men who were talking loudly in Arabic. Too loudly for Richard who was sat next to them! They said they were originally from Somalia. One had lived in Norway for twenty years, another for ten years and another for three years.

We got a busy commuter train south, down the Oslo Fjord to Sandefjord. It still felt very Swedish. We'd have to wait until we got to the West Coast for full on Norway. Mind you, we weren't complaining as the rolling countryside dotted with rust red farms was very pleasant.

SANDEFJORD

In sandefjord, we had a forty-minute walk to Asle's place. I'd decided to get our accommodation as close to the train station as possible in Scandinavia, especially as we were only doing one to two nights in each place but this listing was so much cheaper than everywhere else and he got an impressive 9.7 review rating that I had no choice but to bite the bullet. Richard moaned as we slogged our way out to Asle's place on the edge of town, in a quiet residential area.

Once there we knocked on the door but no one came and opened it. I went to the front of the house where there was an open window and shouted booking.com. A black man with an African accent poked his head out of the window. "There's a code," he told me.

"I don't have it," I replied.

"I'll come down and open the door," he said.

Once in, I realised Zachary from Tanzania wasn't the host. Seconds later, Asle appeared; a very tall, handsome man with long curly grey hair. He was half 1960s hippy and half Viking warrior. He was a warm and very welcoming host. He couldn't do enough for us. He showed us to a small double on the first floor. He'd made-up the king size bed with two single duvets, as requested. Richard is a duvet thief and a nightmare to share a duvet with, although he likes to accuse me of a similar crime!

Asle offered us homemade tomato, cheese and onion pizza. We had only booked a room so this was a big bonus. I could see why he got 10 out of 10 reviews from most of his guests.

Another man from Africa came into the kitchen. "I'm from Tanzania," he told me. "It's in Africa."

"Yes," I know, I replied, feeling rather affronted. "We spent our honeymoon there!!" He introduced himself as Andrew. "I'll remember that," I told him, "because our son is called Andrew." We chatted about the Serengeti and our wonderful wildlife experiences in Tanzania over thirty years earlier. Andrew told me that he and Zachary were communications engineers and working with a Norwegian company for three weeks to learn about airport communication systems. They were returning to Tanzania in a few days.

Later, Zachery proudly showed us a photo of his fiancé who he was due to marry the following October. "We've never met," he told me.

"Never met?" I queried, thinking I'd misheard him.

"No," he said, "it's an arranged marriage. We won't meet until the wedding but we talk on the phone." He seemed genuinely smitten with his telephone fiancé and in this day and age of the video call, who am I to judge? He then announced that we were both invited to the wedding and although he'd only just met us, I think he genuinely meant it!

Richard and I relaxed on the sofas in the lounge for the rest of the evening. Asle had given up his job three months earlier to run his house as a guest house full time. He had eight rooms, including a two-bed self-contained unit in the basement where there was also a bar. If all the beds were occupied, Asle slept in the bar room where there was a large sofa.

His trump card was offering free airport transfers 24/7 to guests. It added up to a great business model. I had wondered why people wanted to fly to a small town one and a half hours south of Oslo but I soon realised that in airport terms, it wasn't an hour and a half south of Oslo, it was, of course, an Oslo airport, served by budget airlines, similar to London Stansted which is nowhere near London!

Asle was divorced and had grown up children. His son, he said, had been a problem child at school but was now a G.P. which was an impressive transformation.

Before we went to bed, we worked out that we were level with the Orkney islands so we still hadn't cleared Britain's most northerly point.

We had a lazy morning after our three-day train marathon. We had breakfast mid-morning in the lounge as Asle offered a range of cereals and fruit, and excellent machine coffee. Luckily, we still had some train milk as he only had oat milk which seemed strange to me but proved to be very popular in Scandinavia. Another downside was that there was no toilet on our floor. The closest toilet was down the spiral staircase. Can you imagine doing that twice in the night? I know I've said it before but it was lucky that we had our travel toilets! Both the oatmilk and toilet were very small issues in the bigger picture! I'd already decided to give Asle a 10/10 review.

Asle had a robot vacuum cleaner, a small black disc that prowled the floor looking for dust and dirt. At one point, it skirted around my feet while we were having breakfast, like a dog sniffing for crumbs under the table. Eventually it said, "Finished cleaning, returning to doc." On close inspection, I concluded that it definitely couldn't compete with a Dyson and a human being but I guess it had a place in the lives of busy or elderly people.

Asle kindly offered to take us out on a tour of the area once he'd finished his chores at about 3:30 PM. He wanted to invite the middle-aged Italian couple who'd recently arrived. They spoke very little English, which must have been hard in Scandinavia. When the Italian woman approached me, thinking I was a member of staff, and asked me some questions, mainly in Italian, I tried to invite her but she didn't understand and they were nowhere to be seen when we set off.

We headed off in Asle's car for a few hours. It felt more like couch surfing than booking.com. We wound our way up through farming country, waving to farmers who were chopping wood. Winter had barely ended but they were already preparing for the next winter throughout Scandinavia. We saw large pallets of firewood everywhere. Asle said he always bought two pallets for the winter at a cost of £300.

In a glade, at the start of a forest, was a burial ground. Istrehagan Burial Ground was an Iron Age site that had teeth like stones of varying sizes that were arranged in a ship like formation. Some were about 4.5 metres high so Asle said it was known as the local Stonehenge. I sort of got the comparison but it was far from the real Stonehenge.

Asle complained that the town was best avoided. He'd been to the shops earlier and said it was mayhem after the public holiday closures. He told us that Sandefjord used to be a centre for the whaling industry and pointed to a sign that displayed a huge tail of a whale. Norway still, controversially, hunted whales. "We only hunt whales that aren't endangered," claimed Asle, trying to excuse a whole nation. After it was banned, a few nations, notably Japan and Norway, flouted the rules, using spurious excuses such as 'we're doing it for research purposes'. Yeah right, nothing to do with the menus of Tokyo and Bergen.

Next, Asle took us to the House of a whaling magnet from Sandefjord. He had no heirs and had millions of unpaid tax so when he and his widow died, it was confiscated by the authorities.

We walked down the long drive to the large brick house. From the grounds at the back, there was a terrace with views of the town and Sandefjord Fjord, from where you could get a free boat to Sweden. "Free!" I exclaimed. "My Mum and dad would have been very jealous!" They lived on the Isle of Wight all their married life and made a career out of moaning and groaning about the cost of the Isle of Wight ferry. When the first space tourist went into orbit, my dad worked out that mile for mile, his trip cost less than the Isle of Wight ferry!

"It makes its money from selling duty free," Asle said.

As we left the house, which was hosting a wedding, Asle asked, "Have you ever gate crashed a wedding?"

"No," I replied. "A few art exhibitions with free nibbles but never a wedding!"

"My wife and I used to do it," he confessed. "As people either know the bride or the groom, no one knows if you're not connected to either one. On one occasion we helped ourselves to the free buffet and made the most of the free bar. Eventually, they said, 'We'd like you to leave now!' We had terrible hangovers the next day!"

We ended our tour at a grassy mound. On the face of it, it was unremarkable but, in reality, it was of great significance as it was where they found the Viking ships now in a museum in Oslo. They were raided by grave robbers in pre-modern times but the ships were too big to half hitch and would probably only have been used for firewood. Luckily, they were left alone until their true value could be appreciated by the history conscious modern era.

In the early evening, a larger than life, in every sense of the word, English woman called Sandra arrived. She collapsed onto the sofa near us and spread out like a large beanbag.

Her life was a mosaic of dramatic and varying experiences. In the words of Richard, "I'm not sure everything she told us stacked up!" but she was certainly an entertaining storyteller. She'd lived in Beverley for seven years so we immediately had something in common. She'd moved to Leeds to look after her parents who were now dead but still lived there. She turned out to be the first interrailer that we'd come across. She'd purchased a two-month pass but had returned home several times to feed her fish. She was fifty nine years old and beyond her parents, she didn't seem to have sustained any long-term relationships, including with her siblings. Thirty minutes in the company Sandra gave us some indication as to why this was! She was rather intense! She'd been married to a Frenchman called Pascal in her early years and they'd run a French restaurant together in London that was regularly visited by Pascal's French friends who were "in the trade". Some worked in the French wine industry and told a story about how they'd once got drunk and labelled bottles of cheap plonk with the labels meant for expensive fine wine and vice versa. They'd laughed at the thought of someone who'd spent a few hundred francs on an expensive bottle of wine, opening it up to find that they had the cheap stuff. "All the educated idiots who praised their expensive wine were unaware that it was not so very different to vinegar!" laughed Sandra. I wasn't sure they would all have been fooled. She had divorced Pascal and they had lost touch.

Another chapter of her life had involved social work. She'd mentored two fifteen-year-old girls who'd gone to prison. "In the past, they sent fifteen-year-olds to prison," she said. "Now they don't go until they're eighteen." I think she meant young offenders' institutions. I never remember under eighteens being sent to adult prisons. In the early 1990s the killers of James Bulger were sent to secure units.

"What did they do to land up in prison?" I asked. "It must have been serious."

"Violence against other children in their children's home," replied Sandra. Their mothers had got pregnant with their pimps. They were very angry all the time.

"I'm not surprised," I commented. "It's hard to imagine the impact of that level of turmoil and insecurity!" Luckily, most children have the anchor of loving parents but these girls had been cast adrift from day one. Sandra said she had fostered them when they came out prison. Her lodger, who was paying good money, had questioned the safety of this arrangement and I had to agree that she probably had a point. Who would want to pay £350 per calendar month to live with troubled teens?! Sandra's role as a social worker made her an expert on education. She contradicted my views on Ofsted and praised the academy system, making me bristle. She probably didn't notice my reaction as she never bothered to ask about my thirty-five years of experience as a teacher! The show was definitely all about Sandra!

Asle very generously cooked us vegetarian curry using a recipe learnt from Pakistani guests and opened a bottle of red wine. "Do I look as if I need feeding up?" asked Sandra, self mockingly. After dinner he invited us to his bar in the basement. "I'll prepare you a White Russian," he said.

"I hope this isn't going to be like a scene from 'Fifty Shades of Grey'," joked Sandra.

"You'll have to wait and see," quipped Asle.

Asle's bar had neon signs, and post cards and banknotes from his guests on display. His White Russians were a superb! Coffee liquid mixed with vodka. When Asle heard Richard was a whisky aficionado, he found him a Scottish whisky. Sandra, very sensibly, started to organise her Sixtieth Birthday Bash at Asle's place.

We slept well! The value of the food and drink which is expensive in Norway had more than covered the cost of the room. What did Asle get out of it? Our scintillating company, I guess!

After a lie in, we went down for breakfast mid-morning. The place was deserted, and the fridge had been completely cleared out, including of our bits and pieces. When Asle appeared, he was surprised to see us. He thought everyone had gone. He offered to go to the shops to get us replacement supplies but I could hardly accept this generous gesture after his great hospitality. Instead, he offered to run us to the station in order to assuage his guilt. It saved us a forty-minute walk so we were very grateful.

THE FAR SOUTH
OF NORWAY

We caught the 12:18 AM train to Skien through deep wooded valleys that had a hint of Norway. In Skien, we were forced to turn around as onward trains that would connect with the line to Kristiansand only ran on weekdays. We, therefore, had to take the train back to Drammen where we had to wait one hour and fifteen minutes for the train to Kristiansand. The 'Silent Carriage' was far from silent, especially when two drunks got on. Our friends in Switzerland would not have been impressed!

I had had to reserve seats in 1st class on an online chat for this intercity train and all subsequent inter cities in Norway. It was free and relatively straightforward but a bit of a hassle, nonetheless.

In Drammen, some young men were whizzing around the station concourse on electric scooters. They were an absolute menace but there were no station staff to berate them and kick them out. I was pretty certain they weren't there to catch a train! Soon after we got to the station our train started to show as delayed. The length of delay gradually ticked up and there was, frustratingly, no explanation. If I could have added 'moose on the line' to my list of reasons for delay, I could have excused Norwegian Trains but I suspected it was a more mundane reason!

The train eventually rolled into the station and departed thirty two minutes late. A young man working on the free tea, coffee and snacks told me, when interrogated, that the train hadn't been able to leave Oslo because the air conditioning hadn't been working. Definitely not as exciting as 'moose on the track'! I concluded that 'Go Ahead Trains' should be renamed 'Go Slow Trains'!

The free snacks cheered me up! Porridge oats, raisins, Ryvita sandwiches and Norwegian Quality Street were all on the menu. I think I could have travelled around Norway on free train snacks, saving myself a fortune, but Richard looked horrified at this prospect when I mentioned it!

On the four-hour journey, the train snaked its way along narrow finger lakes full of small rocky islands covered in pine trees. Their reflection on the water created a round symmetrical image. Pine and birch tree covered mountains rose up in between the lakes and sometimes rocky cliffs were poised at right angles to the lake. A few grassy valleys protected isolated farming settlements. In the distance, there were snow covered mountains.

KRISTIANSAND

When we arrived in Kristiansand around 8:30 PM, it was blue sky and sunshine. Asla had told us it was Norway's holiday resort. Okay, it is the most southerly city in Norway but that still only meant it was on a latitude with Aberdeen. Funnily enough, I've never thought, "Oh I must go to Aberdeen for my holiday in the sun!" It's all relative, I suppose. He did admit that most Norwegians go to Thailand for their sun, particularly in the winter.

It was a fifteen-minute walk through the centre of town that was built on the grid system, to our hotel. It was only when we got to the hotel that I realised that it didn't have a 24/7 reception. You had to download the JustIn App. This could then send a code to your phone number. You had to enter the code into the app in order to access your electronic key. I kid you not! What's wrong with a good old fashioned physical key? Even one of those stupid plastic things you have to stick into a slot with great precision to make sure you get a green light flash up rather than a red one! I felt as if I'd been propelled into the future!

Owing to my age, I didn't grow up with computers. My school acquired a single computer when I was in the sixth form which was the size of a small car. I spent about ten minutes looking at it and that was it! I'm not without I.T. skills but I normally need backup in order to keep up. When I worked, that was in the form of the lovely techy boys (they were normally men rather than women) who would always take pity on me when I needed help and spoke to them nicely. Post work, I had had to rely on my children who were far less sympathetic. "Oh, for goodness sake, Mum! You do it like this!" They'd press an inordinate number of buttons and get me to where I needed to be but do you think I could repeat the process, if necessary? Not a chance!

I now had to find Wi-Fi to download the app I needed in order to receive the code. It all felt very overwhelming. A person at a reception desk was much simpler! I would never again complain about filling in the stupid registration form! After a few deep breaths, I went over the road to the Indian restaurant. The staff there were lovely. "Can I use your Wi-Fi, please?" I asked.

"Yes, of course!" I downloaded the app and, sensing my stress, they gave me a glass of cold water. Having received the code I needed to access the electronic key, I returned to Richard who was guarding the bags outside what, according to booking.com, should have been the entrance to the hotel. It wasn't. A local young man advised us the entrance to the hotel was one street behind and reception was on the street at right angles. We worked our way around to what we hoped was the entrance but we had no luck opening the hotel's main door with the electronic key. After lots of swearing and cursing, Richard happened to touch the key on the phone screen and magically the door opened. Mind you, we still had to get into the room itself so we weren't home and dry yet. We went up to the third floor in the lift, found our room and, hey presto, we were in! We felt as if we had just become members of Mensa!

The large hotel room had a king sized bed that was dwarfed by the size of the room. It should really have been turned into a studio apartment but all it had was a kettle. This element of the hotel we had actually planned for. We had cuppa soup using the kettle and sandwiches.

We checked out at 11:30 AM and left our bags in reception. Yes! It was actually open for a few hours! Julia, the pleasant young receptionist, said we were welcome to leave our bags behind reception. It would close at 12:30 PM but as there was a party in the restaurant, the building would remain open. "If there's a problem, you can ring me as I only live 5 minutes away," she kindly told us, proving a human being is much better than an on-line key!

Kristiansand looked every bit the grande dame of holiday resorts. It was bathed in warm sunshine and covered in a bright blue sky. As if to prove a point, people were sunbathing in their bathing costumes along the waterfront and there was even a small golden sand beach. We passed the fortress and a variety of fountains and statues until we got to the restored warehouse area of classic red and yellow buildings. Most, but not all, were now restaurants. A large cruise liner was parked at the end of town, its image reflected in the modern building with a wave like structure for a roof.

We returned to the hotel to check our bags were still there and that we could access them and then I went a quick look around the nearby old town area of Posebyen. I left Richard grumbling in reception about needing to get to the station and had a wander around the streets full of classic whitewashed wooden houses with colourful flowers in pots, window boxes and small gardens.

We walked back to the train station and from there caught the 2:14 PM train to Stavanger, a three hour and thirty three minute journey. Richard couldn't get his interrail pass to work, which I think can be a common problem. Luckily, the ticket inspector accepted my pass and the two reservation e-mails. Most of the journey was more of the same but as we neared Stavanger and hit the Atlantic West Coast, it flattened out and became more like the West Coast of Scotland. People were making the most of the good weekend weather and zipping around the lakes and rivers in all sorts of crafts.

STAVANGER

O nce in central Stavanger, we had to find our way to our couch surf host. To date, I'd only couch surfed on my own but the high cost of absolutely everything in Norway had led me to look into it as an option. Sixty-five-year-old Joe had accepted my request for three nights. He'd advised me to download the Kolumbus bus ticket app. He said it was cheaper to buy the tickets on there, so I had done this before arrival. It was another example of Norway being run by robots, if you ask me!

We had to take a #16 bus from near the Radisson Blue Hotel which was near the train station. It didn't go until 6:42 PM as it was a Sunday so we had forty five minutes to waste. The large, fragrant smelling hotel reception with soothing music, Wi-Fi, posh loos and, wait for it, free sweets, was the perfect place to while away the time. We felt a bit out of place in this large, expensive business hotel so we sank into the comfy chairs behind the pillars. It was, however, so busy with people coming and going that nobody really took any notice of us.

The bus took fifteen minutes to wind its way up and out of town then along the fjord. We got off at the bus stop Joe suggested but we got a bit confused because some jerk had painted out the last few letters of Joe's street name. As a consequence, we went off in the wrong direction but by a process of trial and error, we eventually worked that out and got back on track.

Joe's house was in a stunning position. It had 180 degree views of the mountains to the south of Stavanger and the fjord. In a message, Joe had said that if there was no answer then he would be around the back, in the garden. This is where we found him with his dad, Rolf. They were having a BBQ, the first of the season, and they invited us to join them. They also offered us red and white wine. Rolf was knocking back the white wine by the tumbler full. I guess the beauty of being ninety-four years old and on borrowed time is that you just don't have to give a damn!

Rolf and his wife lived on the ground floor and Joe lived on the top floor. Joe's ninety-six-year-old mum had broken her hip and was recovering from a hip replacement in respite care. She was due to return home the following Thursday. Joe was sixty-five and worked for the local social welfare department. He was also head of the Norwegian Federation of Trade Unions. This was an impressive sounding title but entirely voluntary so unpaid. He was a carpenter by trade and had worked at a hydroelectric power plant in the past. Although Norway is rich in oil and gas, most of this is exported and Norway uses the energy generated by hydroelectricity. It made sense because it had more than enough raging rivers to power China, let alone keep the lights on in Norway.

Rolf had some amazing stories to tell. He reminded me of why I love talking to people in their nineties. I go back a long way but they still remembered the war and its aftermath, a period that had always been part of history to me. Rolf and his family of 13 lived in eastern Norway during the Second World War. This area was less impacted by the Nazi occupation than the strategically important West Coast. "Did you see any Germans?" I asked.

"Oh, yes!" he replied. "They were all over the place." Out of the eleven siblings, he was the 4th eldest and the only living survivor.

Just as interesting was his two-week hitchhiking trip south through Germany and then over to London in 1946, immediately after the war. He got lifts in lorries. "I was shocked by the scenes of devastation I encountered. Germany was far worse than England," he told me. I told him about my family's experiences of living in London during the war when my grandparents had an Anderson shelter in the back garden and were bombed out twice. How they went with my mum and her sister to sleep in underground stations, and how my mum and her sister were later evacuated to live with their grandparents in Gloucestershire.

I was proud of inter railing around Europe in the eighties; travelling through the Australian Outback; connecting with classrooms in China, Japan and Africa; taking up hitchhiking for a three-week trip in Albania at the age of fifty-eight; and travelling the length of South America but Rolf's travels were something else. Rolf had been a psychologist all his working life, dealing with trauma so I guess this trip had set him on the road to this career.

"How did you meet your wife?" I asked him.

"At the railway station in Copenhagen, she was the prettiest girl there." Sixty-nine years later they were still together. Now that's what I call a great love story!

The next day Joe went off to work before we got up. We had porridge in the lounge and left mid-morning. We walked into town. My theory was that it was downhill and saved us six pounds on the bus fare. Richard's theory was it was one and a half hours of useless torture that he could do without.

We stopped at Ledaal House grounds and Breidabikk House Museum, a typical 18th century house. Both were temporarily closed but were still on the tourist bus route.

Once in the very centre, we had a wander through the old town of Stavanger, full of pretty white dashboard houses. What wasn't so pretty were the hordes of cruise passengers on guided tours through the Old Town. Their home for the week, a monstrosity of a skyscraper, was parked smack bang in town, right behind the quaint old town. Every time I tried to take a photo of one of the attractive old town cobbled streets that wound their way down to the harbour, I was confronted by the cruise ship which rose up incongruously at the end of the street and totally spoilt the effect.

We had a picnic lunch in a small park in the old town that looked over the Valberg Tower, a fire watch tower built 1853, on the other side of the harbour. From his vantage point, the highest in the town, the watchmen had to look out for fires and then presumably shout "fire" loudly before the telephone was invented.

We looked around the Canning and Printing Musuem. Most interesting was the Canning Museum in a disused sardine canning factory that had several tall chimneys. Canning was big business from the 1870s until the 1970s in Stavanger. You could peer into ovens and see how sardines were processed and stuck in a can. The printing section showed the printing of the variety of labels for the small cans. There was a huge photo of women working at the factory. I studied their blank faces and wondered which factory I would have worked in if I'd been born a hundred years earlier.

We then walked down to the harbour, dominated by the enormous floating hotel and looked over at the old classic wooden warehouses, now restaurants and bars. Sadly, the 12th century Stavanger Cathedral, built by Englishman Reginald of Worcester, later known as Bishop Reginald, was closed and covered in scaffolding.

We headed back to Joe's place on the bus where we had dinner downstairs in Rolf's kitchen. Joe cooked Arctic char, a Norwegian fish that is common in the cold water around Scandinavia, which we had with boiled potatoes and carrot salad. He then gave us a tour of Scandinavian alcohol. Linie Aquavit from Lysholm had been matured in oak sherry casks at sea. Even today it is, according to its label, sailed to the other side of the world and back again. I wasn't quite sure what the point of that was but it was strong stuff. Equally strong was the 12-year-old Nissens Reserve. Its label showed a fat drunk man with a long white beard and very red pointed hat, slumped against a rock. He was next to a huge barrel and had a pint-sized glass full of the stuff in his hand. No wonder he was drunk! Finally, we headed off to Iceland for an Einstok toasted porter beer.

When I returned from popping to the loo upstairs, Richard informed me I'd missed Rolf singing. After several tumblers of white wine, he'd burst into song. "I thought he was never going to stop!" joked Richard.

PULPIT ROCK

Having spent £30 per person to go to Pulpit Rock, we awoke to miserable weather. It was cloudy and wet. My heart sank. During breakfast, however, it was suddenly all change and the clouds cleared to be replaced with clear blue sky. My spirits soared. We left at 9:50 AM and got the 10:45 AM bus from outside the Radisson Blue Hotel so we could stock up a few boiled sweets for the journey!

Our route out of the city took us over a large bridge with beautiful views back over the cityscape. The ubiquitous cruise ship could be seen parked up, a different one to the day before.

Next came the longest underwater road tunnel in the world at fourteen kilometres long. We entered bathed in sunlight and emerged under cloud. My heart sank again! We wound our way along a fjord and then up into the mountains. The blue sky and sunshine could be seen bathing the coast but it stubbornly refused to move inland.

Joe had assured us that the path was steep but definitely a path or steps. "So, you don't have to clamber over boulders?" I asked Joe.

"Oh no," he replied.

The so-called steps, built by Sherpas from Nepal, were very uneven and often required a big step up. Steps was an exaggeration; they were boulders of different shapes and sizes. Richard and his two replacement knees, circa 2020, struggled.

I could see Richard was getting upset and it didn't help

when a middle-aged American man announced he'd turned back shortly after Richard had slipped on one of the boulder steps. He was ready to turn back then and there. "Just take it steady," I told him, trying to encourage him to keep going. 'You don't understand," he replied, sounding frustrated. "I don't want to injure myself!"

It was definitely a fine line between encouraging him to push on and pushing him too far. He continued on, slowly and steadily over rocky and uneven steps, along board walks, down short sections and across long stretches of bare rock where prayer flags left by the Sherpas fluttered.

As we got closer and it seemed Richard would make it, he moaned about people who bounded along like mountain goats. Finally, after two and a quarter hours, we made it to the famous Pulpit Rock. I'd seen so many photos of it, I felt as if I'd been there before. Initially, low cloud engulfed the scene but gradually the clouds cleared and large patches of blue sky allowed the sun to light up the landscape and the famous rock which precipitously plunged down into the fjord, hundreds of metres below. Clouds still sat on the mountains further down the fjord but it was better than nothing. All those young people on our bus who had already been and gone had missed out!

I lay on my stomach and peered over the edge into the abyss. It was very dramatic but not for the faint hearted or anyone afraid of heights.

When Richard and I went to the edge of the rock to get our photo taken with the fjord behind, we were barked at by an aggressive middle-aged Norwegian man. "There's a queue," he said abruptly.

"Says who?" I demanded. "We're in the middle of the wilderness!" He made similar demands of other people. Then I realised he had someone about fifty metres away on the path leading to the walk, poised and ready to take a photo of him looking like a right twat. On the count of three, he did a star jump in the air. He repeated this several times, hogging a large area of the rock so no one else could access it. "What do you think I'd get for pushing him over the edge?" I asked Richard.

We had a picnic and then Richard started back down. I walked up above the rock to get a classic view down over the Pulpit Rock and the fjord beyond. I started my descent an hour later than Richard and I only caught up with him near the bottom. Feeling exhausted, we headed for the Pulpit Rock Mountain Lodge and sneaked into the 'guest only area' with lovely picture windows to frame the views for an hour until our bus back to Stavanger at 6:15 PM.

The blue sky had pushed back from the coast to give beautiful views of the fjord on the way back to Stavanger.

Joe was out training for the evening so we made spaghetti for dinner. When Joe returned, we chatted and gave him a card and present, a small token of our gratitude.

UP THE WEST COAST TO BERGEN!

We had breakfast at Joe's and left mid-morning. We got the bus to the centre and had a short stop at the Radisson Blue for the loo and sweets. Our bus left at 11:15 AM from the nearby bus station. Once at the bus station we deposited our bags in the luggage storage below and made our way to the top deck. It was a two to one seat configuration so Richard sat on a single seat a third of the way back and I headed for the front seats as the side windows were heavily tinted which was not at all desirable on the day when there was no sun. A late middle-aged German couple on a two-week trip to Norway occupied the right-hand side seats and a young woman and her bag occupied the left hand side seats. When I asked the young woman to move her bag so I could sit down, she looked at me disdainfully. You would have thought I'd asked her to remove her child from the seat. I looked back at her with equal disdain until she angrily ripped her bag from the seat and stuffed it between her legs. Her thick makeup looked as if it had been applied by her trowel and was more suited to a nightclub than the bus to Bergen. Her feet encroached well into my leg space so I jiggled my legs up and down to make a point.

The four-and-a-half-hour journey was like island hopping.

We worked our way northwards through numerous tunnels and across many bridges. On an island, the smooth rocks that bordered the sea made it look like the West Coast of Scotland. Our first ferry at 12:30 PM was 25 minutes. On returning to the bus, the young woman who wanted two seats to herself, moved further down the bus. 1-0 to me!

It was more island hopping for the next leg, over numerous bridges to another ferry; very sadly in the rain.

The second ferry was also about 25 minutes and then it was a short drive to Bergen.

At Bergen Bus Station, as we waited for our luggage to be unloaded, I laughed at the memory of seeing sacks of potatoes, huge fronds of bananas and crates of ducks being unloaded from long distance buses in South America where buses also acted as cargo lorries.

Our 2-bedroom apartment was supposed to be close to the station but first we ended up going in the wrong direction and then we ended up at the wrong apartment, an apartment that I'd put in favourites before I'd found it was 'sold out' when I went to book it. I always test length of time to accommodation in Google Maps. My mistake was failing to remove it from Google Maps when I couldn't book it.

It was back in the other direction again with Richard moaning and groaning loudly once I'd entered the details for the apartment I had actually booked. Luckily, the apartment I had eventually booked, early that morning, was by far superior, in a fabulous area and much better value so the story had a happy ending!

It was smack bang in the centre of the old town and heavily reduced. Unusually, it had two bedrooms. We spent a few hours chilling out and then headed over to the harbour, a fifteen-minute walk, to see the old warehouses and fortress, as well as the cathedral. We were even treated to a bit of blue sky and sunshine. As Bergen is the wettest place in Europe, with rain 300 days a year, we had to be grateful for small mercies. The seafood restaurants and stalls sold minke whale amongst an array of other fish and seafood.

We stopped at the cheapish Remi 1000 supermarket on the way back and returned to the apartment to eat and use the washing machine. Our smelly clothes were in much need of a wash!

BERGEN TO OSLO

The next morning, we caught the famous Bergen to Oslo train at 11:43 AM. I couldn't get seats in first class for the seven hour and twenty-two-minute journey. "Very disappointing!" I told the man on the chat line.

In reality, seating in first and second class was the same seat configuration in Norway. All you got for being in first on this line was a hot drink. We still got our hot drinks, of course, but it meant a bit of a walk to get them from 1st class.

When walking up to first class, I was able to survey the rest of the train and, in true Scandinavian style, it had a family carriage with a soft play area! As someone who had small children in capitalist Britain where shopping is more important than facilities for the future of our country, I've always been jealous of Scandinavia's great emphasis on social support. At airports, they have terrific play areas for children with aeroplane inspired slides and swings and play luggage carousels to climb all over. My girls and I were always getting told off because at the airports, the only amusement was playing with the samples at the make up counters. We'd smear on lipstick and eye shadow and have a spray of the sample perfume bottles, just to pass the time!

The scenic nature of the line meant moving from side to side and not sticking to my allocated seat. The helpful young ticket inspector said I should start on the left-hand side and then move to the right-hand side to see the glaciers. He also told me which seats should be free for my afternoon of train musical chairs.

We worked our way along fjords that eventually became wide rivers. We had some blue sky and sunshine and as we rose up into the mountains, the rivers became narrower and fiercer, angrily thundering their way down steep ravines and around huge boulders that got in their way. It wasn't hard to see why the Norwegians had decided to harness the power of these fierce watery beasts.

Several hours into the journey, we found ourselves in a white Arctic like landscape. Lakes were still frozen and rivers were only just breaking free from their winter hibernation under the ice. Disappointingly, visibility wasn't clear enough to see the glaciers but it was impressive nonetheless. There were small, stunted trees that still had no leaves on them.

We'd started our inter rail journey at the end of March so as we headed south, spring got into full gear with fields of yellow rapeseed, followed by fields of red poppies in the South of France. In the Loire, the dark gnarly vines were bare but further south they had burst into life with bright green leaves sprouting forth in an ever-increasing riot of nature.

As we headed north to Scandinavia in the middle of May, however, it felt as if we were on repeat. Spring in Scandinavia was several months behind spring in France. There were bright yellow fields of rapeseed that had long ago faded further south, along with daffodils and tulips.

Now that we were up on the high pass between Bergen and Oslo, it felt as if we'd been plunged even further back into midwinter.

As we started to descend the white world was replaced by a vision of green. The Birch trees gained leaves and grew taller; the raging rivers plunged down towards the Baltic, driving turbines that would power the lights of Oslo; and the clouds almost completely cleared, leaving the sun to bathe the beautiful valleys and mountains in sunlight. It was like watching one of those time lapse videos that raced from winter into spring!

I saw two moose in the woods, taking my moose count to three. Richard still had a moose count of zero! I think we all knew he wasn't taking this seriously!

We rolled into Oslo at 7:05 PM and had a fifteen-minute walk to our twin bed studio apartment. When I say apartment, I mean it in the loosest sense of the word! It literally consisted of a of two single beds, a table and two plastic chairs, two electric hob rings, a fridge and a bathroom. Small print said kitchen equipment would be 200 krona extra. People moaned about this in reviews but, luckily, we had our camping gear so used that.

We popped around to a nearby Rema 1000 supermarket to get supplies. Richard fancied one of the weak beers but all the refrigerators with beer in were padlocked. I asked a shop assistant about this. "It's because you can't sell beer after 8:00 PM in Norway!" he said, his mocking smile and tone suggested he wanted to add, "Yeah, I know, it's crazy!" We returned to cook and eat at the small table, with only a squash to sip!

In spite of its foibles, it was a cheap place to stay compared to everything else in Oslo so we decided to stay another night. Going on booking.com, however, I realised it was full as it was yet another public holiday on the following Monday, making it was one of those dreaded long weekend.

We'd decided to head east to Sweden where the weather promised to be far better than the on Norwegian coast so I went online to get seat reservations but was told that it was a Swedish train so they were unable to make a seat reservation for me.

It was at this point that I took back all I'd said about reserving seats on Norwegian trains! Reserving on the Norwegian chatline was a hassle and had me moaning but the Swedish operator didn't have a chatline! Not only did they have no chatline, but they also had no on-line reservations and no station staff. They were totally useless and I went from moaning to swearing! Every time I tried to do it online, I went through the lengthy rigmarole of entering our Interrail Pass numbers but just kept getting 'Something went wrong, try again later!' which was clearly Swedish for 'computer says no!'.

At 11:00 PM I gave up and resolved to go to the station the next day. I was concerned that there were very few seats left on the Oslo to Stockholm train leaving at 2:36 PM. Although there was no public holiday in Sweden, the Norwegians were taking advantage of the opportunity to pop over the border into Sweden for cheaper prices, relatively speaking that is. In particular, alcohol was cheaper and presumably you could buy it after 8:00 PM!

OSLO

T he next day, after a bowl of the tasteless muesli, spiced up with yoghurt, I went off to the station to reserve our seats at the ticket office. A woman in her late sixties said it would be 445 krona (£33) and that there were very few seats left on the train. When I moaned about the bureaucracy and cost, she agreed and, of course, blamed it squarely on the Swedish.

We deposited our bags in bag storage at the accommodation and headed off to explore Oslo. It was a very high hazy cloud but the sun was struggling to break through. It was only ten minutes to the centre where we started in the square near the cathedral which, unhelpfully, didn't open until 4:00 PM. Richard had put his phone in his money belt inside his trousers. Capital cities always had a red flag on them for potential risk of street robbery. There were definitely beggars around the station which often means it is also a prime target for pickpockets. Richard's money belt, however, was too hard to access so he opened up his trousers and secured it around his waist. This involved lots of fiddling around which I observed from the edge of the square. It occurred to me that he looked like one of the many tramps who, under the influence of alcohol and drugs, did unspeakable things in full views. I then realised that the man setting up his Dutch cheese stall was also looking at him and clearly thought he was a tramp. As Richard buckled up and walked towards me, I berated him for the impression he was giving. "Yes," said the Dutch cheese man, realising he was in actual fact a respectable married man, "I thought he was a man of the street!"

We walked down to City Hall on the edge of the harbour where a security guard at the entrance said it was closed because NATO was in town. "I really wish NATO would steer clear when I'm in town!" I told him.

We wandered around the harbour boardwalk which was very pleasant. The spring sun started to breakthrough and people gathered in cafes and restaurants in celebration of the long weekend. There were floating saunas on the water, stacked with wood to power them. Young men emerged the colour of a lobster, climbed onto the roof and jumped into the water, creating a huge splash. Historic steamers and elegant tall ships lined the harbour and their modern equivalents zipped back and forth on the Oslo fjord.

When we walked around to the other side of the harbour, security was tight. Civilian police kept us away from the edge of the harbour. "The Crown Prince is due to arrive," a woman police officer told me. As we continued on, a long cordon had been set up to prevent access to the harbour and a Norwegian frigate. Richard was in his element looking at the huge guns carried by the Norwegian military police. Near the frigate there were American military personnel. How did we know they were American? Because they were characteristically loud! I love the Americans. They are, in my experience, warm and friendly but it is impossible to escape the fact that when they're abroad they're loud! The Americans were there because Gerald Ford was in the area. Not President Gerald Ford who died in 2006 but Aircraft Carrier Gerald Ford.

We photographed the fortress as we walked around it and at one point a local who was clearly bored, jumped out his car and offered to take our photo with the fortress behind us. He was pleasant and chatty but the photo was a disaster because of building work in the foreground, making it impossible to crop out.

There was a marching band in town, probably in honour of their NATO guests. We could hear it but we never quite caught up with it. As we had some time to play with, I decided we should walk down past parliament and on to the palace to see if the band had headed there. Richard grumbled and plonked himself on a bench halfway down the long avenue leading to the palace. I followed the flags fluttering beside the road, up to the palace. Once clear of the long avenue, I got a good view of the full sweep of the palace. It looked suspiciously like the palace at the end of the Mall in London and even had a balcony for waving at the masses.

I passed the equestrian statue of a king. I didn't notice his name but the chances were he was called Frederick or Olav. By now, I had finally caught up with the marching band but I still couldn't actually see it. I went over to where people had gathered, about five people thick, and got some glimpses of it between heads and mobile phones.

KARLSTAD AND A BIG INVISIBLE LAKE!

I collected Richard who was still grumbling and then we retrieved the bags and headed for the station. Once on the train, I got the seat reservations confused as we had them for two legs. This got me chatting to the Norwegian group who I was trying to chuck out of their seats. They were off to Stockholm for the weekend and had London on their list of future trips. Once I'd realised my mistake, Richard and I moved up the carriage to our allocated seats.

We had a quick change in Kil and then it was on to Karlstad, a city on the largest lake in Western Europe. Technically speaking it was on Klaralven River which emptied into Lake Vanern. You had to go a few kilometres further south to dip your toe into the waters of Lake Vanern itself but when you looked at a map of this huge lake which dwarfed the Alpine lakes, Karlstad definitely looked as if it was on the edge of the lake.

I'd booked a hotel a short distance from the station. The hotel still used covid as an excuse for very limited reception hours. Yes, that old chestnut! Where have I heard that before? Just about every customer service outlet in the world! It was, of course, a euphemism for 'we haven't got enough staff'.

The hotel said the room would be open. They would send

a code to get into the building if reception was closed. The Internet had given mixed messages as to whether reception was open until 4:00 PM or 6:00 PM and we'd arrived at 5:46 PM.

It was a relief that someone buzzed us into the hotel which was, surprise, surprise, on two floors of a converted office block. The lift should have taken three people and two hundred and forty kilogrammes but it wouldn't fit us and our backpacks in so we had to go separately. I was pretty certain we didn't have a combined weight of two hundred and forty kilogrammes!

Once out of the lift, we found reception was still open which was good because they offered free sweets! Our room was a quadruple room. It had two single beds and a bunk bed. There wasn't much space once all the beds had been squeezed in but it had an ensuite and upstairs there was a kitchen we could use.

It was fabulous weather so we walked up to the river where we got attractive views of historic buildings reflected in deep blue water. We got supplies for dinner at the supermarket and returned to try and work out how to get to Sodertalje by train the next day. We resolved to take a series of local trains with a long wait at one station. Not ideal but there was no one at the station to get a reservation on an intercity and the online service was still saying 'tough luck, try again later'!

The next day we had breakfast in the kitchen/dining area and prepared for checkout at 11:00 AM. We normally go on the basis that you can push check out by at least half an hour very easily. Our replacement bus to Orebro wasn't until 12:05 PM so it wasn't in our interests to rush. On this occasion, however, the receptionist was knocking on the door at 11:00 AM on the dot. She wanted to close up reception and get rid of us so she could go home. It seemed stupid to shut up shop at the exact time everyone had to leave.

We assumed we could sit in the reception area for a bit until we had to go off in search of our bus, but no, she said the cleaner had to clean the area. "Where are we supposed to wait?" I asked, feeling aggrieved.

"At a café!" she replied, curtly. We left a few minutes later with me already composing my review!

At the station, there were no helpful signs or people to direct us to the rail replacement bus. An elderly Swedish couple who were waiting for a train said we should go to the bus station. "This is the train station," he told me. I resisted saying, "Yeh, I had worked that one out!" as he was genuinely trying to help and, unusually, didn't speak great English. He gave us directions to the bus station, ten minutes away.

We walked to the bus station where we were surprised to find there was a real, living and breathing person. She informed us that the bus didn't go from the bus station, it went from outside the train station. So, it was back to the train station where we found, much to our relief, a replacement bus.

I was really excited about our journey to Orebro, not because Orebro was anything to write home about but because the journey would take us along the north Bank of Lake Vanern, the largest lake in Western Europe. Earlier in our trip, we'd stayed on Lake Geneva, one of the great alpine lakes. It was, however, a tiddler compared to Lake Vanern but it had made a great impression thanks to spectacular mountains that rose up around it.

Sadly, in spite of its record-breaking size, Lake Vanern was a great disappointment! The area was as flat as a pancake and the lake shore was a ragged fringe of peninsulas, making a good view of the lake almost impossible. You were never going to see the other side but you really needed to be in a boat be able to see a wide expanse of water. When we rose up over a very small bump in the landscape, we glimpsed a finger of water between two peninsulas. "There you go," I said to Richard. "We've seen the largest lake in Western Europe!" Most of the one hour and fifty-minute journey was on a boring motorway through mundane forest and farmland. It was all very forgettable!

We got to Orebro at 1:55 PM. Here we still faced about three and a half hours until we'd got to Sodertalje Syd and that included a one hour and forty-five-minute wait at a station down the line! Again, there was no person to make a reservation for the train at the station and online we were still getting 'get stuffed and try again later'!

THE FISHING TRAWLER EXPERIENCE!

Annoyingly, there was an intercity train due that went to Sodertalje Syd. Online, it said it would get us there in two hours. When I went into the station to check the board, a young man asked me which was 'arrivals' and which was 'departures'. He said he was from Algeria and lived in Gothenburg. He had a Norwegian mother. He was very eager to tell me that he'd been talking to a girl from Stockholm for two years. They got on well and he was clearly in love. "I was eighteen yesterday," he told me. "I'm going to see her. It's a surprise!" His excitement was palpable and uplifting to see. I just hoped he didn't get there and find her draped around a local boy.

"Let's just get on the Stockholm train that stops in Sodertalje Syd and see what happens," suggested Richard. I agreed this was worth a try. We made our way over to the platform where everyone was waiting to board. They had a habit of not letting people on the train in Scandinavia until just before it went. A young man had left his phone on the train so they opened the door so he could retrieve it. I took this opportunity to explain our predicament to a ticket inspector. "You're very welcome on here!" he told us.

"We haven't got seat reservations," I warned him.

"Not a problem," he said, heart warmingly. I felt like kissing him but the doors closed again!

The first class complete with drinks, fruit and salted caramel Lindor chocolates was practically empty so taking a chance had paid off. From then on, we ignored the decree that said, 'Thou must have a seat reservation on intercity trains in Sweden'! There was the option to ring the train company every time you wanted a seat reservation but that would have cost a fortune without a local sim so we literally blagged our way around the rest of Sweden and never had a problem. I'd like to give a shout out to Swedish train staff here who were helpful, sympathetic and relaxed throughout our time in Sweden.

Once at Sodertalje Syd, we had to get a train to Sodertalje Central. Unusually, the train wasn't included in our pass. I paid £6 for two tickets, and we went off on a wild goose chase to find the train on the line down on Terra Firma, as opposed to line we'd come in on which was a high wire. It was all very confusing.

We just missed a train and realised there wasn't another one for two hours. Having made better progress than expected, thanks to getting the intercity train, we were now back to square one. It was very frustrating! Luckily the bus came to our rescue. It was twenty minutes rather than seven minutes but one came along within ten minutes and whisked us into the centre. I flashed the train tickets at the driver and he accepted them.

Once in Sodertalje Centre, it was a five-minute walk along the Gota Canal to Ship Windo. It was new to booking.com. It had one 10/10 review. It was definitely a risk but the photos of the old fishing trawler were very enticing. It was certainly unique. Equally enticing was the price. At £13 for a five-bed room, we knew there had to be a catch and it wasn't cod or haddock!

Information on the accommodation profile was poor. We

weren't sure if we had the boat to ourselves or whether there were other rooms. It said ring on arrival and, unhelpfully, there was no WhatsApp number. I pointed out that calling them would be an expensive international call without WhatsApp and worried that the listing might be a scam. We would get there and there would be no boat. My fears, however, were allayed when the owner was good at replying to messages on booking.com. We agreed that I would update them on my ETA which I did when I knew we were on the fast train.

We were met at the boat by Otto in his sixties and from northern Sweden, and his wife Mariana who was from Russia but who had lived in Sweden for twenty three years. They were very pleasant, and we needn't have worried about accessing the boat as it was wide open and had no actual door. In addition, they lived on the boat during the summer. They had a small apartment in town where they lived in the winter. So much for having the boat to ourselves! In fact, it soon transpired that the boat was a maze of different cabins and that it was crawling with other people.

They showed us around. The catch, or should I say catches as there were several, included the room. "Your room is here," they said, pointing to a dark hole that looked like a mineshaft. It reminded me of my visit to a Bolivian mine. We descended gingerly on a vertical wooden ladder into a time warp. The cabin had six small portholes. It looked as if the fishermen would be back on board at any moment and ready to set sail for a few weeks of fishing in the North Sea. Their ghosts were ever present. Two of the five bunks were made-up with duvets for us. They reminded me of three sided coffins.

Accessing them was difficult. It was a squeeze for Richard and quite a challenge as 'agility' is not his middle name.
You had to climb onto the sofa seat that wound its way around the edge of the cabin because there was a huge table in the middle that took up most of the floor space. Along the same wall as the wooden ladder descended, there were cupboards and drawers suggesting they spent a significant amount of

time out at sea catching fish. It felt like a tight squeeze for two of us but I dreaded to think how five burly fishermen rubbed along together. I felt sure the vodka must have been flowing when they were off duty!

Otto, who was a locksmith by trade, had bought the boat ten years earlier and renovated it. It was built in Holland in the 1960s and had been a trawler off the coast of Denmark and Norway in the North Sea and then off the coast of Sweden, in the Baltic. He admitted that as he was new to booking.com, he didn't really know what he was doing.

The boat had a pleasant seating area on the main deck that had been enclosed by glass, conservatory style, but you had to climb onto a pallet to get on and off the boat and sometimes it was a bit of a jump as the boat drifted away from the boardwalk. There was a yacht moored alongside Ship Windo and another large boat in front. Another drawback was that there were no toilets or facilities on board. Well, no shower or toilet facilities that worked. Otto said it was too expensive to get someone to come and take 'the shit' away. The modern toilet and shower block was along the boardwalk, about thirty metres away. I know I sound like an old record but thank goodness for our travel toilets! I think I could easily have drowned on the way to the toilet in the middle of the night!

A positive bonus was a washer dryer that could be used for free by boat occupants so I did a large load during out stay. We sometimes had a washing machine at an apartment but never a dryer! This was an absolute luxury!

In spite of the obvious drawbacks, it was a fabulous experience. Very large ships came back and forth on the canal, using the lock gate visible to the north. The first to come out of the lock was a green ship carrying wood. Next came a ship that was used for transporting cement.

We went to the centre of Sodertalje which was modern and rather like a British new town. Here we got supplies for dinner. Mariana, who taught Swedish to migrants, said the town was 92% Syrian. Whilst it clearly had many Syrians, we also saw many black Africans. Sweden had had a huge influx of migrants in recent years so this was no surprise, especially as the town was relatively close to Stockholm.

We walked back on the board walk running along the canal. When there was no wind, it was like a mirror. The large elegant old steamer, a large antique yacht and some small commercial boats were reflected in the water with sharp and perfectly clear definition.

We sat and had a local beer at the cafe bar near the ship that had outdoor seating overlooking the canal. The weak beer was affordable but the wine, however, was an eye watering tenner for a glass. As someone whose go to alcohol is wine, this was bad news. There was no way I was paying a tenner for a glass of vino!

When we returned to the boat, we went through the engine room where there was a noisy generator and up to the kitchen at the back to cook. It didn't get dark until after 11:00 PM but before we retired to our dungeon, a ship came past all lit up like a Christmas tree. We went up to the top deck to watch it silently float by. The huge ships created surprisingly little wake, probably because they navigated the canal very slowly. It was quite a spectacle!

ANOTHER TANK MUSEUM!

T hat night we slept very well in our womb like cabin, exhausted from continuously being on the move. We had breakfast on the deck and then got the local train to Sodertalje Syd where, after a tight eleven minute change, we caught a train to Strangnas so we could visit the Arsenalen Swedish Tank Museum. The train was crowded, probably because it was a weekend, but it was only twenty seven minutes to Strangnas.

The bus journey from the station to the museum was about twenty minutes and the bus came within five minutes so there was no hanging around. The credit card reader didn't work so the bus driver just waved us on. Strangnas had a huge church tower and windmill to admire on our way out of town.

Richard, the tank fanatic, was delighted when he heard there was a tank museum in Sweden. There are only a handful in the world so to do two on one trip was good going. In the car he has an air freshener in the shape of a tank and the wording 'My other car is a centurion!' It's not, obviously! Parking in our area is bad enough as it is without having to find a parking space for a tank but you get the picture!

There were numerous vintage cars in the car park belonging to the museum. And there was me thinking we had come to see tanks. Once inside, Richard was particularly impressed by the Swedish made tanks he hadn't seen before. One had tracks and tyres! An early version of a hybrid! There was a lorry used to deliver aid from neutral Sweden to Austria once the Second World War had ended. This museum had a mezzanine that meant you could look over the large hanger full of tanks from above which was certainly a different perspective and a change from having the huge, intimidating hulks of metal towering over one.

Yet again, on the bus back to the station, the card reader didn't work so we were waved on. We had a forty-minute wait at a station cafe with views over the rooftops of the town and free Wi-Fi before returning to Sodertalje Syd where we found there was no train due to whisk back to the centre so it would have to be the bus.

When we got on the bus, the driver told me I could only pay for one person with a bank card. Not sure why! He let me pay for one on this occasion but said I'd have to buy a ticket at a machine in future. When I looked at my statement, I found I'd been charged eight pence! Something wasn't quite right there!

We shopped and then walked back to the boat where we had a beer at the nearby cafe bar. Before dinner, we watched the large boats go back and forth. Otto's booking.com profile made him look like a serial killer which was not ideal for a host but, in reality, he was a nice guy who liked to talk. When we were sat on the deck, he would come over and have a chat. He wasn't impressed by the green agenda in Sweden. He didn't mind fitting a heat pump but he considered most of it to be 'bad shit', one of his favourite English phrases.

He was very concerned about immigration into Sweden. He was content with controlled migration, after all, he was married to a migrant, but felt it had got out of control.

When I asked Mariana about the war in Ukraine she said that she wasn't on the side of Putin or Zalenki but on the side of peace. This sounded like a well-worn diplomatic response to me but I guessed that being Russian and living in the west was not easy post the war.

As we sat and relaxed in the communal area, people kept popping up all over the place. Oscar from Sweden was in his thirties. He produced music at a studio in Stockholm at night and was a permanent lodger. He had a dog called Sprout who came and looked longingly our food when we were eating. He was a well-travelled dog who Oscar adored. Like a parent, he thought everyone else thought his dog was wonderful too. He and his girlfriend had lived in a hippy community in Ecuador and she'd bought Sprout as a puppy for $5. They'd paid far more to get vaccinations and to transport him back to Europe. Sprout had lived in Portugal and Spain with the girlfriend after they'd split up, along with their son. Eventually, Sprout joined Oscar on a temporary basis but ended up staying. Mariana told me Oscar had plans to move to Zanzibar because he was sick and tired of being a slave in Sweden, so Sprout could be on the move again.

One rather forlorn looking man who was about our age was sat at the table in the kitchen eating bean stew. He didn't particularly want to talk when I asked him where he was from but he told me he was homeless. "Are they letting you stay here?" I asked, assuming they'd come to his rescue.

"I've booked for four nights," he told me. I got the impression he didn't know where he was going after that. I felt very sorry for this man who was my contemporary and would have been interested to know his back story. He was very shy and reticent so there was no way he was going to share it with me but the psychologist in the me imagined there'd been a breakdown in a relationship and poor mental health.

We went for a walk along the canal and as we returned a fabulous sunset began! In the land of the white nights, it was a late one. As there was some cloud, once the sun descended below the clouds, it backlit them in rich shades of pink and orange. The fluffy pink and orange clouds were then reflected in the wide expanse of water at a point where the canal was more like a lake than a canal. The scene gradually dulled to shades of grey. It was mesmerising but, eventually, I had to give up and go to bed. During the night, loud rumbling indicated that a ship was passing.

We took a mid-morning train to Sodertalje Syd from where it was only twenty minutes to Central Stockholm. I'd chosen the boat with the tank museum in mind but, having Stockholm only one hour away was a big bonus. Accommodation costs in Stockholm were expensive!

As we arrived at the station, we had views of the imposing City Hall, completed in 1923. From here we walked for half an hour along Standvagen waterfront, lined with elegant turn of the century buildings and then crossed a bridge to get to the Vasa Museum.

I'd visited The Vasa on my 1986 interrail trip and it had made a lasting impression on me. This 17th century warship had sunk shortly after its launch. Like Henry the Eight's Mary Rose, it was a vanity project of the all-powerful king. What is it with these men? It was definitely a case of 'my ship's bigger than your ship'. It was too narrow so when the king insisted on two rows of cannon it became unstable and tipped over in the first gust of wind it encountered, very close to shore.

It lay forgotten at the bottom of the sea for centuries when an amateur archaeologist using rudimentary equipment found a piece of oak in the mud and concluded that it must be the wreck of the Vasa. Eventually, this historic ship was raised from the bottom of the sea, an amazing 98% intact and put in a museum for all to marvel at. When I had last seen it, it was in the old museum but a new dry dock had been built with fabulous walkways at various levels so one could view its many ornate carvings close up. A huge lion holding the Vasa dynasty shield leapt from the bow of the ship. There were many more examples of the king of the beasts who symbolised regal power. They were on the port hole flaps and most impressively stood proudly on the royal crest on the intricately carved stern castle which had carved figures from the top echelons of society to lowly women peasants, all the subjects of the mighty king.

Roman emperors further emphasised the King's power and there was a Polish king hiding under a table to emphasise to the king's Polish cousin that he had no claim to the Swedish throne which, incidentally, he did if he had wanted to push the issue!

The whole boat sinking episode, ironically, did the opposite to bigging up the king and made him look like a right idiot! Luckily for the guy who designed the ship, he died before the ship sank so the king had no one to blame or make a scapegoat.

We went on the free tour and watched the film, then we spent ages admiring the carvings and the artefacts found with the ship. Only thirteen people died when it went down as it was so close to the shore. Their skeletons, shoes, fragments of clothing and personal items were on display.

We had a picnic at the museum and then walked around to the old town, passing the royal palace with young guards on duty who certainly didn't have the discipline that the guards at Buckingham Palace display. They don't move a muscle but these young men looked around and shuffled from one leg to another.

We wandered through the old town to Stortoget, the main square with handsome town houses, painted in deep primary colours. Stortoget means Grand Square and it didn't take much imagination to picture merchants and peasants coming and going in medieval times. Back in 2023, it was bustling with people sat at cafes enjoying the sunshine.

We passed the Riddarholmen Church with its filigree style cast iron steeple on our way back to the train station. It is one of the oldest buildings in Stockholm and was originally built as a Greyfriars Monastery. The monastery was dissolved after the protestant reformation and it became a Lutheran Church but today it is only used for burials and is the final resting place of many Kings and Queens of Sweden, owing to its proximity to the Royal Palace.

The café bar was closed so we had our own beer on the

decking outside. We were approached by a man who said we couldn't drink our own beer there as the café bar could lose its licence. It seemed a bit over the top as the café was closed but we were on our last swig. "Don't worry," I told him, "we're finished!" We ate on the back deck of the boat and then went for a walk along the canal.

UP THE EAST COAST OF SWEDEN

T he next day we left the boat feeling it had been a great experience but that enough was enough! We got a train from Sodertalja to Uppsala where we had a tight twelve-minute change. The stress of this wasn't helped by the fact that Platform One, where we had to catch the train from didn't lead off the same tunnel as the other platforms. We had to go up, around, down, up again and then feel our way to platform 1, owing to a lack of signs.

The section up to Sundsvall was stressful because there weren't many free seats. I sat next to a young woman speaking very loudly into her mobile phone. Some pointed looks didn't do the trick, so I put on one of my podcasts at full volume and she seemed to get the message and tone it down a bit.

At one station, she got off the train, leaving her large bag next to me. Unattended luggage is a concern in the U.K. On public transport and at airports, you are constantly warned not to leave your luggage unattended and report any unattended luggage. This had got into my psyche so I was worried. She didn't look like a terrorist and she had smiled very pleasantly at me as she left but it made me feel uncomfortable.

I went to the train door, trying to decide whether to mention it to a guard. It wasn't the sort of bag you would just leave behind! At the train door, I found she was having a quick fag just outside! Panic over!

I enjoyed the fruit, salted caramel Lindor chocolates, tea and coffee as the train sped through lots of trees and past numerous lakes. There were a few glimpses of the Gulf of Bothnia out to the east which I'd never even heard of! I just thought it was all the Baltic but the turned out to be all sorts of gulfs and seas!

We regularly saw large birds that looked like small emus from a distance in the fields. They had long legs, long necks and bustle like tails. It transpired that they were cranes that migrate from Spain in the spring. They gather in large numbers at Lake Hornborga in central southern Sweden which is supposed to be quite a spectacle, before dispersing.

SUNDSVALL

I t was a short walk to our hotel room in the centre of Sundsvall. "I sent you a message," said the receptionist, very abruptly. "You booked the last economy double".

"I booked a twin," I told him.

"You requested a twin," he said with a sarcastic emphasis on the word 'requested'. Customer service was clearly not his forte! "It's two beds put together."

"Well, that's very disappointing!" I told him.

"I can cancel your booking," he said, probably thinking that he could stick up the price and make more money now rooms were selling like hotcakes!

"No, thank you. I don't want the hassle of making another booking and walking somewhere else," I replied.

Ironically, I would probably have thought the two beds put together was the twin I'd requested. This was not an unusual arrangement. Then there was always the review! I didn't tell him that because he came across as the sort of man who would cancel the booking for the hell of it, if threatened with bad review. I'd save 3/10 for later! A quick search of the reviews indicated my gripes were pretty common place!

We had a rest in the room which was very small and dark but had an ensuite. We then went for a wander around Sundsvall which had lots of attractive turn of the century architecture and a statue of one of the many kings called Gustavus. We had beer and pizza at prices that were similar to the U.K. so no complaints there.

Breakfast at the hotel was an unhelpful 7:00 to 9:00 AM so we went down at 8:30 AM. It was a typical Scandinavian spread with good coffee so we were happy. We chilled out in our room until the 11 AM checkout, the awkward receptionist having point blank refused to entertain the idea of giving us a later check out, and then put our bags into the bag storage. The reception closed between 11:00 AM and 3:00 PM but our train wasn't until 3:57 PM so we could retrieve our bags and head for the station when reception reopened.

It was high cloud cover as we climbed up through the forest with good views of the surrounding area. Information boards described the flora and fauna around us.

At the top, a folk band was entertaining a group of older people who could trace their roots back to the Vikings on a covered stage.

The open-air folk museum was full of small school children in yellow high vis jackets. They swarmed all over the place, making taking photos quite difficult. When I went into the stable which was combined with the hen house, they pounced on me and jabbered away in Swedish. "I don't speak Swedish," I told them. "You'll have to speak English." Being Swedish, this was no problem. A little Muslim girl in a headscarf took my hand and they asked their questions again in English.

"Is that a real horse?"

"I think it's a real horse that's been stuffed," I told them, looking more closely at it.

"What about its eyes?"

"They're glass,"

"How do the hens get out?"

"They've a door at the back. If you look around outside the hen house, you may find an egg they've laid." I remembered a similar discovery with my own small children. It was like finding gold!

The sun started to poke through the clouds. Richard and I found a traditional café-restaurant at the high point, overlooking the surrounding valley, town and coast where we had a hot chocolate and used the free Wi-Fi.

We walked back down through a much quieter open-air museum now the kiddies had returned to the classroom. In the centre of town, we found a large group of older students who had been released from the classroom. It was a tradition in Scandinavia for graduating high school students to dress up in silly sailor hats and go out drinking. They milled around, drinking, chatting and enjoying the feeling of having been released from their textbooks! We left them to it and made our way back to our hotel to collect our bags and head for the station.

NORTH TO UMEA!

The journey north to Umea was only two hours and thirty-six minutes. As we journeyed north, we entered a sea of trees spreading across rolling countryside and punctuated by lakes. Where trees had been cleared, it was a rocky landscape. Railway sidings in central and northern Scandinavia were full of waggons piled high with logs from the pine and birch forests. From time to time, flatbed cargo trains shot past loaded with huge metal bars, presumably from the iron ore mines in Lapland; and v-shaped mineral wagons clattered down the line to the smelting plants further south.

Our hotel in Umea was near the station. It was very pleasant, spacious and modern. We had an ensuite bathroom and dinner was included so we had chorizo stew in the light and modern restaurant. The whole set up and feel of the place was a total contrast to the hotel the night before but, sadly, we arrived at 7:00 PM so didn't have much time to enjoy it, especially as the only train out of Umea was at 6:22 AM the next morning. This meant we had to be up at 5:30 AM. We'd were told we could fill a bag at the buffet breakfast which started at 5:00 AM to take with us. The hotel clearly revolved around the early train.

There was a bit of confusion with the woman on breakfast duty the next morning because she directed me to reception when I asked for a bag to fill. She followed me down and pointed to a prepared bag. This was for people who left before 5:00 AM and was rather sparse.

Eventually, she got it and gave me bags for Richard and I to fill with the generous spread. We managed to fit in a quick coffee and raced off to the station where we found the train was delayed by thirty minutes!

To pass the time, I walked down through the centre of Umea to the wide river where there was a park and some turn of the century buildings. Outside one of these grand buildings was a model of a shiny rust orange Panther. I wasn't sure of the significance! Then, in the new part of town, I passed a restaurant called 'Bastard Burgers'. It was certainly a strange place!

Once back at the station, the delay had crept up to an hour. That was an hour of lost beauty sleep that I was never going to get back! When the train rolled in at 7:20 AM, we realised there was no first class so we couldn't even consul ourselves with a nice cuppa. It was a night train that had travelled through the night (I was going to say darkness before I realised that wouldn't be accurate!) from Stockholm so many of its compartments were sleeper compartments.

We found a four-person seated compartment with glass panel doors that had plenty of space for our luggage. Richard stayed there and I moved around to get views.

EVEN FURTHER NORTH TO LULEA!

We arrived at Lulea, a name that really did sound as if Father Christmas lived nearby, at 11:00 AM. I'd booked a hotel that sent a code to access the hotel and our room. It was definitely a thing in Scandinavia and clearly a cost cutting measure but it felt very 1984. It would be emailed to me.

The night before, feeling exhausted, we'd decided we'd like to stay on an extra night at the hotel in Umea and just chill. I contacted the hotel in Lulea via booking.com and requested to move my booking forward a day. I told them in a message that I had an early train so would need a rapid response. Booking.com, however, responded by saying I'd get a response in 24 hours. Fat lot of good that was!

When we found a cafe to download the code, once in Lulea, I discovered that instead of a code, I had a message to say my booking in Lulea had been moved to the next day! Typical! We were now several hundred kilometres north of the hotel in Umea where we had wanted to spend an extra night and I was rapidly realising that Booking.com was just a big computer that couldn't deal with any nuances!

We found the hotel which was in a windowless basement and as we were there early, at 12 noon, we found that actual living and breathing people were on the premises. They were far more helpful than the computer! They contacted the head office as it was part of a hotel chain and moved my booking back. If I had contacted booking.com, I would just have got a computer response saying, "We'll get back to you in 24 hours" and no code to access the room. I would have had to rebook for that night and pay again!

They gave me a code and we got into the room which was like a prison cell without a window but at least it wouldn't get light coming in at 2:00 AM. It was a double and a single bunk bed. We had breakfast food from the last hotel for lunch and dinner but got free coffee from the machine, a perk that one of the helpful hotel staff pointed out to me. "€4 for you," joked his side kick.

There was a seated area outside the room and it was quiet until the early evening. Most guests were a similar age to us but there was a group of youngsters who came back from the shops with alcohol. "I hope you're not going to have a party!" I commented, only half-jokingly.

"Not after 10pm," they told me, which was the time guests were asked to observe quiet time. They told me they were from Kiruna in northwest Swedish Lapland. They were heading south to Umea for a pop festival, keen to make the most of the long summer days.

"Are you going to camp?" I asked.

"No," they told me. "It's too cold but some people are going to camp. It's normally warmer at this time of year. We're going to stay in a hotel."

I told them about my trip to Kiruna to see the Northern Lights. It had turned out to be a wild goose chase but was an interesting place for winter orientated activities.

"It must be hard living there in the winter when it gets light at 10:00 AM and dark at 2:00 PM," I observed.

"Yes," they said. "There's lots of depression in the winter. The miners who go down the mines hardly see any daylight all winter." True to their word, they were very quiet and if they had a party, I didn't hear it.

We were struggling to find out whether there was a train up to Haparanda, on the border with Finland, or whether we had to take a rail replacement bus. There was no rail link to Finland. We knew that at least. This seemed rather absurd, thinking about it, because Sweden and Finland both had railways running north to their borders; they just didn't connect. It's not rocket science!

Anticipating that there would be no person to help us interpret the array of information and misinformation on the Internet at the train station, we walked up to the tourist office. I was sceptical as to whether it would be staffed by human beings resident on Planet Earth but it was and we were helped by the wonderful Sanna, who confirmed we had to take a bus and printed off the timetable for the bus to Haparanda. She said we then had to take another bus from there to Kemi in northern Finland where we could connect to the Finnish train network and printed a timetable off for that bus too. It made me feel nostalgic for the good old days, before the internet, when tourist offices were the bread and butter of travellers. Most have now closed and Saana said the Lulea tourist office was in danger of being closed. They were a dying breed!

It was wet, damp, cold and miserable but we had a walk anyway to blow out the cobwebs over to the waterfront on the other side of the peninsula. Here there was a huge crane for loading and unloading and icebreakers sat further around the bay.

With the cold Arctic wind biting at our faces, we returned to the hotel to hunker down in what felt like a nuclear bunker! Mind you, at least we didn't have to brave a trip to the supermarket because our breakfast bits sustained us for dinner and breakfast the next morning! It's amazing what you can fit into a paper bag!

We had to manually download our journey to the Interrail app. We got the 10:20 AM bus to Haparanda, a two-hour and thirty five minute journey. I managed to bag the top deck front seats either side for Richard and me but a man wanted to sit next to Richard so he moved to a single seat further back. I stayed put and luxuriated in the rolling panorama presented by the wide front windows. Like most trains in Scandinavia, the bus had free Wi-Fi, in a flip with further south where you could get station Wi-Fi but not free train Wi-Fi. Yes, France and Switzerland! I'm talking about you! In Scandinavia, free Wi-Fi could sometimes be accessed at station cafes and restaurants but not always!

My moose count went up to five. A track led down to the road and an animal stood looking at a fence along the road that blocked its way. At first, I thought it was a reindeer but, as we got closer, I saw it had a best mate, a bit further up the track. This young animal, who looked very hesitant as our coach thundered past was clearly a fresh faced, juvenile moose.

At one of the bus stops, I watched a red squirrel who was, in fact, very orange, scamper across the track and head for some pine trees. This meant my red squirrel count was now up to two on this Interrail trip!

Once at the bus station in Haparanda, in Sweden but within spitting distance of the border with Finland, there was no sign of the 2:30 PM bus to Kemi in Finland. The bus station staff were Swedish and they nonchalantly showed me a timetable that had bus times to Kemi. It only showed a 3:00 PM bus. "Is there a 2:30 PM bus?" I asked.

"No idea," he said. "Nothing to do with us." The good folks of Facebook had already warned me that the process of getting over the border was long and laborious. Another bizarre complication was that although we were in Sweden, the bus times to Kemi were posted in Finnish time, one hour ahead!

We got talking to John from Leeds, the man who also sat at the front of the bus. He too was heading to Kemi. Like us he had a first class Interrail Pass. He wished he could have done three months but couldn't afford it. He'd been travelling with his wife who'd recently returned to Brussels where they now lived. He didn't explain why. He had about ten days to go and was heading through Finland and the Baltic States and then west via Poland and Prague, back to Brussels. He'd been up the Norwegian coast, an area we'd avoided because of the weather. When pressed about the weather, it became clear that we'd made the right decision!

Unlike us, he'd planned his trip meticulously. On a long journey from Bergen to Oslo, there had been a fire on the line which had led to delays. This had caused problems because he had booked a sleeper train to Trondheim with a connection in Oslo and the delay meant connections would be missed. Passengers in this situation were invited to go to the restaurant car where they would be rebooked onto later connections. This was a disaster for John who had a string of bookings for travel and accommodation, relying on him being on the Trondheim sleeper train. He explained this predicament to the staff. As he frantically wondered what to do, an announcement came over the tannoy, "Would John Smith please get off the train now!" He and his wife jumped off the train where they were met by train staff.

"Run to platform 8," they were told. "The Trondheim sleeper train gets in in five minutes, you'll have to be quick." It transpired that they were at Oslo Airport Station. The Trondheim Sleeper had already left Oslo Central but made a stop at the airport. Train staff had cleverly worked out that they could board the train there instead. They slept well on the Night Express to Trondheim after all their trials and tribulations!

As there was an hour and a half to kill before the bus, I went outside to observe the birds who were nesting on a grassy area and on an old car park near the station. Well, it was either that or visit the most northerly IKEA store which was directly opposite the bus station.

As I walked close to them, they rose up into the air. Arctic terns and black headed gulls whirled above me, squawking loudly in an attempt to protect their ground nests. The nests were hidden in the grass but over in the car park, which was next to a small lake, there were many more gulls. The nests there were clearly visible on the tarmac and on builders' rubble that had been illegally deposited. They formed a noisy swarm above me, very annoyed that I was disturbing them, and I instinctively put my arms up to protect my head from attack. Small nests made of grass and sticks contained two to three brown speckled eggs. I wasn't a threat, just curious, but it would have been an easy meal for an Arctic fox or weasel!

FINLAND!

As we boarded the 3:00 PM bus at 2:00 PM Swedish time, we found that we had to pay for it as it wasn't included in our pass. €7 each felt very expensive when we were used to just flashing our passes! Richard thought the female driver looked like a Bond villain, Colonel Rosa Klebb, a Soviet counter intelligence officer in 'From Russia With Love'. We kept well away from her shoes where she kept her poisonous blades, just in case!

Richard watched enviously as John, the other interrailer, swung his forty-litre backpack onto his back to board the bus. Richard had what he described as a hate-hate relationship with his seventy-litre backpack which was full of camping gear; camping gear which we were yet to use and with the not so tropical temperatures, it looked as if it would turn out to be our worse ever packing mistake! I'd never been able to pack light, even when I didn't carry my potential bed for the night on my back. I had written in my 1982 Interrail diary that I had packed everything but the kitchen sink, so time had obviously not influenced my packing habits for the good. I have friends who can get away with packing the equivalent of what will fit in to a supermarket carrier bag but I always seem to return with half a backpack of stuff I haven't worn or used. I probably need packing therapy!

On the bus, I got talking to Albert, a delightful Finnish man who said his six times great grandfather was English. He'd travelled to Finland to work in the factories there in the 1880s. Britain's Industrial Revolution meant his expertise was probably valued in Finland's textile factories that had some catching up to do.

I asked him about the bright green berry with a gold lion cap badge that he was clutching. "I'm a reservist in the army," he told me. "When I was younger, I spent time up in Lapland training as part of national service". We talked about Finland's recent entry into NATO because of the threat of Russia since the invasion of Ukraine. "In Finland, we think the Russians are spineless," he said translating from the original Finnish and certainly not mincing his words!

Thirty minutes later, we were in Kemi. Here I realised that my downloaded directions to our hostel were from the train station, not the bus station. I went into the station burger bar to ask a very large and jolly manager who, in the absence of any customers was doing her books, if I could use her Wi-Fi. She couldn't get onto the Wi-Fi but offered me her phone to use. "Can I use your hotspot?" I asked.

"I'll try" she said, "but I'm useless at technology." She was, indeed, useless with technology and failed to work her hotspot but she told me the train station was over the road so it was problem solved.

It was a ten-minute walk to the hostel where we had a twin room with shared facilities. We sat in the conservatory style dining area and enjoyed the free filtered coffee and juice before we went to the supermarket for supplies. We got reindeer soup and ate it in the basement kitchen. Even though we hadn't seen any reindeer so far on this trip to Lapland, at least we'd eaten Rudolph!

Our room had a sauna right opposite. The unit with a WC,

changing area and bath/shower could be locked so it became our own private sauna. It's a common myth that the Swedish invented the sauna but it's simply not true. It was the plucky little Finnish Kingdom who invented the famous sauna. To be fair, it was part of Sweden at the time and the sauna remains popular all over Scandinavia so it's an easy mistake to make.

SANTA LAND!

T he next morning, we had a bit of a lie in but it didn't feel like a lie in after losing one hour when the time went forward an hour in Finland. We caught the 9:36 AM to Rovaniemi, a one hour and twenty-seven-minute journey. We didn't want to tackle the long hack south to Tampere, after the long journey up the East Coast of Sweden, moving on every night for three in a row, so it made sense to book an extra night.

In spite of having a booking confirmed and evidence of payment, however, the woman on reception said she hadn't got my booking. "Well that's your problem" I told her, "I've paid and got a booking.com confirmation". Then, all of a sudden, she had a lightbulb moment and found my booking so all was well.

The journey up to Rovaniemi looked interesting when viewed on a Google Maps as it followed a huge river. Sadly, although it looked like a train line in close proximity to the river on the map, in reality, it was a train line enclosed by trees with the odd glimpse of the river. There was some blue sky and sunshine to light up the forest on the journey to and from Rovaniemi but once in Rovaniemi itself it was low grey cloud.

The station had a steam train on display, beloved by many

Scandinavian stations. It was a twenty-minute walk to the centre of town which was 1960/70s concrete jungle and full of fast-food restaurants and bars. Like many of its counterparts in Scandinavia, it reminded me of a British new town. We walked out of town and along a wide river that seemed to turn into a lake. At times, it felt as if Finland was more lake and river than land! One only needed to look on a map to confirm this theory!

Rovaniemi was clearly a Jekyll and Hyde sort of place. It was marketed as a Winter Wonderland where families with very deep pockets could go and meet Father Christmas and visit the elves' workshop. Photos showed heart-warming and idyllic scenes of snowy forests where reindeer pulled colourful sleighs. It was a total contrast to the drab grey place I was looking at on a mid-summer's day.

Mind you, Rovaniemi did have one thing going for it all year round. It was smack bang on the Arctic Circle. I'd crossed the Arctic Circle line a few times but it was Richard's first time. I always got a thrill when I crossed one of the seven big hitting imaginary lines marked out on Planet Earth. The only one I hadn't crossed was the Antarctic Circle. I'd been over the international dateline twice, going to and from New Zealand. It's possible to arrive before you leave and lose a whole day of your life! I'd been over the Equator and Tropics of Cancer and Capricorn multiple times and, of course, I'd lived near the Greenwich Meridian most of my life, so I'd lost count of the many times I'd transected that one! As we walked through Rovaniemi town centre, we crossed the Arctic Circle about where there was the aptly named Arctic Burger Bar.

Disappointingly, the only sign of Christmas was a tacky window display with some Christmas soft toys so we got an early train back than planned at 13:10AM and made hot chocolate back in the hostel conservatory to make up for not being able to conjure up the spirit of Christmas!

LOTS OF TREES AND LAKES ON THE LONG JOURNEY SOUTH!

When we went to have breakfast in the dining area, we found a large group had commandeered the coffee machine. Now this wouldn't have been the crime of the century if they had just got on and poured their coffee when brewed but they didn't and seemed oblivious to the fact that anyone else, namely me, might desperately need a coffee. As the time ticked away to the departure of our train, I tried to encourage them to pour their coffee so I could get on and inject myself with much needed caffeine but it fell on deaf ears. My next request for them to pour their coffee was not so polite and my tone betrayed my irritation. The woman who seemed to be in charge looked at me indignantly and went over to her group to complain about me. As an English speaker who has never managed to master another language, I've always been a bit jealous of those who can slag off the opposition in another language. "I may not be able to speak Swedish," I told her, looking her confidently in the eye, but I can speak tone of voice and body language!" I gave up and went down to the basement kitchen to fire up the coffee maker down there before running to the station to catch the train!

Finnish first class turned out to be complicated. Oh, a bit like everywhere else, with the exception of Switzerland. You didn't need a seat reservation but on busy trains, it was advisable. It was impossible to get one at most stations as they had no staff. I tried the chatline, but I was told I would have to ring up and pay for a seat reservation. We decided against this and resolved to just go for it. If all else failed, we could sit in second class with 'the peasants'!

Over planned John had rung and paid for a seat reservation, but the thought of doing this every time we wanted to board a train sounded onerous, plus, I dreaded to think what the cost of all those calls would be with no local sim card.

Being gluttons for punishment, we decided to go for the fully booked 10:40 AM. Even second class was fully booked! A member of the public at the station had told me that some seats were always reserved for the train staff and that I should I asked the ticket inspector to point out these seats. It sounded like an emergency option!

At the train station, I asked the only member of staff I could see a question about how full the train was likely to be that morning.

"I drive the wood train," he told me, pointing to the goods train loaded with wood that was about a mile long in the siding.

"Ask the train staff when it comes," he told me.

Richard and I got seats in Exstra for about an hour until Oulu. Then the musical chairs began. The ticket inspector helpfully told me which seats in second class were free for the train staff. Richard went down there but I stayed put in two seats that had been reserved from an earlier station but not occupied. "They may be in the restaurant car," said the ticket inspector who had looked the seats up for us. I took Richard down drinks and after about an hour and a half, he returned to Ekstra on the basis that the reserved seats were still unoccupied, and it was unlikely that they were in the restaurant car.

TAMPERE!

We rolled into Tampere after five hours. On balance, we'd been lucky in Ekstra for most of the journey considering the train had been billed as 'Fully Booked' that morning.

We walked to our apartment in the centre of town, over the 1929 bridge with huge and dramatic statues that reminded me of the great statues of the Soviet Era. Tampere's Industrial heritage was very evident everywhere. Tall brick chimneys and factories lined the river between two lakes and rapids were created by the power of the water descending from one lake to another through a narrow channel.

Our apartment had four keypads, into which we had to punch a code we'd received. It all seemed rather over the top and made me feel as if I was entering an American top security penitentiary full of lifers on Death Row! It was a pseudo apartment. Let's face it, a kettle and a microwave don't constitute an apartment! The only sink was in the bathroom so you had to wash your face in the same sink as you washed the dishes. Not very hygienic! It was basically a hotel room badly disguised as an apartment. In reviews people said it was like a Finland to Sweden ferry cabin. They definitely had a point. The wall to wall plastic bathroom unit looked as if it had been taken out of a cabin and put in the hotel room (I'm sorry, apartment!) that was previously, of course, an office block. They probably got a job lot!

We went to the local supermarket and got knocked down sushi and stuffed peppers that we could heat up in the microwave. A three-course meal with wine was definitely off the cards but Richard treated himself to a beer! For a moment, I was celebrating because a bottle of wine in the supermarket was similar to the price of a bottle in the U.K. My euphoria, however, didn't last long because, on closer inspection, I realised it was a mere 5% proof, making it low alcohol. I decided to wait another couple of weeks until I could have the real deal 12.5% wine! Overall, Finland seemed more expensive than Sweden, in spite of having the euro.

TANKS FOR NOTHING!

Mid-morning, we walked to the station and got a commuter train to Parola, forty minutes to the south. Parola is a very small and very insignificant place with one significant exception in that it has a tank museum. Now for most people that wouldn't be enough to elevate it to 'significant' status in any way, shape or form but for tank fanatic Richard, it was practically the centre of the universe. Three tank museums in one trip had to be a record, especially as there's only about six of the darn things in the whole of the world!

It was a thirty-minute walk to the Parola Finnish Tank Museum. Halfway there we crossed a motorway junction where there were two tanks, one pointing south and the other pointing north, presumably to advertise the tank museum. "It must be a shock if you're driving along and suddenly find a tank pointed at you," joked Richard.

The museum had a King Tiger Tank on loan from Bovington Tank Museum. Like a rock star, it was on tour! Another star attraction was the armoured train that looked as if it was straight out of a World War Two movie. The museum also had two sheds and two covered areas full of tanks and armoured vehicles. Richard liked the fact that it had a bias towards Finnish tanks and was like a kid in a sweet shop. He left with a panzer t-shirt and promised to wear it when my pacifist friends came round!

On the way back to the station, we admired the colourful array of lupins which reminded us of our trip to New Zealand. We were back in Tampere by mid-afternoon where we returned to our 'apartment' to relax.

In the evening it was a bright blue sky so we went out for a walk around Tampere. We found our way to where the river widened out on its way to the lower lake and sat and had a local beer on the deck of a boat that had started its life as a German river barge. We then walked through town and along the river to the art nouveau fire station designed by a very successful female architect, Wivi Lonn. Her fame led to much jealousy amongst male architects who wanted her to marry as then she wouldn't be able to practice any longer but she never did marry. Pretty pathetic really when viewed through the prism of liberated 2023 but one forgets how far we've come! It was rumoured that she was a lesbian; I bet that really pissed them off!

We walked over the weir and then passed a factory that was now a museum and shops. As with much (but, sadly not all) of Britain's disused industrial architecture, it had been given a new lease of life.

COUCH SURFING COMMUNITY!

C heckout the next day was at 11:00 AM but the cleaning lady let us last stay longer. She said she finished at 4:00 PM so she generously said we'd have to be gone by then. We stayed until 12:30 PM because Johanna, our couch surfing host, messaged to say she was home and that we could make our way there. We had a coffee at Expresso House, found all over Scandinavia, and then walked to Johanna's home, about twenty minutes on the other side of the train station. Two days earlier, Johanna had replied 'maybe' but by then I'd booked the apartment so we delayed for two days rather than just move on and I'm so glad we did as it turned out to be a unique and very Finnish experience, the sort you can't get in a pseudo apartment in the centre of town.

Johanna gave us a warm welcome and was very easy to get on with. She immediately put us at our ease. She lived in a community with her husband Mikko and their children. Their wooden home was over a hundred years old. It was one of about forty houses encircling an inner courtyard. Originally, these houses had been for workers in the shoe factories. Their small three bed apartment had been two apartments on inception and each had housed two large families. They didn't have bathroom facilities back in the day. They went to the sauna once a week to wash. I think our family of five who enjoyed the space of a five-bed detached would have killed each other in such cramped conditions!

Johanna's family home had tall elegant tiled fire places so typical of the Nordic countries that it felt like a museum. Just to emphasise this point, there were bullet holes from the 1918 Civil War, fought between White and Red Finland during its transition from Grand Duchy of the Russian Empire to an independent state, in the bedroom fireplace.

Johanna worked part time at a health technology company and was also an activist supporting refugees. The family had an Iraqi Kurd living with them for a period of time on his arrival in Finland. They said he had very little education in Iraq but was clearly very intelligent and had learned Finnish quickly and soon learnt to read and write. He had recently finished university education and was considered to be part of the family.

Johanna and her family were vegans. She cooked us spinach pancakes, a popular Finnish speciality. She said her husband Mikko had once had fifty in one sitting when he was at school! I think they were small ones but evenso!

She took us on a tour of the community which was very much based on sharing resources. There was a woodwork workshop with expensive tools. "Aren't you worried they'll be stolen?" I asked.

"Oh no," she said. "There's a high level of trust in Finland." There were unchained bikes. As someone who had had her chained-up bike stolen from outside Basildon train station only a few months earlier, when the thick chain had been cut off with bolt cutters whilst I was at the opticians, I was very jealous. If I'd got hold of the bastard who stole my bike, one of the community's chainsaws would have come in very handy.

They had a room full of large chest freezers. There wasn't room for a freezer in the apartment and as everyone grew fruit and vegetables at the communal gardens about one kilometre away, they needed plenty of freezer space. Again, theft was not a problem.

Finally, we looked around the social centre where there was a party room, a communal sauna and a swap shop. It all seemed to work fabulously well. I wasn't sure if it would work where I came from!

We had a wander around the area of wooden houses, which was unique as most of their generation had now been demolished in favour of apartment blocks. A hare sat on the grass verge. When we expressed surprise, Johanna told us they see them all the time. When we told her about the urban foxes that stroll around our area, as bold as brass, it was, of course, her turn to express surprise. They don't have any urban foxes. I guess there wouldn't be any hares if they did!

HELSINKI!

We had breakfast with Johanna and then caught the train to Helsinki at 9:00 AM. Ekstra was crowded with business people so we had a limited number of seats to choose from and Richard ended up going downstairs to second class. A man in the seat in front of me wanted to pull down the blind which, in turn, blocked my view. When I asked him not to and pulled it back up, he said, sounding rather disgruntled, "There's nothing to see!"

"I've never done the route before so I'm sure that won't be the case." Okay, he had a point to a certain extent as there were lots of trees which must be pretty boring for your average commuter but for a newbie like me, there were some lake views and the view of the 13th century Tavastehus Castle reflected in a lake near Hameenlinna which was fabulous.

On arrival into Helsinki, we didn't have to go far to find one of Helsinki's top sights. Helsinki Central Station, my favourite station on the trip, was an art nouveau gem. One of its claims to fame is its forty eight meter high clock tower which was the first of several designs that finally ended up as the design for the 1922 Chicago Tribune Tower, America's first skyscraper no less! The exterior of the building is made of granite and there is a huge archway over the entrance which is flanked by two giant and Soviet style statues carrying globes to illuminate the building at night. Sadly, as it was never dark when we visited in midsummer, we didn't see the façade lit up! Johanna told us that the city authorities put various colourful sleeves on the statues to mark big events such as the Eurovision Song Contest and the Olympics.

From the station, we walked to the harbour where we got a twenty-minute boat across the archipelago to Suomenlinna Fortress Island. Originally, the fortress was called Sveaborg which means Swedish Castle. Built in the 18th century, it was designed to deny the Russians access to the Baltic Sea. This was a miserable failure because during the Swedish-Russian War of 1808-9, the Russians strengthened and expanded it before it passed into Finnish hands and was renamed Finnish Castle. A large ferry sat waiting to go overnight to Sweden and smaller boats zipped around the blue waters, dotted with rocky outcrops.

Once on the island, we had a wander around the Naval Academy that still trains fresh faced recruits. A large colony of barnacle geese was also on standby, at the ready to defend their young, very cute fluffy chicks. They honked loudly at us as we passed, especially if they thought we were getting too close. There were hundreds of them, along with swans with signets and grebes with chicks.

The military museum had interesting displays about the plethora of obscure Finnish wars. Not only was there the Civil War, the Winter War and the Continuation War, there was also the Lapland War. Even Richard hadn't heard of the latter war so it had to be obscure!

Part of the military museum was a submarine you could tour. Vesikko Submarine was launched in 1933 and saw action in the Winter War and the Continuation War, during which, it sank the Russian merchant ship Vyborg. As I walked through this cramped, tube-like vessel, I reflected on how I could never be a crew member on a submarine; it's far too cramped and there are no views. "I'll stick to being an aspiring train driver!" I thought.

At the top of the hill, there was a lighthouse church. The tower had a lighthouse on the top. It brought a whole new meaning to the light of God! The interior of the church was so plain that I was almost starting to hanker after a bit of baroque by the time I'd finished looking around it but outside there were huge cannons and metal ship chains forming a perimeter fence which was much more eye catching and made up for the barren interior.

Once on the ferry back, we met a German American couple. I praised them for speaking their own languages to their four-year-old child. "You'd be surprised how many don't," I told them. It means you have the great advantage that you can learn a language without any effort whatsoever; and I should know because I've been trying to learn French, German and Spanish for years which has taken great effort and reaped little reward! In addition, you don't end up with the problem that your child can't speak to one set of grandparents! Can you imagine that? It happens but it can all be avoided with very little effort!

On our journey back to Tampere, we met our first of several officious Finnish ticket inspectors. He provocatively took hold of our phones to scrutinise them. "Photo ID," he demanded, very abruptly. We showed him this and he scrutinised it. It felt as if he was trying to catch us out. He then said, with what seemed like great satisfaction, that although our passes were in order, we'd have to go downstairs because we were in Ekstra.

"But we've got First Class Interrails," I told him, fixing him with a determined stare. "My understanding is that that entitles us to Ekstra class."

"Oh," he said, clearly flummoxed. "I've never heard of First

Class Rail Passes."

"Well, there are plenty of us," I said triumphantly. He took hold of our phones again and scrutinised them. With nowhere else to go, he returned our phones.

Now this is really the part where he should have said, "I sincerely apologise for being a Trumped-Up Little Job's Worth!" But, unfortunately, all we got, of course, was, "Well help yourself to tea and coffee!"

"Oh, we've done that already!" I told him gleefully, with more than a hint of 1-0 to us!! As he disappeared off to terrorise more passengers, Richard and I called him all the names under the sun, mostly not printable.

Back at Johanna's place, we met her husband Mikko, who'd returned from a work trip and son Osmo who had already finished school for the summer. Mikko was clearly highly intelligent and enjoyed talking about history, politics, culture and just about anything under the sun! We had Finnish summer soup, a tasty cornucopia of vegetables, with salad, bread and cheese for dinner.

At around 9:00 PM, Joanna and I went to the communal sauna. Twice a week, on a Wednesday and Saturday there are two sessions, one for men and one for women. Men were 6:00 to 8:00 PM and women were 8:00 to 10:00 PM on this particular day.

The reason for the divide is that you have to go in absolutely starkers. Now this doesn't bother the Germans where Richard and I once went into a mixed sauna with swimming gear on and nearly caused another World War. My German was good enough to know that, on entry, our fellow sauna goers were not happy that we were clothed. Richard just upped and left but I persisted. They politely told me that it wasn't allowed to go into the sauna with clothes on. You could only go into the sauna au natural. "Well, I'm here now," I said, "so I hope you don't mind if I stay". I figured the damage was done! I'd broken a cultural norm and whether I left immediately or waited for ten minutes, it wouldn't matter too much by that stage. After all, having a sauna isn't like going to church and spitting on the Madonna or sitting in a mosque and drawing a cartoon of the prophet. Or is it? They were perfectly pleasant and we had a nice chat in English about life in general.

As Finland is the birthplace of the sauna, I was thankful to have Johanna to guide me through sauna etiquette but it wasn't long before I was inadvertently breaking the rules of the sauna. We showered in the shower area just outside the large wood fired sauna and Johanna gave me a small towel. I assumed this was for mopping my brow but, on entry, when I put it beside me, she told me I needed to sit on it. Of course, from a hygiene point of view, that made perfect sense.

There were six females, including us and a girl who was about eleven years old. "From what age can children use this sauna?" I asked.

"About six months," they told me. I was shocked. I expected them to say about ten years old.

"When I was pregnant, there was a sign on the sauna saying pregnant women couldn't use the sauna. Is this the same here?" I asked.

"Oh, no!" they said. "Women give birth in the sauna here!"

Tiitu, who was a writer and illustrator and who had produced an excellent graphic novel about the town and the community that Johanna had lent me to read, was one of the women who had joined us in the sauna. Her husband was also called MiKko and she described how his grandmother had gone to the communal sauna once a week; and that this was her only opportunity to bathe in the absence of a bathroom at home. The women spoke perfect English even to each other as if it was the most natural thing to do. It's the norm in

Scandinavia but I still very much appreciated the gesture!

We had a break halfway through and sat, wrapped in a towel in one of the communal rooms and sipped on Mikko's homemade apple cider and blackberry juice. These drinks had originated from communal garden harvests of previous years. They'd been lovingly bottled and stored for just such an occasion as this when all that sweating in the sauna required liquids to be rapidly replaced!

The sauna is cleaned and operated as part of the community's rota of jobs. When I asked if there were any slackers who didn't play their part, Johanna assured me that there weren't. I guess playing your part was a part of buying into this wonderful community and if you didn't then it just wasn't for you.

Finland regularly achieves the accolade of 'Happiest country in the World'! I was sceptical. All that darkness in the winter leads to alcoholism and strict controls on the stuff. Wine is sold at a strength of 5%! That would be enough to make me unhappy! But, having spent some time with Johanna and her community, I got it. It wasn't just about the high level of trust, it was also that the Finns valued what they had. They were 'glass is half full' people and that made them happy. Us Brits like nothing better than a good old moan so we were never going to come top of that league but I decided to try and learn from this Finnish Philosophy and count my blessings more often!

A LOCAL TOUR!

We got up at 8:00 AM so we could have breakfast with Johanna and MiKko before Mikko left work for work at 9:00 AM. Mid-morning Johanna and I went out for a walk. It's always good to get a local's perspective and Joanna was an excellent tour guide.

It was, unfortunately, a cloudy day. We walked through a park and then through an area of communal gardens which added some colour to the grey day. Each garden had a house that looked big enough to live in. Johanna assured me that people didn't live in them but that some people spent a significant amount of time there during the summer; eating and drinking during the long days of summer. I guess they were equivalent to the British beach hut!

We crossed a bridge to another area of communal gardens and here we found Johanna's family garden. It was rather overgrown from the burst of growth that takes place in the spring so she pruned her rhubarb plant and pointed to the apple trees from whence came the apples responsible for Mikko's potent apple cider.

I was keen to see some of Tampere's notable and rather unusual churches. We started with the most unusual. Locals call Kalevan Church, the grain silo and I could see exactly why. There were no other words to describe it. Inside, it was beautiful in its simplicity. Towering narrow windows of simple glass, stretched up to the oak ceiling high above which undulated from one end to the other. Far below the pews radiated towards a pine organ.

Nearby was the solid, chunky Scandinavian art nouveau cathedral. It's grey blocks of stone merged with the pewter grey sky. Inside, it was a much more colourful affair. It had huge stained glass windows featuring knights and dragons as well as a kaleidoscope of patterns. Organic art nouveau patterns decorated the pillars, columns and archways; and the murals included nude children and the wounded angel being carried by two young boys. It was Lutheran with a twist of Scandinavian creativity and sexual liberation. The Catholic Church would definitely not have approved, but then again, they do have lots of naked cherubs on display who are, strictly speaking, angels but look remarkably like small children with wings!

We had the added bonus that various police choirs were practising for a concert. Mikko was in a choir so it was obviously a popular local activity. Johanna told me that the Finns go a bit mad in summertime. One can hardly blame them when they have such a long, cold and dark winter. She said orienteering is very popular and they have hundreds of festivals from country music to welly throwing. My personal favourite was the Wife Carrying Festival. I'm not sure you'd get away with that in the U.K. today. I mean, it's wrong on so many levels! We shopped for groceries and I insisted on paying. "You can only pay if you make sandwiches to take," said Johanna.

We had lunch back at the house. Osmo practised his English on us and Mikko said he'd really enjoyed chatting and wished we'd had longer to chat. It's amazing how strong connections can be made in such a short time.

After lunch, Johanna took us for a tour of the highest

esker in the world. In reality this record-breaking geographical feature was a small hill with good views of the two lakes either side of Tampere. An esker is a mound of gravel; glacial deposits dumped during the last Ice Age. Over the millennia, it has grassed over and about a hundred years earlier, it had had some prime real estate built on top of it. The colourful wooden houses had stunning views of the lakes. As the clouds were clearing and the sun was becoming ever more dominant, we were able to enjoy views of the lakes with blue sky. From the elevated position of the esker, we could see the islands that dotted the lakes as we wandered around the ridge, trying to get the best views through the tall pines that populated the hill. Someone had put clothes outside their house for anyone who wanted to give them a new home. I snapped up a pair of trousers and a nice black top. Joanna said second-hand shops were very popular in Finland. Sounded like my sort of place!

Johanna drove us to the viewing tower, assuring us that we had enough time to go up the tower and then get to the train station for our 4:00 PM train to Helsinki. The ever-improving weather picture meant it really was worth giving it a go, in spite of the clock ticking down!

We bought tickets and had to wait for the lift to come down. Mind you, I wasn't complaining. It was quicker than using the stairs when there was a time pressure! The views from the top were well worth the high blood pressure! Not only could you see the two lakes but you got a bird's eye view of the city of Tampere. "You can see where the river runs," said Johanna. "You just have to trace the line of chimneys." There was no time to stop at the cafe on our descent but I did take a quick photo of its beautiful geometric ceiling.

We had 19 minutes and 20 seconds to get to the train station. Johanna 's sat nav and frequent red lights added to the tension. As we approach the station with 7 minutes and

4 seconds to go, we found the entrance to the station blocked by a taxis. With the clock ticking down rapidly, Johanna managed to pull just into the entrance to the station. We jumped out and grabbed our backpacks from the boot of the car, thanking Johanna profusely for all her kindness, in the absence of the time to give her a hug and a kiss.

We raced to the entrance of the station. Once through the doors, we expected a large board with train times and platforms on it. There was nothing. The tunnel with platforms leading off it was ahead of us but there was still no board. We had 4 minutes and 15.2 seconds to go. "Wait here," I told Richard and I raced back to the entrance and down the corridor to the right. This, thank the lord, had a board displaying the train times and platforms. Luckily, the Helsinki train went from platform one, at the start of the tunnel. I ran back to Richard and we hurried up the ramp onto the platform. We have 2 minutes and 49 seconds to spare as we saw the train approaching the platform.

BACK TO HELSINKI!

Thankfully, there were seats in Ekstra. I didn't fancy playing musical chairs after our train dash adventure. It wasn't long before we were relaxing with a complimentary tea and coffee! We got into Helsinki central at 5:30 PM and got the underground train out to Urhellupulsto, a part of the modern Garden City of Tapiola, which is in Espoo, a sister city to Helsinki. This huge conurbation all merged into one. Confused? Think Leeds Bradford!

It's hard to get a couch surf host in a capital city. Accommodation is expensive so they get lots of requests! I sent out multiple requests and I was pleased to be accepted by Elias.

Elias couldn't have been more different to Johanna and family! Looking at the smiling profile photo, I thought Elias was a woman but on closer inspection of the profile page, I realised Elias was a man. He said he was on the rainbow spectrum. We exchanged WhatsApp messages and he sent me excellent directions to his place which was close to the underground station.

He said he wouldn't have much time to spend with us and that he was shy. This was fine by me. When I travelled solo, I enjoyed the company but on this trip, I had Richard. My request always mentions my desire to meet locals as a way of learning more about the history and culture of a place.

It's important not to give the impression you just want a free Airbnb! In most places, I can offer couch surfers the chance to practise their English with me, being an English teacher and all that, but in Scandinavia, they speak better English than most English people.

When we arrived, Elias let us in. He had just taken his dinner out of the microwave. He showed us the room and then fled to the two-seater sofa, clearly not wanting to engage. He gave us a key so we could come and go as we pleased. The bed was a king size but very low. There was hardly any other room in the bedroom. We had to push a wooden box into the corner to give us better access. Elias had tossed his clothes and bedding on top of the box. He was thirty-nine so nearly middle aged but lived like a student. He didn't clean! Mind you, who were we to judge? He was offering us three night's accommodation in a great location so we had no right to complain. After all, if we didn't like it, we could just go and find a hotel.

Elias was watching QI, a popular English quiz show, one after the other. I didn't feel comfortable not having at least a quick chat so I went into the lounge to say how grateful we were. He spoke English with a Glaswegian accent. He'd lived in Greenock for six months where he'd worked for IBM. He said speaking with a local accent meant he was less likely to be stabbed. Three of his colleagues had been stabbed when out on the town! I knew things were bad in Glasgow. I mean, we've all heard of the 'Glasgow Kiss'; but I didn't realise they were that bad! He said he spoke Finnish with the northern Lapland accent! He spent six months there too.

He described himself as a bit autistic. I had already worked that one out! He was an artist in the broad sense of the word. He played the violin and was learning Japanese. He had been visiting Japan when the pandemic broke out and Japan hit the headlines because people were confined to a cruise ship where there had been a major outbreak.

He was a computer games designer and thought the best life was an online life! Um! He was also a tattoo artist. An example of his work was plastered across his neck. I'm not a fan of tattoos. If my kids want to wind me up, they tell me they've got a tattoo. This is just a joke. They don't want to be written out of the will. But each to their own and even I can appreciate the artist nature of a tattoo.

If this is where it had ended in the case of Elias, then that wouldn't have been anything out of the ordinary. But it wasn't. Twelve years earlier, he had had his eyes tattooed black. I'll give you a few moments to think about that! On his couch surfer profile under 'one amazing thing I've done' he'd put 'I've got my eyes tattooed black.' Amazing is not how I would have described it. Talking to him gave me a chance to observe this very strange phenomenon. "Why?" Was all I could think. It made him look like something out of a zombie apocalypse movie or a James Bond villain. I don't use the word freak lightly but it made him look like a freak! On the other hand, I'm always up for a new experience and I've never met someone with tattooed eyeballs before. The part of me that wasn't appalled was fascinated! When I asked him if anyone else had had their eyeballs tattooed, he said, "Yes. Twenty to thirty people, mainly from Germany, have had it done. We are being monitored to see if it will cause us to go blind." What a risk? He would have been my son's age when he had it done, 27 years old! I wanted to ask how his mum had reacted and if he had any regrets but decided against this approach as it would probably have given away my prejudice and disapproval!

Something deep down inside made me a little uneasy. I knew I wasn't being logical but the phrase "follow your instincts!" kept invading my mind! I sent Kathryn,

Elias' couch surfer profile details and his address details. She had access to our booking.com details so if we went off grid, she had a point of reference for speaking to the authorities. Unfortunately, by sending her Elias' profile she also got to see a photo of him, complete with neck tattoos and tattooed eyes.

"You are joking?" she messaged back.

"No," I told her.

"I think you need to rethink your decisions!" she lectured. "You must have concerns about this person or you wouldn't be sending me these details."

"No," I lied. "I always send dad my couch surfer details when I travel solo." That bit was true but I didn't feel I needed to send Johanna's details to Kathryn, especially as I was with Richard.

"I think you've been watching too many American movies. Will you stop overreacting?" I told her. "He's babysitting for his nephews aged four and seven-years old tomorrow! I won't sleep if you carry on like this!"

As one couch surfer correctly said, "you get what you get." If I'd been on my own, I wouldn't have stayed there as he only had one review from a woman. It was positive but she'd only stayed with a friend for one night. Probably a case of read between the lines. My rule is about five positive reviews from women and recent, if solo.

"I'm not cooking here!" said Richard, referring to the unhygienic state of the place. We went to the supermarket over the road to get crisps and beer to go with our sandwiches. As we went off to sleep about midnight, Elias was starting a night of gaming. It was still light which went a long way to prevent my active imagination going into overdrive. I'm not sure it ever got dark.

A DAY IN HELSINKI!

We awoke at 7:00 AM, glad to be alive. Okay, that may be a bit melodramatic. My sense that I was overreacting the night before seemed to be true in the cold light of day (as opposed to the cold light of night!). A downside of Elias' place was that he didn't have Wi-Fi. A bit strange for a gamer! He let us hotspot but it wasn't ideal as we didn't have a local sim.

We crept around as Elias was sleeping on his two-seater couch. It didn't seem like a comfortable option. It was very kind of him to give up his bed for us, especially as he hadn't murdered us in our sleep, but I just didn't get why he couch surfed. I suspected that, in spite of being on the verge of middle age, he wanted young couch surfers who would make him feel young. He was a bit of a Peter Pan. We clearly didn't fit that bill but he had still accepted us, for which we were grateful.

We didn't rush out as we'd arrived quite late. We had breakfast in the room and then crept out about 10:00 AM so as not to wake Elias. Elias' shower was far from ideal. The seal on the floor was broken so water seeped under the bottom of the shower unit and flooded the bathroom floor. It could have been a really nice flat with a bit of TLC but it was seriously neglected.

There was free Wi-Fi on the underground so I could message Kathryn to say we were still alive and well. It was only twenty minutes to the centre of Helsinki but at €3.10, ticket prices felt astronomical compared to the free overland train travel we were enjoying with our passes.

On the way to the National Museum of Finland, we met David, father of the couple with the four-year-old we'd met on the boat to the fortress island a few days before. "I recognise you by your camera," I told him. Although he was German, he had an American father who had been in the forces in Germany. He spoke English with a German American accent. His American wife's father was of 100% Finnish descendant, so they had decided to visit Helsinki. It was his father-in-law's first visit to the land of his ancestors!

The National Museum of Finland was not exactly the British Museum. They didn't have all those colonial delights acquired (some would say stolen!) from across the globe when the sun never set on the British Empire. Finland was a very young country, by contrast, that had previously been part of the great empires of Sweden and Russia. Nevertheless, it was worth a few hours. The Scandinavian art nouveau building was interesting. A bear sat on the steps up to an ornate doorway. A stone bear that is, not a real one! A Tsar's thrown used by the Russian Tsar when he was visiting the Russian controlled Kingdom of Finland and some Viking artefacts found in Finland, caught my eye.

At lunchtime, we walked through central Helsinki to Market Square (Kauppatori), a famous outdoor market by the waterfront. Here they had 'cooked to order' moose burgers with chips for €15 each. "Have a seat," she told us, "and I'll bring them round." She was warning people who were picking up food from the counter to keep their hand over their food so enterprising seagulls couldn't swoop down and steal from their plates! Seagulls at the English seaside are notorious but in Scandinavia they seemed to take aggressive behaviour to a whole new level!

The moose burgers were delicious! Very succulent! We kept our eyes out for seagulls on the prowl. It's not often you get moose on the menu and we didn't want to lose it in one fell swoop!

After our burger, we walked up to the Helsinki Cathedral which sits on a platform like a large, tiered wedding cake. Inside it was very plain, in the Lutheran tradition. In total contrast was the Upenski Cathedral, the Orthodox Cathedral. The impressive brick built Orthodox Church had multiple towers and spires topped by thirteen gold cupolas. Inside, it was a riot of altars, icons and crosses. The intricate patterns on its arches were set against block marble and there was a preponderance of gold embellishments.

Following on our theme of having a beer on historic ships with lots of character, we had a drink on a red and white lighthouse ship. It was pre-war and sank during the Second World War but was brought up from the seabed and given a new lease of life as a bar. We sat in the warm sunshine overlooking the old warehouses, now bars and restaurants, and watched boats coming and going!

We returned to Elias' place. At his underground station, a very long escalator rose up towards a panelled perspex opaque window which dispersed the bright sunlight. It was like a scene out of a sci-fi movie and very in keeping with the modern feel of the area.

Elias was out. He had told us he was going to play board games with friends for the evening. Like Johanna and family, he had a huge set of shelves full of board games. It was clearly a popular pastime in Finland. Some might say an obsession judging by the number of board games they both owned. We could only scrape together about 10, including Monopoly, Uno and Scrabble. Which self-respecting household didn't have those famous games? In Finland, however, it seemed to be obligatory to have fifty to a hundred! Johanna had run out of space for them all!

Elias didn't have a kettle so I boiled water in a pan. It wasn't until I smelt burning that I realised it had boiled dry! That's what happens when you're used to a kettle that turns itself off. Also known as a modern safety feature! I would have felt bad if I'd burnt his flat down!

In the event, Elias didn't return until the next day. We got a pizza and beer from the supermarket. Most places only have a hob and no oven so Richard relented on his proclamation that he wasn't going to cook at the flat. We relaxed, enjoying having the place to ourselves!

TURKU!

We were up early and left at 7:30 AM to get the 8:36 AM to Turku. Confusingly, we had to go to Kupittaa, the station before Turku because of engineering works. Our train was due to go from platform 11 but when no train arrived on platform 11 with minutes to go, I realised the first half of platform 11 had been boarded off. We went further up to investigate and had to go around the board to find the train. Signs, as is often the case, were not clear and it would have been easy to miss the train!

After this difficult start, however, things improved. As it was a weekend, Ekstra class was wonderfully quiet. We settled in and had tea and coffee on the train as it raced across the southern part of Finland towards historic Turku, one hour and fifty minutes east of Helsinki, in the pleasant sunshine.

Once in Turku, it was a twenty-minute stroll to the centre of Turku, the former capital of Finland. I say centre but it didn't really have a centre. It was stretched out along the river. We started with Turku Cathedral which was burnt down several times over the years. I had a look at the museum with its many medieval treasures that had survived the fires. Intricately inscribed bibles were juxtaposed with huge silver candle sticks and gold chalices. The robes of long since buried priests had survived remarkably well.

During the long walk along the river we had many historic

boats to look at with the star of the show being the Sigyn, a three masted merchant ship built in Gothenburg in 1887. There were also small naval vessels that caught Richard's eye. We stopped for a picnic on a bench overlooking the river. Huge cranes stared menacingly at us from the opposite bank.

There was a wedding going on at the castle and photos were being taken. The castle had been heavily restored and in parts it was like Disneyland. You had to work hard to find what was the original but it was an impressive building, none the less, and certainly had a classic Scandinavian appearance. You would never get this hard edged, angular and chunky looking castle confused with one of the fairy tale chateaux in the Loire! The oldest part of the building dates back to the Swedish Era of the 1200s since when it has had many guises from luxurious palace, the seat of government, administrative centre and warehouse to, of course, the ubiquitous prison!

On the long walk back to the train station, we took the free chain ferry across the river and then stopped on a barge boat for a beer. The staff told me the boat had been a river barge working up near Helsinki. When the company who turned it into a bar acquired it, it had been used as a brothel for a number of years. "We found booths on the bottom deck!" they told me. Every boat tells a story!

We got the 16:31 PM train back to Helsinki and encountered our second out of three officious Finnish ticket inspectors. My pass was taking a while to load which often happened. With this in mind and on the advice of Facebook aficionados, we always took a photo of the ticket when we first generated it. These photos have been accepted by every ticket inspector the length and breadth of Europe in the last nine weeks of travelling but this job's worth refused to accept this screenshot of the day's ticket, dated 7:30 AM that morning. If he thought I had the I.T. skills or time to fake that, then he was sadly deluded. "I'll have to turn my phone off and reload it," I told him, hoping this would send him on his way but no.

"I'll come back," he said brusquely and disappeared.

Once I'd got it up and running and ticking away in real time, he was nowhere to be seen! I had to keep clicking on it to ensure it didn't disappear. Thirty minutes later, he was back. "You took your time," I told him. "You're stressing me out!" I continued! He looked unconcerned about my mental health as he checked my pass! "Satisfied?" I asked, unsure if he'd get British sarcasm. "Yes!" he said, curtly and off he went.

Back at Elias' we had the place to ourselves again and had more reindeer soup.

BACK UP NORTH!

We had to be up early and straight out for our 8:19 AM train. Elias was awake and on the sofa, so we were able to say goodbye and thank him. We left a card, a London themed bag and stickers.

At the train station, a homeless man was asleep on a bench and a few others were just waking up. Our return journey back up through Finland followed a central route via Kuopio and Kajaai. Our route down through Finland had been down the western side of the country so the idea was to take a different route back for variety. A few hours longer but quieter and easier to get a seat in Ekstra. In the event, the route was different but the view certainly wasn't! It was trees and lakes on repeat the whole journey. I tell a lie, I spotted a few hills off to the east at 3:47 PM! I was that surprised. If our week and a half in Finland had taught me anything, it was that it is very flat! Well that and the fact that it had a lot of trees and lakes!

On the first leg of our journey, we encountered Mr Job's Worth Mark 1 again, the same ticket inspector that had demanded to see and inspect everything, right down to our shoe size! "Are you on the return journey?" he asked, clearly recognising us.

"Yes," I told him. Now you'd expect that as he recognised us and had already checked all our vital statistics, he'd be able to give it a break and take a day off but no, true to his Mr Job's Worth title, he scrutinised everything! He was clearly after 5 gold stars and the 'Mr Job's Worth of the Month' award!

It was a very pleasant, sunny day but even the bright sunshine couldn't penetrate the forest floor in places where the dense vegetation was at its thickest. We were often travelling through a corridor lined with trees that blocked out views even of the sky. It reminded us of driving through Victoria in Australia. There a road went through a forest with trees the size of skyscrapers towering above us on each side of the road. It took three boring hours before we emerged from the forest. For me, the joy of a road or rail trip is the view so three hours of having it blocked by trees is a form of torture! The equivalent of waterboarding in my book!

Compared to some of the longer journeys we'd done it was relatively straightforward. It basically consisted of two 4-hour legs with a change of trains in Kuopio. What could possibly go wrong? Signal failure, that's what! About an hour before we arrived in Kuopio, the train started to go at a snail's pace. We had a "short transfer" of only ten minutes and it didn't take a genius to work out that we were going to miss this connection. There were some announcements in Finnish but none in English. "They probably said, we're stuffed," I told Richard. "Mind you, we're on a train to the middle of nowhere to catch a train that departs from the middle of nowhere. Who is going to be on that train if it's not people from this train?" Sure enough, I was right. I nabbed the ticket inspector who confirmed my suspicions.

"The train to Oulu will wait for this train. It will be further up the platform." In the end, it was a smooth transfer in Kuopio but we arrived into Oulu about thirty minutes late. Luckily, we'd booked a studio apartment near the station.

OULU

We dumped our bags and went to explore Oulu which, unlike most towns in the northern regions of Scandinavia, had some pleasant turn of the century architecture. It was bright sunshine and the locals were out on the town. We walked down to the Gulf of Bothnia, where there were lots of old historic warehouses, some now cafes and restaurants. As we returned, I was getting frustrated because I still hadn't found the City Hall; a grand, ornate yellow building. When I googled 'Oulu images' it featured prominently so I expected it to be posing as the centre piece of city. Richard had started to get frustrated, keen to get back and have dinner.

Telling Richard, he could go back to the apartment if he liked, I resolved to continue the search. I just couldn't understand why I was struggling to find it but with persistence, the sort of persistence that really pisses Richard off, I found it, hiding in plain sight. The reason I couldn't find it initially was that it was totally covered in scaffolding because it was being tarted up for Oulu's moment in the spotlight when it would be European Capital of Culture in 2026!

BACK TO SWEDEN!

We settled on an early start from Oulu as we had two unpredictable bus journeys on our route. It was a re-run of our border crossing from Sweden to Finland but in reverse. It had been rather laborious on the way over and we predicted it would be rather laborious on the way back!

It was one hour to Kemi and, horror of horrors, there was no Ekstra class as it was a sleeper train that had ploughed its way through the light night from Helsinki. I'd got far too used to Ekstra class! "So, there's no free tea and coffee?" I asked the ticket inspector. We hadn't made coffee at the apartment as we thought we'd get it on board. I must have looked distraught because he took pity on me, and said that if we showed our passes in the restaurant car, we'd get free tea and coffee! This worked a treat and it was good to see not all Finnish ticket inspectors were mean and nasty!

Once in Kemi, we crossed to the bus station where we had to wait until 10:55 AM for a bus over the border to Haparanda in Sweden. The waiting room was locked up so we had to sit outside. It was quite warm in the sun but not in the shade where the seats were located.

Back at Haparanda bus station, we gained an hour which we soon lost because we had to wait just over an hour for the bus to Lulea. We decided to pay the ground nesting gulls and Arctic terns a visit. I went first while Richard stayed with the luggage. As before, I was very much an uninvited guest but I wasn't the only uninvited guest. This time there were other people out with their cameras.

When I crossed the grassy area terns and gulls rose up into the air and screeched loudly above my head. One Arctic tern swooped down and pecked the top of my head, forcing me to wave my arms about frantically above me. The grassy area provided good cover for the nests. I only found one tern nest with eggs by watching a tern fly up into the air. I had to be very careful where I trod as I didn't want to tread on a nest. Concentrating on what was below and above was stressful!

By way of contrast, over on the tarmacked area, the black headed gulls' nests were very visible and easy to observe. Many of the green speckled eggs that were in the nest one and a half weeks earlier, had turned into speckled brown fluffy chicks. With the gulls screaming blue murder above, I could get very close to the nest with up to three chicks. Some chicks who were out of the nest, hid in undergrowth but they would have provided a perfect smorgasbord lunch for a hungry Arctic fox! One chick was still picking its way out of an egg. All I could see was a hole with a small beak poking through.

In spite of the warming weather, the bus was cold. I got a good view at the front of the single decker but I was too cold to enjoy it. "Is the air con on?" I asked the driver. "It's a bit cold."

He didn't understand 'a bit.'

"It's too cold," I said, in order to be more specific.

"I'll look at it at the next stop," he told me. When he did adjust it, the temperature was fine. "It was eighteen," he said, "and I've turned it up to twenty-one." It felt more like eight degrees to me!

Once in Lulea, we crossed to the railway station and sat on a bench on the platform in the warm sunshine. I got a beer and an ice cream from a nearby supermarket and we watched a number of mile long cargo waggons and container trains go up and down the line along with passenger trains. A young trainspotter stood on the platform, eagerly recording train numbers and photographing the trains. Apparently, the politically correct term these days is 'rail enthusiast' according to the many 'rail enthusiasts' on Facebook! He waved at the train drivers and many waved back. One of my all-time favourite students, Jake, was a trainspotter. Sorry, 'rail enthusiast'! He'd gone on to get his dream job working for the railways at Kings Cross Station in London! I wondered if this young man would end up working as a train driver, ploughing his way up and down Sweden in the future. I was guessing there wouldn't be many jobs at his local station which didn't seem to employ anyone and where machines did all the work. Mind you, will trains be automated by the time he's old enough to work?

It was only twenty-nine minutes to Boden, a nondescript town like so many 'up north' but we'd booked a night at one of the few historic buildings in town. The hotel was now a budget hotel but it had been a bank in the past. It had a huge safe where they now put the cleaning equipment! It was a bit faded and had shared toilets but it seemed to want to be a posh hotel, providing free chocolate on the pillows, slippers and bathrobes. We had a huge room which was good but, unfortunately, the huge room came with two huge windows. Normally, I would welcome a light and airy room but with 24/7 daylight and flimsy curtains, this didn't bode well for a good night's sleep.

There was a fridge but no kitchen, according to the booking.com details. As it was a Monday, most restaurants were closed but we did manage to find one that was open and got good reviews. We had a large pizza that we shared and two large beers. It wasn't any more than we would have paid at home. Either Sweden had got cheaper or Britain had become more expensive. I suspected it was probably the latter!

Back at the hotel, I went in search of the free fruit offered in the dining area as advertised in reception and what did I find next to the dining room? Yes, you guessed it, a kitchen! Mind you, in the fridge there were some breakfast leftovers that included scrambled egg and meatballs. A sign said, 'help yourself,' so I did. I filled my food container for later. I can forgive anything when free food is on offer.

SWEDISH LAPLAND

There isn't a train I wouldn't take, no matter where it's going!
Edna St. Vincent Millay

T he breakfast buffet for a budget hotel was fabulous. It had hot and cold food, freshly squeezed orange juice and good coffee. There was enough for a packed lunch for the train! What more could a girl want?! Afterall, I figured it would only end up in the fridge as 'help yourself'. The only train out of Boden, a one-horse town, to Narvik was at 10:31 AM. It would take seven hours to cross remote Swedish Lapland then enter Norway.

Now we were back in Sweden, we had the issue again that we had to reserve a seat but the only way to do that was to make an international call on my mobile every time we wanted to get on a train. As I've said before, on our busy schedule, this wasn't realistic. We'd found that on our way up through Sweden, there were spare seat and ticket inspectors hadn't questioned the fact that we didn't have a reservation, which, incidentally, you had to pay for so we'd probably saved ourselves a fortune.

We were a little concerned when we arrived at the station and found that the platform was packed. Where had all these people come from? It was the middle of nowhere! I had a wander up the platform and observed that many were hikers with backpacks and tents. I got chatting to a group of French speakers who were going hiking in Abisko National Park. I'd read about a long-distance trail there so I guessed most of the people on the platform were also heading there. "You sound as if you're from France," I said.

"No, were from Belgium." I apologised for my faux pas but they didn't seem too bothered. People often ask me if I'm from Australia and that does bother me. Not that I've got anything against the Australians. I lived there for a year and taught in a country school. It was a great experience. Okay, they are a bit too obsessed by sport for my liking but it was 2005 and we beat them in the Ashes cricket series, our first win in twenty years, so that wiped the smile off their faces! No, it's because I've been perfecting my Queen's English for years so I don't take kindly to my accent being confused with an Australian accent. I mean, have you heard Dame Edna Everage speak?

I asked some train staff about how full the train was likely to be. They were going on the train waiting to go to Lulea but said they thought it would be busy but not full. "It's the holiday season now," said a buxom woman with blonde hair. "Many people are travelling." The summer holidays had started at the beginning of June in Scandinavia which was bad news. I'd aimed to avoid school holidays since retiring as a teacher but in vain! "We've had lots of Interrail travellers," she told me, "because of the 50% off sale!" They said there was no first class on the train to Narvik which was a bit of a blow!

When we boarded, Richard found a single seat at the back of the last carriage. I noticed a glass compartment so went in there. A man with a baseball cap, a goatee beard and workman's shorts gabbled something jovially at me. People often mistake me for a local and speak to me in one of the Scandinavian languages. This was very different to most of the world where I certainly didn't look like a local. "I'm an English speaker," I told him.

"I was here all on my own and now I have company," he said in English. We both had company fairly soon as the carriage started to fill up. Amongst others, we were joined by Talita who was twenty-one years old and had recently graduated. She was going to Abisko National Park to work in a hostel for the summer season. She enjoyed hiking so could make the most of her time off. She was Dutch but had moved to north Gothenburg with her parents at the age of nine.

She kindly let me use her hotspot to book an apartment in Narvik. I'd held off booking accommodation, worried that there would be a problem getting the only train of the day. "I'll book it when we get on the train," I thought. Then, much to my horror, there was no train Wi-Fi, a luxury I'd got used to during Part Two of our Interrail trip. We now faced arriving in Narvik at five o'clock with no accommodation and the prospect of finding somewhere to get Wi-Fi and book accommodation. Initially, Talita's internet didn't work but she said we could try when we got to station where we would wait for ten minutes and where there may be reception. Luckily, there was and I booked an apartment.

We were also joined by Milan, a twenty-nine-year-old man from Czechia. We talked about the Czech Republic recently changing its name to Czechia. "I travelled there when it was Czechoslovakia," I joked. "Before you were born." He was a geography graduate who worked in mapping. Like us, he had a three-month interrail pass. His Ukrainian girlfriend also had a three-month pass but had decided to join him for only seven days; reluctantly would have been my guess! What a waste!

We were now four weeks into our Scandinavian trip and hadn't even come close to pitching the tents we were lugging about with us in our backpacks. Milan, on the other hand, had been camping on most of his Interrail trip which he'd started about the same time as us. When he wasn't camping, he'd stayed with friends. To add insult to injury, he didn't even have a large and heavy backpack like us. It was very much a medium sized backpack! The reason for this was that he wasn't camping in a tent but under a tarp. He showed me a photo of his yellow tarp and then dug it out to show me. It was the size of a pakamac and I had to admit that I didn't think that would work for me!

We travelled northwest, across Swedish Lapland where rolling hills made a pleasant change from the flat landscape of Finland. The train stopped frequently but if I'd thought Boden was a one-horse town, I ain't seen nothin' yet! There were small settlements with a few houses! Mike, who I'd christened Mike the Miner, because he worked at the mines in Kiruna and regularly travelled on the line said, "Nothing happens in these places. See that tractor, it hasn't moved for five years. That Mercedes has been in that exact spot for three years."

Mike the Miner was a larger-than-life character and held court in our twelve-seat compartment. Some may have enjoyed his lively banter but other people moved out so they could find a quieter spot. Mike was originally from Finland but had moved with his parents to the East Coast of Sweden, near Umea. In the nineties, when the Finnish economy was struggling, many Finns had moved to Sweden.

He was an excavator driver at the mines in Kiruna and did seven days on and seven days off. "The money is good," he told us. He had two daughters and one had just hit the teenage years. "She's become like a different person. Really moody and angry," he said, clearly struggling to understand this new phase. "I just don't get her! I can't say anything without her biting my head off," he commented forlornly!

Mike the Miner had a top tip that he was keen to impart to us. Buy a coffee for 22 krona at the start of your journey and you can top it up for free for the rest of the journey. It soon became clear that Mike had other incentives for frequent trips to get a top up. "The woman in the cafe is like a pirate," he said. "She's got dreads and a bandana. Oh, and big tits." He put great emphasis on the words 'big' and 'tits' and added an extravagant mime, in case we didn't get the picture. A few hours into the journey, having heard Mike the Miner relay the story several times, I decided to go and check out 'the pirate' for myself. She was, indeed, just as Mike had described her: bandana, dreads and very buxom. She could have been Johnny Depp's female twin.

Mike's 22 krona deal didn't seem like a deal to me at all, having enjoyed free tea and coffee on tap in first class throughout Sweden. I told her I had a first class pass and that on the train in Finland, if there was no first class, you could go to the cafe and get free coffee and tea. "We don't do that in Sweden," said the woman, "but I'll give you free coffee." She kindly poured me two cups and I returned to the glass carriage community to report I had checked out 'the pirate' and she was a lovely lady. I thought it wise not to mention she'd given me a free coffee!

Besides not being very politically correct, Mike the Miner was also not very diplomatic. When the topic of conversation got onto the high price of beer, Milan from Czechia said, "Czechia beer is cheap."

"It is," said Mike, "but it tastes like salt water mixed with piss!" If mild mannered and pleasant Milan felt offended at having one of the national icons of his country insulted, he didn't show it. All beer sold in Sweden was a weak 3.5%! Perhaps that was the problem!

As we travelled northwest across Swedish Lapland, the trees became small and feeble. The thick forests were replaced by open, grassy areas. "It's called a myr," said Mike the Miner.

"It's a swamp. It's covered in cloudberries. Later in the year it turns yellow because of the yellow berries. People from Thailand come and pick them to sell when they're ripe."

As we climbed into the mountains, snow-capped peaks appeared. In tandem with this, angry rivers full of tossing and turning meltwater tumbled down the mountainside and under the railway line.

Mike pointed out Malmberget Mountain which was still striped with snow from the previous winter. It translates as Ore Mountain as it's a source of iron ore which is mined and exported.

In the area of Abisko National Park, the train wove its way around some large lakes. Some smaller lakes were still frozen and there was lots of bare rock covered in snow and ice. You certainly knew you were well above the Arctic Circle!

The horn of the train was constantly being blown. This was a frequent occurrence in Scandinavia but here it was double the frequency. "They're trying to keep the reindeer off the tracks," said Mike the Miner. "The Sami insure their reindeer for one million krona each. They then go, 'Oh no, my ten best reindeer were on the tracks and got hit by a train!' It's a very good payday," he continued, sounding very cynical.

Richard, who hadn't seen more than a few hares so far in Scandinavia, proudly proclaimed he'd seen a whole herd of reindeer. My only sighting was three reindeer who were dangerously close to the tracks. "They're really stupid animals," said Mike. "They wander into the middle of the road and lick off the salt."

Mid-afternoon, we rolled into Kiruna. When I'd been there in the winter, it was covered in snow and the slag heaps looked like dramatic snow-covered mountains. We'd been dog sledding and out on a skidoo through snowy forests and across frozen lakes. It was a winter wonderland. Looking out at it from the train in the summer, however, it was a depressing place. The slag heaps were ugly dark brown muddy mounds. It was from here that the cargo waggons we saw along the way, radiated out.

Mike said the unmarked carts contained gold. "Isn't that a security risk?" I asked.

"Not really," he said, "it's unprocessed so the waggons are full of big lumps of earth."

Once Mike had left the train, ready to jump straight into his mega machine, the carriage became far more subdued. The scenery, however, was far from subdued. As soon as we crossed into Norway, we hit a classic fjord. A sandy beach marked its start, far below and then it filled with water as we travelled along the lip of it, way above, all the way to the sea. Ribbon like waterfalls crashed down the opposite side of the fjord as the precipitous views intensified.

NARVIK

Milan and Tanya, who travelled on to Narvik with us, were going to camp for the night. Milan had shown me a photo of a wild camping site but as we got off the train and the cold Arctic air bit, I was glad we were heading for an apartment.

It was about fifteen minutes to the old wooden house and our ground floor apartment. We had a code to get in and 'free to take' leftover breakfast food we could heat in the microwave for dinner so most of our time was spent relaxing after our long train journey.

The double bed had three walls around it and was off a corridor/storage area. It was fine for one person. The two-seater sofa in the lounge was not a sofa bed so I had to get my mattress out. I also had to get my eye mask out which I had packed in anticipation of the long white nights, because the blinds on the windows were useless! It wasn't all complaints, however, as we were able to wash clothes in the washing machine.

Checkout was at 11 AM the next day but about 10:00 AM, I walked down to the bus station to check that the times of the buses to the Lofoten Islands corresponded to those online. Only two a day went from Narvik to the islands and we'd already missed the first bus so there was no room for error.

It was overcast and an Arctic breeze hit my face. I wondered how Milan and Tanya had got on with wild camping. I felt chilled to the bone just thinking about it!

Once at the bus station slash shopping centre, I couldn't find a human being to confirm the bus times but there was a timetable on a board that corresponded with the Internet timetable so that would have to suffice. It didn't surprise me that there was no living, breathing person at the bus station in automated Scandinavia. I went to double check with the woman at the flower shop. She confirmed there was no person and no information office but she kindly looked at the bus timetable on the internet for me, just to confirm what I had read was correct and that there were no messages in Norwegian like, 'Only runs every other Sunday in August'! She was Norwegian but spoke English with a working-class English accent, having lived in Bedford for ten years.

The bus wasn't until 3:50 PM so we had time to spare. I messaged the apartment owner to ask if we could leave our bags in the hallway and collect them at 3:00 PM. The reply was an abrupt "No! Haven't you checked out yet?" We started packing up when he appeared. "We have other guests arriving."
"But check-in isn't until 4:00 PM."
"They have an early check in. They have left luggage at the train station."
"But we're going by bus!" We packed up and walked to the bus station with me composing my negative review on the way!

We went and sat in the food court of the shopping centre attached to the bus station. We fitted in well because it was full of O.A.P.s having a coffee and a natter!

As we had a few hours to twiddle our thumbs, I went off to the supermarket to get supplies, calculating that it may be more expensive and more difficult to shop on the islands. I got some beer but when I checked the bill, I'd been charged for an extra can. Each can comes with a deposit so two amounts appear on the receipt. That made it a long list and worth checking. I got an extra beer from the shelf that I had, after all, paid for but didn't want because they couldn't refund me on my card; and they chucked in one for free when I kicked up a fuss!

When I emerged from the supermarket, it became clear that I was about to take my life in my hands. A young woman coming up the street was under attack. A large gull, the ones that are the size of an albatross but far more aggressive, had swooped down and was dive bombing her. She had a bag and that seemed to be the object of the attack. Once she'd beaten it off, it came after me! Perhaps it was after that extra beer I'd got for free! It seemed to sit on top of a chimney pot and target shoppers. It was obvious that Scandinavian gulls had evolved into monsters that probably snatched babies and flew off with them to swallow them whole!

I'd been advised to download the Norland Bus App. That morning, whilst still on the apartment Wi-Fi, I had downloaded the app and paid £56 for two bus tickets to Kabelvag. It seemed astronomical but, on reflection, it wasn't bad for a four-and-a-half-hour journey. Unlike the bus app in Stavanger where you had the option to pay and then activate later, I realised that my ticket had been activated. It would run out 45 minutes after we boarded so, technically, we'd have no ticket for three hours of our journey. Oh, the joys of modern technology!

When we boarded, the tickets, that were still active at that point, refused to load. The fat, friendly driver didn't seem bothered so I relaxed about the ticking time on the ticket. Ten minutes later, it loaded and I took a screenshot but it was never checked.

As Narvik was the end of the train line, Milan had been talking about returning to Boden on the train to go south or taking a bus to Bodo. I recommended he and his girlfriend take the seven-hour bus through the Lofoten Islands and then the free for foot passengers ferry to the mainland. He'd obviously taken my advice because they turned up for the bus.

"How was the wild camping?" I asked.

"Oh, okay," he said, unconvincingly.

"Was it cold?"

"Um, yes, but there were some buildings so we got some shelter from the wind."

"Oh, that's good to hear," I told him, thinking at the same time, "sounds horrendous!"

THE AMAZING LOFOTEN ISLANDS!

The weather improved and blue sky and sunshine broke through as we wound our way around the fjord and on to the Lofoten Islands, a chain of islands and mountains that have been on my bucket list for a significant length of time. Photos of divine looking red fishing huts hanging over fjords with mountainous backgrounds grace many a glossy travel magazine. It's always blue sky and sunshine. Unfortunately, this is not the reality. It pisses down with rain for over 300 days a year and you can't see a thing! We intended to head up the Norwegian coast in early June, after we'd done the southern area of Norway which enjoys much better weather. I'd monitored the weather on a daily basis and the weather symbols were constantly dark grey clouds and rain. We decided to head for sunny Stockholm instead. Three weeks later, as we travelled up through Finland, I'd notice there was a good weather window coming up. At least three days showed full and uninterrupted sun. We decided to go for it!

Views back inland and over to the Lofoten Islands with beautiful towering peaks still covered in snow, started to appear. As we headed south on the Lofoten Islands, I noticed that Milan and his girlfriend were fast asleep and missing the sublime views. "So much for wild camping," I thought.

The road was punctuated by tunnels and bridges in order to navigate under and over the many fjords and inlets. One bridge over an inlet gave us fabulous views of rocky, flat, green inlets surrounded by turquoise water. It could have been a scene from the Caribbean. Similar turquoise waters were to be found throughout the islands on our five days there, giving out very unexpected tropical vibes so far above the Arctic Circle!

We continued to wind our way down fjords, always with mountains rising up precipitously. The mountains throughout the islands displayed attractive patterns and shapes. Some looked like the turrets of a castle and others were folded, fan like. Most were various shades of grey, depending on the light and shade. Many were still decorated with significant bands of snow, in spite of the fact that we were racing towards midsummer, now just over a week away.

We stopped at a bus stop every few minutes and in the last third of the journey, clouds started to descend. They swirled around the peaks, the tips of which sometimes appeared above the clouds. Sometimes they sat like hats on the top of the mountains and on other occasions they came over the mountain tops and descended menacingly, like an invading army. Whilst they were interspersed with blue sky, it was atmospheric but once they'd seized the skies and dominated, it was oppressive. It is something we are used to in Britain so I didn't need to travel to this remote part of the world for cloudy conditions!

We stopped for fifteen minutes at the airport and fifteen minutes in the capital, Svolvaer. Only twenty minutes after leaving Svolvaer, at 8:20 PM, we were dropped off at the Kabelvag Holiday Houses and Camping Ground. It was a short walk from the road to the reception. Here we were met by a larger-than-life owner who said we had two options. He gave us the keys to look at both options. Our original cabin was on stilts. It had a terrace overlooking the lake, connected to the sea on the other side of the road. It was very quaint and like all the buildings, had hair in the form of moss and grass. The kitchen cabin even had several small fir trees growing on its pitched roof. Inside, the cabin was small and only had one bunk bed with little headroom. The other cabin wasn't so quaint but it was more spacious and had two single beds. We went for the second one but we went and had a beer, sat on the terrace of the first cabin so we could enjoy its better view.

We didn't get to the kitchen to cook until about 9:30 PM owing to our late arrival. It was small, crowded and badly equipped. When Richard couldn't find a pan, I notice the young German man next to me was eating from a pan. "There's no crockery or cutlery!" he told me. I had to go and get the camping set out so we could use the plastic plates and cutlery it included. It was the one piece of camping equipment we'd actually used more than once on this trip, but we he hoped (well I did!) that the Lofoten Islands would be the moment we got to camp in the wild! We'd even brought a gas bottle for the camping stove in an outdoor shop at the Narvik bus station shopping centre so we really were, good to go. Someone just had to tell the weather to get with the programme!

The young German man had cycled all the way from Kristiansund, just north of Bergen, not to be confused with Kristiansand in the south of Norway. He'd, of course, had dreadful weather but he was still camping. "Doesn't the 24/7 daylight up here bother you when you're camping?" I asked.
"No," he replied, "a much bigger problem is the birds singing all night." It must be very confusing for animals who don't have a watch to rely on. How are they supposed to know when it's time for bed?

NOT THE WEATHER
WE WANTED!

As predicted, it was cloudy. If the weather forecast for that day was correct, we hoped it would be correct for the next three days as it forecast sun, sun and more sun! We decided to give ourselves a day off. Scandinavia had been exhausting with lots of single nights and long train journeys. We weren't complaining, that was just the nature of the sparsely populated northern region of Europe. The scenery had been worth the effort but there were few places where you could base ourselves in one place and radiate out, as we'd done on Part One of our trip.

We slept late and lazed around, watching Netflix and surfing the net! It was wonderful. Later in the day, there were signs of an improvement in the weather so we went out to stretch our legs and blow out the cobwebs. We followed a path up behind the campsite to see mountains being slowly unveiled as the clouds lifted.

The campsite was encircled by mountains on three sides. Where there weren't mountains, there was water. This was a typical landscape on the Lofoten Islands. The grassy path was squidgy with water and the moss and lichen grew thickly on the rocks. We crossed the road and walked through local housing to a harbour. As we double backed to the campsite, we watched a thick white bank of cloud coat the mountain slopes to the South. It reminded us of the ice wall in 'A Game of Thrones'!

We had dinner about 5:30 PM so it was quieter in the kitchen/dining area. When I was doing the washing up, I got chatting to Bert and Ditta from Holland. Like us, they were sixty years old but this is where the comparison ended! Whilst we'd been sat back letting the train take the strain, they'd spent the last four weeks cycling from Kristiansand in the far south of Norway to the Cape in the far north of Norway. The weather had been so bad up at the Cape that they'd been blown off their bikes.

There was me thinking we were hardcore travellers! In my view, they were totally insane but for them, it was clearly about the cycling challenge! When I mentioned we lived in Yorkshire, we got onto talking about the Tour de Yorkshire, a Yorkshire version of the Tour de France.

On my way back to the room, I was watched the colourful array of birds on the bird feeder which included a magnificent red breasted bull finch, the like of which I hadn't seen for years. I tried to observe from distance and not disturb them so it was a surprise when they got very skittish and flew off to the branches of the tree above. I soon realised, however, that it wasn't me who'd spooked them but the enormous fluffy cat who strolled out from behind the tree, tail erect in the air and as bold as brass. Mind you, the bird life soon got its revenge on this ball of fur because it wasn't long before an equally enormous seagull started swooping down and harassing the cat, even pecking at its head on one of its low swoops over the frustrated cat who seemed to be used to the ire of the furious gull.

During the day, we'd contemplated how we would see the

islands in this train free part of the world. The train pass had been very useful getting us there but was now useless. The bus option was expensive and inflexible. They ran infrequently and didn't go off the beaten track. A bus-hitchhiking combo was a possibility but would still have been a risk, stressful and time consuming. We didn't want to get stuck in the middle of nowhere. On the basis that the weather was going to be perfect for three days, we decided to splash the cash and try and hire a car. We just hoped they weren't all booked up.

I went to reception where the receptionist rang a local car hire company for me. I asked for their cheapest car. He said they had cars but he wasn't in the office so he didn't know exactly what. "130 Krona a day," he said.

"That's expensive," I told him. In early June, when the weather was dreadful, it was 80 Krona a day.

"I can do it for 120 a day."

"110 a day," I said, "and you've got yourself a deal!"

"Oh no," he said, "I can't do it for that! I said I'd have to put up prices this summer. I can do 115."

"Okay," I said. I didn't tell him I would have paid 130 Krona a day! We agreed we'd be picked up at the campsite at 8:30 AM the next morning. "I just hope the weather is going to be good," I told him.

"Oh, I don't know about that," he responded. "It will be okay weather."

"Okay! If I'm paying 345 Krona for a car, I need good weather," I told him.

"This is good weather," he replied, matter of factly. It was cloudy and any hint of sunshine had disappeared. I just had to hope the weather forecast was correct. I guessed he wasn't obsessively checking the weather forecast every hour like me.

HERE COMES
THE SUN!!!!!!!!!

As I drifted in and out of sleep during the night, 'night' in the loosest sense of the word; I was confronted by the sunbeams trying to penetrate the blackout we'd set up over the curtains and door to try and keep the cabin as dark as possible. Towels, coats, leggings and socks were all employed to lay over flimsy curtains and cover the glass strip down the door.

At 7:30 AM, I drew back the curtains and was presented with a perfect blue sky and sunshine. My heart leapt with joy. All it had to do was stay like that for seventy-two hours! As we went towards reception, we were met by a very large Viking from Lofoten Car Hire Company. He wasn't the boss who I'd spoken to the evening before so I couldn't berate him for predicting 'okay weather'.

Our driver said they'd only been experiencing damp and cloudy weather to a great extent in more recent years, as the climate has changed. "The Northern Lights were amazing last winter," he told us. "They went on for most of the season. Sometimes there was a few nights' break and then they were off again. I've got a friend who's an expert and he said the solar activity is going to be even better in 2024 and peak in 2025."

"Are you Lofoten Islands born and bred?" I asked.

"Oh yeah," he said, enthusiastically, "I've never wanted to move away. I love it here," he continued. "When I had children, we had plenty of babysitters," he said, in a nod to the community spirit and 'everyone knows everyone else' spirit of island life.

"Yes, I know," I said, "I'm an islander too." Mind you, I'm not sure I'd want to live on an island where it's dark 24/7 for several months and light 24/7 for several months, in spite of the divine scenery.

Once all the paperwork was down, our first stop in the car wasn't a spectacular viewpoint but REMA 1000 supermarket. Once we'd filled up with groceries, however, we headed straight for the harbour and seawall at Kabelvag, a pretty and colourful fishing village.

It was breezy and fresh but we hardly noticed. The sunlight sparkled on the water and the perfect light led to snow-capped mountains being reflected in the waters of the harbour: dispersed only by the wind whipped ripples in places; thick patches of light brown seaweed, above and below the water; and a wooden pier that projected out into the harbour. A large red fishing hut in colourful Kabelvag, now transformed into a restaurant, announced we were 68.13N and 14.30E.

We walked along the seawall and admired the snow-covered mountain range on the mainland, out to the east. It was idyllic and the contrast to the day before was massive.

At Lofoten Car Hire, I'd asked the best places to see the midnight sun. The closest was at Gimsoy, near the golf course. "There's a bench up there," he said. "Go in an anti-clockwise direction around the island."

We decided to go and check it out for later. As we drove south into classic Lofoten Island territory, we were spellbound by the scenery. One mountain rose up like a fairy tale castle and was perfectly reflected in a lake and another rippled its way down the spine of the islands. I may be romanticising them in the midsummer sunlight because they were also giant walls of solid, dark grey rock that towered above us, mainly untouched by human hands.

We crossed from the large island of Austvagoya, the northernmost and largest island to small Gimsoy on the long-arched bridge. Traffic lights on top of the bridge gave an opportunity to observe the strong currents that swirled around the many islets in the channel and the colourful fishing boats coming and going. Once off the bridge, we looped around and went underneath it, leaving the E10 that is the main thoroughfare down the length of the islands.

The more minor but good quality road hugged the coastline, as was the case in much of the islands, and took us past one of the many stock fish drying racks so we stopped for a closer look. Hundreds of fish were hanging, rather gruesomely, from the racks. I walked beside and under them. Their wide-open mouths gave me glimpses of their inner workings and their spines formed a pattern, the length of their bodies which still had fins and tails attached. The breeze whistled through them, making a rustling sound as if it was a giant percussion instrument. When I tried to break a piece off one of the fish, I was unsuccessful. It was rock solid.

Further along the coast, we found the golf course, bench and the stage that was ready to host the midnight sun's performance. The sun was still high in the sky but by midnight, we hoped, it would descend to just above the horizon to give us one of the greatest shows we had ever seen or would ever see.

We carried on around the island and re-joined the E10 to pass over another arched bridge onto Vestvagoya Island. Hardy looking ponies inhabited some of the grassy fields beside the road. We stopped to get a closer look at one who came over to greet us in the expectation we were there to feed it. Delicate, long clouds started to sit on the mountain tops and I hoped this wasn't the start of a decline the weather.

THE TOP BEACH
IN EUROPE!

S hortly after Leknes, the second largest town, we headed northwest towards two of the top beaches on the islands. We had no plans to sunbathe. It was still far too cold! This was sort of the place I had imagined we would be camping but we'd given up on that idea and rented the cabin for a few more nights, all visions of waking at midnight to open the tent door and gaze out at the midnight sun crushed. It was a good idea on paper but, in practice, it was too cold!

The first beach, Haukland Beach, was voted Lonely Planet's 'Best Beach in Europe'. As we drove down the campervan clogged roads, Lonely Planet's name was mud! If only they had just left it alone in its remote obscurity, we would have had the roads to ourselves, but no, they had to splash it all over and here we were, unable to go more than two minutes without battling with a German campervan head on! Every campervan and his dog seemed to be heading down there.

It was hard to find places to pull over and photograph this award-winning spectacle. We could see why it had earned the accolade: a crescent sweep of white sand and a mountainous bay gave it a Caribbean vibe. That is, until you got out of the car and felt the temperature! Some brave souls were even sunbathing or playing beach games. Totally mad if you ask me!

We parked up and went for a wander. Forget the Caribbean, it could have been a beach on the West Coast of Britain! A river carved a path through the sand to the beach and sheep grazed in the area. I felt as if I had been transported to the Gower Peninsula!

A short drive through a tunnel, holding our breath and hoping we didn't meet a campervan coming in the other direction, as some of them were humungous beasts; and we came to equally beautiful, according to my judgement, Uttakleiv Beach. Much of this beach was covered in large boulders that looked like huge sea turtles resting on the beach. In the background, white sand stretched around to a jagged mountain range that guarded its far flank.

There was a large rock with a small heart-shaped rock balanced on top. Perfect for Instagram photos! A huge, flat, bright green, grassy area extended behind the beach to a round mountain fringed with green but with snow still sprinkled on the top.

Many people chose to camp here as it was one of the wild camping spots where you could see the midnight sun. The trouble was, since the pandemic, wild camping with no facilities had come with a price tag which rather defeated the object of wild camping.

On the way back north, we turned off towards Henningsvaer. Here, we parked the car and crossed its wide river. From the bridge, you could see colourful fishing boats moored up and the ubiquitous mountain in the distance. The town had some 19th century houses but it was crowded so we didn't linger.

THE MIDNIGHT SUN!

W e returned to the cabin in the late afternoon, elated that we'd had a wonderful day of unadulterated sunshine and with high hopes of putting a big tick on the bucket list at midnight. With a midnight road trip planned, it was important to have some rest and relaxation before we set out. Twenty-four-hour daylight plays havoc with one's body clock. Darkness is a time to sleep. In England, even during mid-summer, there's always roughly six hours of darkness that adds structure to one's day. The white nights of the Arctic were very confusing. Normally, I know roughly what time it is, even without looking at my watch but here, I didn't have a clue.

On our arrival back, the camper vans were rolling into position around the campsite. Most were retired Germans who were our age and even older. Richard made a few inappropriate jokes about German campervans recreating the 1940 invasion of Norway.

We ate early evening. As we ate our meal in the kitchen, we got a strange feeling that we'd woken up in a German retirement village. I love the Germans. Some of our closest friends are German and all our children lived there for a year but that didn't mean I wanted to live cheek by jowl with them, or British O.A.P.s, come to think of it! Cooking wasn't a problem but getting access to the single sink was. The camper vans cooked in their camper vans but took a large bowl of washing up to the kitchen where they queued to wash up and take over the single sink. It wasn't really their fault. I blamed the campsite. It was intensely irritating that the campsite didn't have outside sinks they could use.

As we got ready to go on our midnight sun road trip at 11:30 PM, I noticed that the local mountain was bathed in sunlight. It was a very good sign. It took us about thirty minutes to get to Gimsoy where they were playing golf in the midnight sun. Just because you can, I guess, but it was weird. Really weird. Cows sat chewing the cud in fields. We weren't the only people at our favoured spot. Two elderly French women had set up a tripod to capture the witching hour of midnight. What exactly do witches do during the midnight sun? We parked next to them and counted down the minutes to midnight.

At the stroke of midnight, we felt jubilant. A huge orange orb was suspended low on the horizon, well above the water. It was less dramatic than a sunset but, of course, much rarer. We recorded the moment on camera multiple times and took a selfie. The French ladies took a photo for us on my phone and theirs. We chatted in Franglish and Monica said she'd e-mail me the photo. She entered my e-mail address. "There you go," I said to Richard as they drove off, "I said the French were lovely people."

I had to persuade Richard to stay until 1:00 AM so we could see the sun at its lowest point in the sky before it started to rise again. He didn't really see the point, but he humoured me. The beer and crisps we'd brought with us probably helped!

At one point on the return, we got the sun poised above an inlet and framed by mountains either side, it's shimmering orange tail on the water. They say that the best photos are always taken at dawn and dusk when the sun is low in the sky. This was definitely true for us because we had dusk and dawn all thrown into one. The reflections in the water were fabulous. I felt like a professional landscape photographer even with my humble little iPhone. We drove back, getting back to the campsite at around 1:40 AM. On a quick trip to the toilet block, I could hear birdsong all around the campsite and observed birds flying from tree to tree.

We were greeted on our return by the enormous fluffy cat. Unhelpfully, the dodgy cabin door lock locked from the inside and wouldn't open. At 2:00 AM, I was climbing out of the window to unlock the door with an enormous cat opportunistically trying to break in!

THE STARS OF
THE SHOW!

We decided to have a late start on a day when, technically, we'd had a very early start. Confusing? Yes, I know. When we started to wake at about 9:45 AM the enormous cat jumped on the windowsill and scraped its paws down the window in a "let me in" sort of way. "That cat looks evil," said Richard. I couldn't disagree.

We had breakfast and watched the campervans roll out. It was a much warmer day, so some had got their chairs and table out to sit and eat in the sun, reluctant to move on.

At midday, not to be confused with midnight in these parts, we set off to the most southerly point you could go to on the road. Almost but not quite, the southernmost tip of the islands. Moskenesoya Island has most of the superstar attractions featured in the glossy travel magazines. We had to drive for over an hour to reach them but, oh boy, was it worth it. On a map, Moskenesoya Island looks like Atlantis; more water than land. As we drove through the spectacular scenery of interconnecting mountain ranges, fjords and rocky coastlines, the rorbuer fishing huts were the stars of the show. The red huts of Hamnoy fishing village were followed by the yellow huts of Sakrisoy. Reine wasn't quite the grand finale but it felt like it. From the vantage point of a bridge, high above, we admired the rorbuers encircling the fjord and the mountains, fit for a Tolkien novel, which formed a spectacular backdrop. And all this bathed in glorious sunshine and temperatures of 25 degrees celsius. The car had already paid for itself!

By the time we reached A, which had a small circle symbol on the top of it and was the end of the road, what would normally have been a wow moment hardly registered. It was the same with pretty, Nusfjord, a fishing village. It is possible to have too much of a good thing?!

As we drove back, we praised the impressive infrastructure. The remote southern tip was accessed by a series of bridges and tunnels. All were feats of incredible engineering and must have cost a fortune. In poorer countries, such places would take days to reach, not a few hours. Sections were worthy of a high-speed car chase in a James Bond movie; roads cut into the cliffs and bridges weaving across rocky inlets would have been perfect.

At Flakstadoya, the double bridge really evoked James Bond being chased by several black Mercedes, motorbike assassins and menacing helicopters. We couldn't resist and set off to recreate the scene. Sadly, our hire car didn't quite hack it but we could but dream!

Back at the campsite, whilst we were preparing dinner, a couple came in and set up a table for dinner and then left. "Must be Germans," I said joked. "It's the equivalent of putting your towel down on a sun lounger first thing in the morning!"

MORE SUN!

W e awoke to another beautiful day. We loaded our backpacks into the car and checked out. We'd decided to head north to see an area that had clouded over on our journey south from Narvik to Kabelvag.

We stopped at a viewpoint on a fjord just north of the capital, Svolvaer. Steps went up a hill to a viewing platform that afforded commanding views over the fjord, complete with reflections of the snow-capped mountains that surrounded it. The midsummer light really showed the beautiful Lofoten Islands at their best. Off to the north was a safe haven for colourful fishing boats seeking refuge from the ferocious seas that surrounded the islands. In the current calm conditions, it was hard to imagine the storm force gales that regularly swept across the Atlantic Ocean and angrily battered this defenceless little island chain. Hopefully, we would be long gone on the road south before the next one hit.

Continuing on, we came to a viewpoint where, far to the north, a particularly high mountain had glaciers tumbling down its steep slopes. They shimmered in the fjord. Waterfalls, swollen with meltwater, cascaded over cliffs. Once we reached Gullesfjord, well on the way to Narvik, we turned west on the 85 to explore the islands that didn't feature in the glossy travel magazines. We headed towards Storland and went just beyond for about half an hour before we soon realised that there was a reason they weren't featured in the glossy mags. Whilst the area was perfectly pleasant, it just didn't have the wow factor of the E10 Highway islands. We turned around and double backed so we could explore some of the more off the beaten track roads that radiated off from the E10.

The FV868 road took us down the side of Tengelfjord. It was a bit of a hidden gem so less well trodden. A few savvy campervans had already bagged prime spots and got their table and chairs out to settle in for a long white night. We had a picnic overlooking the fjord and then noticed a medium sized cruise ship coming down the fjord. It was a notable sight amidst the towering cliffs of the fjord. Its passengers were all up on the decks to enjoy the sublime views. We managed to keep pace with it as we drove south before it did a sharp turn and disappeared down a side fjord.

At the far end of the fjord, we turned west and crossed onto Arsteinen Island. From here, we travelled down its eastern shore on the FV872. The white sands, turquoise waters and rocky inlets transported us, once again, to the Caribbean and now the weather had warmed up to a balmy 25 degrees Celsius, less imagination was required!

We retraced our steps to the E10 which we re-joined for a short distance before turning off to the west onto the 82 for a coast hugging experience combined with a helter skelter of a road that weaved in and out of small fjords. Still, clear water formed perfect mirror images. One mountain, coated in velvety green looked like an arrowhead when reflected in the water. Another striking scene was a mountain range with various sized peaks. Small green mounds at the front and large rocky peaks at the back reminded me of a family photo. Their reflections in the water below combined to create diamond shapes.

I was finding it hard to pull myself away from the treasures of these magnificent islands but Richard was getting edgy as we had an 8:00 PM bus to catch to the ferry. We re-joined the E10 and arrived back in Svolvaer with time to spare.

Once back in the capital, we found a petrol station to fill up with diesel. When it didn't seem to work, I went in to ask for help.

"Oh, we've run out of diesel," an attendant told me.

"A sign would help," I told her. Luckily there was a petrol station over the road that hadn't run out of diesel.

Richard dropped me at the bus station with the luggage and then returned the car. The car had been great value for money thanks to the glorious weather! It proved to be a gamble that had really paid off!!!

Richard had a short walk back from the car hire office and whilst waiting for the bus, we had a reunion with the cruise ship which was moored alongside the bus station.

The bus south was a re-run of the spectacular route we'd travelled in the car at our leisure the day before. I wasn't complaining. I'd decided you can't get too much of a good thing when it comes to the glorious Lofoten Islands in good weather. We changed bus in Leknes and then trundled south.

We'd stopped at the ferry terminal the day before to check the Internet timetable was correct and that the boat to Bodo departed at 11:45 PM. "Yes, it does," confirmed the young man sat outside a porta cabin.

"And the bus arrives at 11:20 PM so connects with the boat. Is that correct?"

"Oh, I don't know anything about the bus!" he replied.

When I now checked with the bus driver that the bus arrived at the Moskenes Ferry Terminal at 11:20 PM, he confirmed it did. "And it connects to the 11:45 PM ferry to Bodo. Is that correct?"

"Oh, I don't know anything about the ferry," he replied.

"Just no joined up thinking!" I thought, in exasperation.

FAREWELL TO THE LOFOTEN ISLANDS! WE'LL MISS YOU!

I n the end, it all went smoothly and we boarded the boat at 11:45 PM without so much as a ticket! Foot passengers were free. This was a glorious treat in a land of sky-high prices. My island-living mum and dad would have been very impressed!

As we sailed away from the beautiful Lofoten Islands, they had a few more surprises in store. The sun had ducked down behind the mountains of the Islands and now backlit them so they appeared to be a long black spine like that of a dragon or a dinosaur. The edges glowed orange as the ferry sliced through the still, inky black and orange-tinged waters, sending ripples off across the sea.

As we travelled further from the islands, the sun popped up between the mountain tops and sent a long orange streak across the water. Over to the south and the east, the skies turned pink and purple.

The idea was to get a few hours beauty sleep before the boat docked in Bodo at the very uncivilised hour of 3:00 AM. My strong desire to sleep was tussling with my equally strong desire to see one of the greatest shows on earth that Mother Nature could put on.

We each bagged a row of seats to lie flat on so we had the potential to get some sleep. No doubt the campervan occupants weren't bothered because they would just park up in their vans and sleep on disembarkation.

At one in the morning, I went out onto the deck for a final look, the sun being at its lowest in the sky. There was a bit of a stir and people were peering over their railings at the water below. When I went to look and see what all the fuss was about, I saw a large shark fin slicing through the water beside the boat, probably the fin of one of the many basking sharks that frequent the waters around the Lofoten Islands which are rich in plankton, its primary source of food.

I managed to doze off but couldn't help taking a peek, every so often, through the window at the archipelago we passed through towards the mountainous mainland.

We drew into Bodo harbour in broad daylight. Thankfully, there was a warm waiting room so Richard and I, along with a single woman who was a cyclist, could carry on sleeping in there. We got our inflatable mattresses out and used the free toilets.

At 7:00 AM, Richard woke me up because the woman who operated the Thai restaurant in the waiting room wanted to open up. The cruise ship from the day before was sitting outside. No doubt they were all waking up in their comfy cabins and heading off to breakfast. I tried not to think about it as we had a quick wash in the toilet and then headed over to the train station.

Annoyingly, the train to Trondheim didn't depart until 12:27 PM. A cup of stewed filter coffee at the train station was an astronomical £4 so we decided to bite the bullet and wait until we could get free fresh coffee on board. I carried on sleeping on a bench and before I knew it, we were boarding.

BACK ON TRACK
FOR A SCENIC
JOURNEY SOUTH!

Trains, like time and tide, stop for no one
Jules Verne

We weren't disappointed when it came to the coffee. The smart modern train had a smart modern coffee making machine. I had a cappuccino and added an espresso to it. I swiftly followed this with an encore. The shot of caffeine certainly woke me up so I could enjoy the famous scenery on the Bodo to Trondheim route, a nine hour and forty six minute journey, making it the longest single journey without changing on our inter rail trip.

I settled into my window seat for the long haul and appreciated the chance to catch up on my diary whilst enjoying the view. We had a picnic and the time flew by.

As the train travelled west along Saltfjorden, high snow-capped mountains were visible on the far side and small fluffy white clouds were reflected in the still waters. The tide was out so mudflats stretched out to the water's edge, intersected by channels of water running through them and patterned by pools of water and exposed rocks.

After a few hours we slowly climbed up onto a high plateau where snow still lay on the ground and wide, ferocious rivers raced through the boggy ground. It was a desolate yet starkly beautiful place.

I popped to the loo more than a few times on this long journey with free coffee, tea and hot chocolate on tap. I'm always moaning about the long queues outside women's toilets compared to no queues for men's toilets but I was finding that unisex train toilets could be occupied for an inordinate amount of time by men. My theory is they are on the loo on their mobile phones, and I have evidence for my conclusions based on extensive studies of how long my son and husband spend in the toilet, having disappeared in there with their mobile. And don't get me started on the smell!

On one occasion on this journey, I was queuing for what seemed like for ever but was probably about ten minutes outside a toilet. It had been occupied when I got there so the person in question could have been on the loo for longer than ten minutes. I was accompanied by a Norwegian woman who asked me what on earth they were doing in there. "Goodness knows!" I said, "They're probably on their phone." Several minutes later, she asked me to knock on the door. "Are you okay in there?" I asked. There was no reply. Several minutes later, I suggested she knock and ask in Norwegian.

Several minutes later, an indignant young man emerged. "I haven't been long," he claimed.

"Yes, you have," I laughed because let's face it, it was a joke. "We were concerned you'd been taken ill." It was either that or he had a serious case of constipation. Mind you, one glance at what he clutched in his hand gave us the real answer!

We followed the wide rivers down through the boreal forest that stretches around the northern part of the planet and on to the fjords further south. As the sun sunk low over the Trondheim Fjord, we rolled into Trondheim City at 10:30 PM, keen to find our bed for the night. After breaking the record for the longest train journey, we managed to break the record for the shortest walk to our accommodation. It was just three minutes to our hotel that was practically next door to the station. And what a three-minute walk it was. The sun was shining directly on the facades of the colourful warehouses which were perfectly reflected in the river, on the opposite bank of the river. We even got a hotel room opposite this spectacle and an ensuite! We felt as if we were in heaven! Forget the pampered cruise passengers! This would do us!

TRONDHEIM

Checkout was a very respectable noon, and our train wasn't until 1:18 PM so we had some breathing space. After breakfast in our room, I set off to explore Trondheim and Richard opted for some R&R in the hotel room.

I'd been to Trondheim on my 1986 Interrail trip but the only memory I could rake out of the annals was a statue of Olaf, the Viking King who'd brought Christianity to Norway. He was huge and on a stepped pedestal.

I walked up to the main square where I found the statue which was nothing like my memory. He wasn't huge and he wasn't on a stepped pedestal. I think I was merging two memories, the other being of an image in Iceland which I visited a year earlier. A quick search on the Internet suggested that that wasn't on a stepped pedestal either but in front of the cathedral with a stepped facade. It's funny how your mind plays tricks on you. I'll be reading this in forty years' time (I hope!) and not remember half of it as I recorded it here! I had revisited most of the places I'd gone to on my first four Interrail trips in my teens and twenties but I'd never returned to Finland or the northern area of Norway and Sweden, thus time had created a gaping chasm!

The Nidaros Cathedral was a surprise. It's 800 years old and it looked as if it should be in France. It's a classic gothic Catholic church, although it's now a protestant church. Rows of stone saints and kings on the outside contrasted with the simple wooden Sami inspired wooden altar on the inside.

I walked down to the old bridge and admired the colourful wooden warehouses on the Nidelva River, before wandering back through the old town, full of colourful wooden houses and busy pavement cafes. I returned via the supermarket to get supplies for our train journey which was a mere four hours and thirty-seven minutes. When I struggled to find the supermarket, I asked a group of young men for directions. They were manual workers on a break, their overalls stained with oil and paint, and they struggled to communicate in English. They discussed my dilemma in Norwegian and when one bravely tried to direct me in English, his mates cruelly sniggered at his efforts.

BACK TO CIVILISATION!

As we progressed south on the train, it felt as if we were returning to civilization and leaving the more wild and remote north. Farmland started to become more prevalent than wilderness. Bright green pastures contrasted with blue sky and red farmhouses once again.

Sadly, it clouded over by the time we reached Lillehammer which was a shame because it was in a stunning location. We had planned to travel directly to Oslo but since our visit there to see the sights, about three weeks earlier, prices had rocketed so we had had a rethink. We didn't want to visit Oslo, we just wanted to stop over and continue south to Malmo the next day. Accommodation in Lillehammer, two hours to the north was much cheaper so Lillehammer it was.

LILLEHAMMER

Google Maps claimed our accommodation was a fifteen-minute walk from the train station. What it failed to mention was that it was up the side of a steep mountain that rose up from a long, narrow, glacial lake. The famous 1994 Winter Olympics ski jump was just above our accommodation and by the time we'd lugged our heavy backpacks up the mountain, we felt ready to compete in the next Olympics! Weightlifting probably!

We'd been given a code to access our studio apartment and told not to go upstairs. When we found the property, we spotted a door with a code panel on it. I put in the code and entered. It looked rather lived in. A Russian woman appeared and although she spoke little English, it became clear that our apartment was the door with a code panel around on the other side of the building, and past yet another door with a code panel. I wasn't sure how on earth we were supposed to find the right door with such dreadful directions. Our apartment had a great view thanks to our tiring climb so it wasn't all bad and we settled in and had pasta and a rest.

SOUTH TO SWEDEN!

"Well at least it's downhill," I said to Richard as we prepared to return to the train station for our onward journey to Malmo at 11:14 AM. When we were navigating the steep downhill slope, however, we both agreed the "downhill" was just as hard as the "uphill".

"The uphill was tough on the lungs," commented Richard, "but the downhill is hard on the joints!"

We hadn't made coffee at the apartment; preferring to wait for the complimentary coffee on the train. It was, therefore, a bit of a shock to find it was a local train with no first class and no free tea and coffee! We have become very used to the perks of our firstclass rail pass, and some may even say reliant on it!

When the ticket inspector came round, I double checked the situation with him. "No," he said, "there's no first class and no buffet car, just the drinks machines." Machines required credit card payment but our friendly ticket inspector said he'd get us a coffee and true to his word, he returned a few minutes later with our coffee.

"You're a lifesaver!" I told him. "You're much nicer than Finnish ticket inspectors."

"Oh yes," he said, "they're very strict." He had a thick bushy moustache, warm eyes and a peaked cap. We chatted about problems with train strikes in the UK. "It's privatisation there, isn't it?"

"Yes," I replied, "but the government has just taken one train company back into public ownership as it was so badly run."

"That's bad," he said. "We have similar problems here in Norway!"

We had a respectable forty-four minutes to change trains in Oslo. As there was no station seating, we went and sat on a mezzanine in Starbucks so I could get our water bottles refilled. "Have you been camping?" asked a young man opposite.

"Sore point," I told him. "We had intended to camp but it was just too cold and too difficult."

"I like wild camping," he told us.

"Where do you camp?" I asked.

"I live south of Oslo and there are lots of lakes where you can just find a spot and pitch your tent in the middle of nowhere. I love being out in the wilderness all alone. It's so peaceful."

"Sounds wonderful," I said, wistfully thinking that that was how I'd envisioned our camping going.

Sixteen-year-old Christian said he was about to specialise in I.T. at school. "I'm really into programming," he said. "I've already got patents on several pieces of software I've developed."

"Wow," I said, "I'm impressed. You'll go far! I'll look forward to learning that you've become Norway's Steve Jobs!"

Our journey to Gothenburg had first class but no free tea and coffee for the three and a half hour journey. Like many trains in Scandinavia, it was billed as an intercity but stopped in every one horse town along the way. I doubted that they knew what a city was. France had the right idea. TGV from Paris in the north to Bordeaux in the south in two hours with

NO stops, not stops every five minutes!

We crossed the border into Sweden and on arrival in Gothenburg, we had to get the dreaded rail replacement bus again. On our way up it had been an hour by bus north of Gothenburg but now it was a twenty-minute journey south of Gothenburg. At least we knew the drill this time. We walked around the corner to the bus station and were directed onto a bus by train staff. It was an earlier bus than on our schedule, so we hoped we'd get an earlier train but five minutes after getting on this bus and climbing steep stairs to the top deck, we were asked, along with the other passengers, to transfer to the single decker next to it. We still left earlier than scheduled so our hopes of an earlier train remained high.

There was a train waiting to leave when we arrived in Molndal so we hopped on, pleased that we may arrive in Malmo forty-five minutes earlier than expected. We checked with a young man in the carriage that the train was going to Malmo and he assured us it was going to Malmo.

Off we went, a few minutes later, trundling ever further south on our three-day continuous train trip when the ticket inspector came round to look at our passes. "This train only goes as far as Falkenberg, you'll have to get off there and catch a train down to Malmo."

Our hearts sank at the realisation that we'd have to get off after an hour on the train and wait for what was probably our original train at Falkenberg. "I hope the train to Malmo won't be full by the time it reaches Falkenberg!" moaned Richard. The young man who'd given us the false information, kept his head down.

Luckily, by way of compensation, Falkenberg had an indoor waiting room and free Wi-Fi to keep us occupied before we boarded what was our original train.

MALMO

As we neared Malmo, we could see Denmark off to the west in the fading light. After two weeks of white nights, it was strange to be back where it got dark, well at least for a few hours. We arrived in Malmo at 21:51 PM and had a thirty-minute walk to our accommodation. The Malmo hostel reception desk had closed at 21:00 PM so they'd sent a key to the JustIN app. We'd successfully got into our room in Kristiansand using this method but I still felt nervous. It was with much relief, therefore, that I'd opened the app to find the key had been sent whilst we were in Falkenberg, but I wouldn't be able to relax until we were safely in the room.

Once at the hostel, the key worked a treat and the room was spacious and close to all the facilities. When we chucked our bags down, it was safe in the knowledge that we'd booked four nights in one place so wouldn't have to lug them around again for a while. We settled down to relax and when I looked out of the window at midnight, it was actually dark! The first time it had been dark for well over a week!

A DAY TRIP TO COPENHAGEN!

After our three-day train marathon, we were in no hurry the next morning. We had a leisurely breakfast and headed for the station. I'd worked out from reviews of the hostel that we didn't have to walk all the way to Central Station and that Triangeln Station was closer. I wished I'd worked that out a bit sooner as we would only have had to lug our backpacks for fifteen minutes rather than thirty minutes the day before, but better late than never!

We arrived at the station early, at about 11:00 AM. As trains went every twenty minutes to Copenhagen, we had the potential to get an earlier train. Malmo was the perfect place to get cheaper accommodation and visit more expensive Copenhagen, a popular capital city, if you had a rail pass because it was only just over thirty minutes to Copenhagen by train.

The trains were delayed so we ended up getting a delayed train at about the time we were scheduled to get our original train. Richard got a seat but I ended up standing for part of the journey, the first time I'd had to stand in nearly three months. I got chatting to Kristian who was in his fifties and stood next to me. He and his wife lived in a small town, Ystad, southeast of

Malmo. It was where the Scandi drama 'Wallender' was filmed, starring Kenneth Branagh. "We were living in England at the time and Kenneth Branagh and his wife considered our property as a place to rent. Unfortunately, his wife thought it was too far from the centre." Kristian and his wife were going to Spain for a long weekend.

"The train delays were caused by Denmark," said Swedish Kristian. In my experience, where there are delays on cross-border trains, it was just a case of blame the other country. "We always use Copenhagen airport," he told me. "It's much closer than any Swedish airports."

Once we'd crossed the longest road and rail bridge in Europe and arrived at Copenhagen airport, passengers poured out of the train and I was able to get a seat before a new crowd boarded.

When we arrived in Copenhagen, we walked through the busy centre. It felt as if the whole world was there. I could hear languages and accents from all over the world. As one of the top capital cities in the world, it was like a honey pot for international tourists. On this sunny midsummer's day, it felt like London, Paris or Rome. Its popularity was reflected in its prices. When Richard decided he wanted a coffee, we discovered a humble latte cost £6.23. "We're not paying that," we both agreed. It was going to take a while to wean ourselves off free train coffee but sadly, that ship had sailed. Or should I say, train had left the station?

At colourful Nyhavn, Copenhagen's 17th century waterfront, we sat on the deck of a barge and had a beer. It was cheaper than a coffee and provided a quiet corner to escape the crowds and enjoy the views of the historic merchants' houses. We got chatting to a Scottish couple in their late 60s. I assumed they were a couple, but they were just friends who valued companionship when they travelled. She was a widow and said she also travelled with girlfriends. It made perfect sense.

Nearby was the main canal. As we crossed to the other side, we could see three enormous cruise ships parked up, from which tens of thousands of passengers had spilled earlier that day and were now swarming everywhere!

We wandered over to the King's Garden, a park with some formal gardens. Rosenborg Castle looked resplendent sitting high up on a pedestal, above the gardens; and the locals and tourists alike were having picnics, playing games and promenading around the many paths that crisscrossed the park.

On our way to the Kastellet, the former citadel of Frederikshavn, we walked through the 19th century workers houses, long rows of back-to-back terraces. Workers from the Burmeister and Wains Shipyard who saved money into a building society could win the right to rent one of the properties in a lottery; an early example of the humble council house.

At the Kastellet, which dates back to 1625, we crossed the moat and entered via a gate guarded by soldiers. They were very young and probably doing the compulsory military service that all Danish men have to complete. I'm not sure how they get away with that in these days of equality. In Israel, men and women have to do military service but they can opt to do community service instead.

We passed long rows of red barracks as we walked to the central parade ground where there were elegant 18th century yellow administrative buildings. We then climbed up onto the star shaped ramparts and walked a third of the way around them so we could see the huge windmill.

We left via the opposite gate to the one we'd entered and walked a short distance down to the main canal to see the

354

famous Little Mermaid. Here I had to push my way through swarms of cruise ship passengers and graduating high school kids in sailors' hats. One mischievous student climbed up and put his hat on the Little Mermaid. I've seen her twice before but it has to be done on a trip to Copenhagen.

We caught the train back from nearby Osterport Station which saved walking back across Central Copenhagen. We were up to 20,000 steps and had aching feet so it was a wise move.

Once back in Malmo, we went to a nearby supermarket. At the supermarket, the man at the checkout said, "I love your English accent."

"Thank you," I replied. "I love your accent too, where's it from?"

"Lebanon," he told me. "I came to Sweden when I was seventeen and I'm fifty-three now." We discussed the trials and tribulations of Lebanon, Bekker Valley wine and the recent economic woes as a result of the grain silos collapsing. "It's very corrupt!" he said, dolefully.

A MALMO AND
LUND COMBO!

I went off to explore Malmo's old town in the morning, leaving Richard at the hostel. My 1986 memories of Malmo were of a huge town square filled with tall colourful merchants' houses. Much to my horror, I found this wonderful place simply didn't exist. The old town of Malmo was actually rather mundane when viewed by my 2023 eyes. It had a few attractive buildings but none were colourful merchants' houses. There was an imposing equestrian statue of the 17th century King Karl X Gustav who reclaimed the province from Denmark and a modern installation of a town band which I don't remember being there in 1986. When I looked it up on the internet, I discovered it was erected in 1985!

I could only conclude that my memories of Trondheim and Malmo had got intertwined to create a semi fictional place in my mind. Even so, I stuck Malmo Memory 1986 back on the shelf of my memories. It had lived with me for too long to be ripped up. I added Malmo 2023 as a separate and very different memory. Perhaps I was travel weary after three months of seeing acres of spectacular sights in Europe. Don't get me wrong, I'm not complaining but three months of travel in our amazing continent can be a little overwhelming just by the sheer wealth and diversity of history, culture, food, architecture, languages and landscapes. I know I'm biased as a proud European but, take it from me, you can't beat Europe! Go anywhere in the entire universe and you'll never find anywhere that is so special in so many ways!

I wandered over to the nearby Saint Peter's Cathedral where I met Abdul with his family who were picking fruit from a tree near the cathedral. "They're mulberries," said Abdul. "Only the black ones are ripe," he told me, handing me a handful to try. "There used to be a much bigger tree here but it was struck by lightning."

He told me he was from Jerusalem and it wasn't long before we started talking politics. "The Americans could solve the problem with the stroke of a pen," he told me, very emphatically.

"I think it's a bit more complicated than that," I responded, shocked that he saw the solution as being so simple. He'd lived in Sweden for many years. His son, who was about twelve years old had been born in Sweden. He'd visited Jerusalem regularly but his Palestinian wife was not allowed to return. He had a Jordanian passport as East Jerusalem had been under Jordanian control when he had been born and he'd got his son a Jordanian passport. In those few sentences that described his family's situation, he had demonstrated that the situation was far from simple!

Inside the 14th century brick gothic cathedral was a large wooden retable above the altar, the largest of its kind in northern Europe. Most impressive was the Kramare Chapel. Here, in the early 20th century, ceiling murals have been restored in order to give a glimpse of the fabulous medieval artwork that had been covered by Puritan white paint after the Reformation. Some of the murals and gravestones in the floor featured men in impressive doublet and breeches.

I had a wander around the castle with its huge moat guarded by red round towers. The Parkland around the castle was full of Swedes celebrating Midsummer's Day. Many were having parties and women wore beautiful floral crowns, often made of real flowers. Midsummer's Day is the second most important holiday in the Swedish calendar after Christmas and this was very evident here.

In the afternoon, Richard and I took the train over to Lund, one of sweden's oldest towns, having been established in the year 990. In addition, it also has one of Sweden's most prestigious universities. Founded in the 13th century, it is now amongst the top one hundred universities in the world, making it a bit like a Swedish Oxford or Cambridge.

After a short, fifteen-minute train journey, we wandered through cobbled streets and parkland, past university buildings. The biggest jewel in Lund's Crown is the cathedral which dates back to the eleven hundreds. It wasn't hard to find, thanks to its two chunky stone towers. Inside we found an opulent altar and beautiful carvings on the choir stalls which included Old Testament men and a ram's head. The colourful 14th century astronomical clock was restored in 1923 and the cool crypt below the church was decorated with patterned pillars. Here lay the remains of bishops, medieval knights and lords; in fact, anyone who was anyone!

Outside was an information board next to the 15th century library with a stepped gable. It said the cathedral was part of the Pilgrims' Way that stretched all the way to Santiago in Spain. When Queen Margaret had been travelling through Lund in 1387 with her son, Olof, he unexpectedly died aged seventeen years old. It said she'd buried his heart in the middle of the cathedral beside the picture of 'Mary-in-the-middle-of-the-floor'.

Fearing I'd missed this important grave, I returned to the

cathedral and asked where it was at the reception desk just inside the main doors. "No one knows," they said. It had obviously been lost in the mists of time.

We looked around the old town and passed back through the large square with the attractive Scandinavian art nouveau buildings, near the train station, before heading back.

RETURN TO COPENHAGEN!

With continuing good weather, we decided to return to Copenhagen for a day of castles and palaces; something this regal capital had in spades. Thankfully, the train wasn't late or overcrowded.

This was our fourth trip over the world-famous Oresund bridge. Irritatingly, when you travelled over the bridge, you couldn't see the long span of the bridge. Nor could you see it when approaching it by train. I asked the ticket inspector if there was a station where you could get off and see this magnificent bridge from a distance but he replied that there wasn't.

Not one to give up, I sat on the right side of the train, looking back towards Sweden, and squashed my face right up against the window. At last, there it was, its two towers thrusting skyward. I'm sure it wasn't the best view of the bridge which could probably only be obtained by a coastal road trip up the Danish or Swedish coast, but it was better than nothing. The bridge opened in 1999 and featured in the Scandi smash hit drama, 'The Bridge', so it's a bit of a diva in its own right!

As it was a midsummer holiday weekend, the sailing boats were out in force on the channel of the same name, and I could see the famous and very weird Malmo Turning Tower to the northeast. This twisted skyscraper is the tallest in Scandinavia and a modern architectural masterpiece.

We got off the train at Osterport Station so we could finish walking around the star shaped ramparts of Kastellet. With our first castle conquered, we walked over to Amalienborg Palace which is, impressively, four palaces in one, arranged around a square. Queen Margaret II, the longest serving monarch in Europe since the death of the Queen Elizabeth II, occupies part of the palace and the rest is used for official engagements. The soldiers of the royal guard with tall bearskin hats and blue uniforms were standing guard. Like in Stockholm, they didn't compare to the guards of Buckingham Palace.

Next we returned to Rosenborg Palace. This palace, which from the outside looked like a fairy tale castle, was inhabited by the royal family until 1720 and then used as a summer retreat. It became a museum for some of Denmark's greatest cultural treasures in 1838.

Once inside, its opulence was very evident. It was ornate on over drive, particularly in the marble and baroque reception rooms. The fireplaces were huge and very decorative, and the ceilings dripped with plaster cast cherubs and coats of arms.

The Knights' Hall housed decorative coronation thrones used from 1871 to 1940; and the famous Rosenborg tapestries which have adorned the walls since 1693. Exquisite porcelain was also on display, including the famous floral Danica Service.

The piece de resistance, however, was the Danish Crown Jewels in the basement. Crowns, orbs and sceptres were on display, dripping with rubies, sapphires, emeralds and diamonds.

Finally, feeling rather jaded and as if we'd already

seen one castle and palace too many, we walked over to photograph eight hundred year old Christiansborg Palace which is the seat of the Danish government. It houses parliament, the prime minister's office and the Supreme Court; and several sections are still used by the royal household. It was open to the public but we'd had our fill of castles and palaces for one day so it would have to wait for another trip.

On our way back to the closest station, we passed the round tower which is 36 metres high and was built as an observatory in 1642. Having sat opposite the birthplace of Denmark's famous son, Hans Christian Andersen, when we had a beer, we now discovered that this tower featured in his famous story, 'The Tinderbox'- "eyes as big as the Round Tower". Once back at the station, we found it was full of people with backpacks and camping gear, off on a midsummer trip.

In Malmo, we went to the nearby supermarket to get pizza and beer for dinner. "That's really expensive," I said to Richard.

"Yeah," he agreed. It was only then, that we remembered we were back in Sweden where it was 13 Krona to the pound, not 8 Krona to the pound as in Denmark. Hopping over borders and back again in one day can get really confusing!

THE FINAL FURLONG BEGINS!

Having stayed at the hostel for four nights when most guests only stay for a night, I persuaded the manager to give us a free breakfast. I chucked in a 10/10 star rating as part of the negotiations! It was a basic buffet. There was the usual Scandinavian cold spread but nothing hot if you don't count the coffee. I wasn't paying for it, however, and I'm not one to look a gift horse in the mouth!

We were scheduled to catch the 11:33 AM train but managed to get an earlier train for the short hop to Copenhagen Airport where we had to change to catch a train across Denmark to Frederica, on the east coast of Jutland. I'd hoped we'd be able to get an earlier connection but this hope was soon dashed after a quick look at the departures board. The next train was the one we were due to be on and departed from Platform 2. Confusingly, there were signs to Terminal One and Terminal Two but no indication as to what platform we were on. I mean, it's not much to ask! We had to take the escalator up to the main station concourse, just to determine we'd been on the right platform all along so needed to go back down to the platform we'd originally arrived on!

The good news was that free tea and coffee were back

on the agenda. And, even better, there were top notch sweet treats! It felt like the last hurrah!

First class was practically empty when we boarded. Whilst some people would have booked a seat, it wasn't obligatory and the ticket inspector assured us that it was unlikely to be full.

It was unlucky, therefore, when a woman and her husband got on and approached the seat where I was sitting. "You have this seat reserved?" I asked, getting up to move to one of the many other seats. So far so good.

"Don't you have a reservation?' asked the large middle-aged woman.

"No," I said, expecting that to be the end of the matter.

"You need reservation," she told me, assertively and with kind of authority that suggested she had a PhD in Railway Management.

"No, I don't," I replied, starting to feel mildly irritated. I'd moved out of her seat without question so why was she so worried? "I've got a train pass," I told her.

"Oh," she said, "you can't travel in first class with a train pass." Not a word of a lie! I'd navigated first class using a train pass throughout Western Europe for three months now so I thought I knew a thing or two about how it worked. Who did she think she was, a bloody ticket controller who gives out fines to people trying to fare dodge?

"I can," I spat out as I went and sat well away from her. When the ticket inspector came around ten minutes later to inspect our VALID first class rail passes without question, I eyeballed her and she eyeballed me back, clearly unhappy that rail pass riff raff could travel in first class and that we hadn't been kicked off the train.

The journey was like island hopping. Having crossed a huge waterway to get from Sweden to Denmark, there were several more waterways to cross. It felt as if the whole of

Denmark was out on the water, enjoying the midsummer sunshine. The undulating farmland felt far removed from the dramatic, mountainous scenery of north Norway that we'd left behind only a few days earlier.

Our final leg, down to Flensburg, just over the border in Germany was an hour and twenty two minutes. We arrived at 4:00 PM and it meant the end of our six-week Scandinavian Odyssey!

GERMANY

I'd never heard of Flensburg until our 2023 Interrail trip. Another Interailer had praised it and it was a convenient stop on our way back to catch the boat. It was a twenty-minute walk to our hostel but it was right on the water in the centre so worth the long walk with our backpacks.

As we emerged from the station, I was trying to figure out which way to go using Google Maps. A woman kindly came over and asked me in German if I needed help. I replied in German and told her I was English. I thanked her and said I was fine. "That's good," she replied in English. It reminded me that, unlike the Scandinavians, the Germans don't speak fluent English as a rule, so I'd have to dust off my German. I normally enjoy practising my French, German and Spanish and can get frustrated when people reply to me in English but I was travel weary and in no mood to practice my German. At least, I comforted myself, it was just a one-night stop and then we'd be in Holland where they all speak the Queen's English.

When we got to the Flensburg harbour area it was buzzing with people out enjoying the weekend and the warm early summer sunshine. Our hotel was recently refurbished. It had started life as a seamen's mission where seamen working on cargo ships had stayed. It was very trendy with distressed fixtures and fittings, and smooth concrete floors. We had a large corner room with a pleasant view of the harbour.

I met a sixty-eight-year-old German woman, Angelica, in the kitchen. She'd spent three weeks cycling around Denmark. Interestingly, she'd cycled up the Oxen Trail, a route her great grandfather had used for its original purpose, to take cattle to market. "Would you like some butter?" she asked. "I'm going home tomorrow." I didn't want to turn down this kind offer and even less so when I realised it was a nearly full pack of Lurpak. It's so expensive in the UK these days that they security tag it!

We had dinner and a beer at a table on a terrace overlooking the courtyard, and then in the early evening, we walked to the other side of the harbour. The low sun lit up the many historic sailing ships and classic yachts and their bright reflections painted the water. We had another beer in the courtyard before we went to bed so we could use up the beer we still had from Scandinavia and then hit the hard stuff. It's probably illegal to sell such low strength beer in Germany! Our good friends in Warstein where there just happens to be a very famous brewery and where beer is a second religion, would be appalled!

THE NETHERLANDS

Our train didn't depart until 12:15 PM so we had a leisurely breakfast. The woman preparing breakfast for guests who'd paid for breakfast kindly gave me fruit and coffee when I went to make porridge. When she put left over salad and feta on the 'free to take' shelf in the fridge, I boxed it up to have for lunch on the train. Who needs to pay €10 for breakfast, is what I say?!

Soon after we set off for the station, it started to rain quite heavily. It was grim but made us realise we'd generally been very lucky. We hadn't been rained on like this since France in April.

We got to the station with thirty minutes to spare and were feeling like drowned rats. I was in no mood for any messing so when I found a young man had parked his bike up against the only spare seats at the station, whilst he fed money into the nearby ticket machine, I wasn't best pleased.

"Is this yours?" I asked.

"Si," he said, moving it.

"Gracias," I replied. We had a chat in Spanish! He was from Morocco but had been working in Barcelona for a year.

"So, you speak Spanish?" he asked.

"Some Spanish," I said. "I spent a year travelling in South America. You have to speak Spanish there."

As on the way up to Scandinavia, the route through Germany and Holland was very bitty. We had to endure three changes on the six-hour journey to Groningen.

In Scandinavia, we'd regularly done four to nine hour journeys without a single change but the network had gone from a few lines on a map to a spider's web of connections owing to the increased density of population. We comforted ourselves with the fact that once we got to Groningen, we'd be home and dry as it was only two and a half hours to Rotterdam from there. We didn't want to speak too soon, however, because strikes and cows on the line were still possible!

The first train from Flensburg to Hamburg was fine. We sat upstairs in what felt like a panoramic carriage as the large windows sloped around on to the ceiling. The landscape in northern Germany is similar to Denmark. Norwegian wow factor, it didn't have, but it was perfectly pleasant in a "Jerusalem", the song, sort of way.

The second leg from Hamburg to Bremen was hell on earth! It was just under an hour but it felt like five hours, and it was a rundown old train. We found a space for our backpacks but not for us very easily in first class. Richard went off to second class and I headed for the only spare seat.

As I went to ask the man in the aisle seat if he'd move so I could get in, a young woman in the seat opposite asked if she could take that seat as she was struggling to travel backwards. "Yes, fine," I told her. "I'll just double check that there are no spare seats up there." It doesn't bother me which way I travel but for some people who get motion sickness, I understand it can be a problem. There were no seats further up so I returned to the spare seat vacated by the young woman. The fierce frau who'd already got up once to let the young woman out, wasn't best pleased. As I shuffled past her, sarcastically asking her if she expected me to stand, I had to revert to English as my German vocabulary doesn't extend to argy-bargy on trains! Before I'd even sat down, she threw my coat over to my side. I didn't even have free coffee, tea and fondant fancies to cheer me up.

I could see why people moaned about German railways on Facebook. It was hardly the German powerhouse we had come to expect! "The Hamburg to Cologne route is always very busy," the ticket inspector told me when he came around.

I got chatting to the young woman who had swapped seats. She was travelling from Berlin to Brussels, a journey that was even longer and more complicated than ours.

At Bremen, with Richard down in second class, there was no way I could get the backpacks off the overhead luggage racks by myself without knocking someone out as the bag fell off, so I employed a man who kindly helped me with the job in hand, rather than wait for Richard to turn up.

We had a rather sharpish twelve-minute change in Bremen but the next train was like the first train, a modern double decker with the panoramic windows. When a woman came around asking who wanted tea or coffee, I assumed it was all part of the service. It was, therefore, a surprised when she wanted to charge us. "Oh, you can forget that," I told her, too used to free coffee on trains to start paying for it.

Whilst first class was a pleasant oasis, there seemed to be only a single toilet for the entire train and that was down in crowded second class! One irritating girl who was about thirteen years old, British and had purple hair was talking very loudly on FaceTime to her friend. Her new age hippy parents were oblivious to how annoying this was for other passengers. When she came up to first class to give her friend a guided tour at full volume, I gave her the kind of hard stare that I'd perfected over 35 years in a classroom. She got the message and returned to her hippy parents in second class.

A pleasant distraction on this leg was the Rensburg High Bridge. This transporter bridge and viaduct is an impressive iron structure that is from another era as it was constructed between 1911 and 1913. The train approached it in a giant loop that gave great views of it, unlike the Oresund bridge in Scandinavia, and then it rose up to cross the bridge that straddles the Kiel Canal.

At Leer, we had to catch a fifty-five-minute rail replacement bus over the border and into Holland. For several years the route had been a bus because a boat took out the bridge. On Facebook there were rumours that it would soon be rebuilt but not in time for us. As we crossed into Holland, the landscape became Dutch flat as a pancake.

In Groningen, we walked through the centre for thirty minutes. It was immediately clear that this city wasn't a Dutch classic but, like Flensburg, it was a convenient stop on our return journey. Our hotel was in an old paint making factory, complete with brick chimney. It's always good to see industrial heritage preserved when so much has been demolished.

We had a kettle in our room so we had cuppa soup and rolls before going out for a wander. Luckily, the sun was setting so the canal was lit up. Elegant mansions and merchant warehouses were reflected in the canal's still waters, along with a classic church spire. The next morning, without the benefit of the sunlight, the canal looked very mundane. We stopped for a drink in the main square where historic buildings intermingled with 1960s brick office buildings. It was a planning disgrace! What wasn't a disgrace was the alcoholic content of the alcohol and the cost of wine. I had my first glass of wine for six weeks and savoured every sip! Richard had an 8.5% German beer.

POLDER COUNTRY

Our journey from Groningen to Rotterdam would be our last. I felt sad in some ways but in others we recognised that we were getting jaded and that it was time to go home. It's psychological. When you know the end is insight, it starts to drag. We were now travelling through places to get home rather than pausing to experience and enjoy the culture, history and scenery of a place.

"I just want to get home now," said Richard, who is less adventurous than me. "It's been great but I need a break."

"Yes!" I agreed. "We need a holiday!" I had been concerned that Richard may not have had the resilience for three months of continuous train travel. After all, it's very hard. I'm a bit of a travel junkie so it feeds my addiction but Richard, whilst he enjoys travel, is not as obsessed as me. When we met in our twenties, the extent of his travel was minimal compared to me. Being married to me for 34 years had changed all that but he still passed on travelling for months in South America and Southeast Asia with me. I was, however, wrong about him not having the stamina for three months interrailing! He had coped remarkably well. He had a bad relationship with his backpack throughout the trip and was never going to let me forget I'd made him pack all that camping gear that we never used but he'd lost lots of weight thanks to lugging his nemesis around for three months so, as I pointed out, "It's not all bad!"

We walked back through Groningen to catch our 13:19 PM train to Rotterdam. Bikes rule in Holland. You have to have your wits about you because some people cycle very fast so crossing cycle paths means you take your life in your hands! I'm a driver, cyclist and pedestrian so I can see things from all perspectives!

In Groningen, there were bikes parked all over the pavements. It felt like a Dutch version of Ho Chi Minh City! At one point, the pavement narrowed to single file because of parked bikes. Just before I entered it, a man with a long ponytail, swept past me and then literally pushed Richard out of the way and into the bikes. "Oy!" I shouted after him, angrily.

"You should look behind you," he snarled back.

"Rubbish," I shouted.

"Shut your mouth," he shouted back, peppered with a few swear words and whilst flicking a rude hand gesture. Needless to say, I didn't shut my mouth and I did get the last word in but it's not printable here!

I'd like to say, our final train was a state-of-the-art, modern train fit for the 21st century but, sadly, it was tatty, dirty and probably began life in the last century. It wasn't, however, all bad because there was a first class that for much of the journey was not crowded and when I went through the second class compartment to the toilets which were covered in graffiti, sprayed all over the walls and mirror, I realised second class was far grimier.

By the time we got to Utrecht, the train was stuffed to the gunnels. It was so full, the passengers from second class had to stand in first class.

ROTTERDAM

On arrival in Rotterdam, we went to double check where the bus to the P&O Ferry Terminal went from at 5:00 PM the next day. It had been six weeks since we'd been dropped off and there had been quite a few miles added to the clock since then! To be fair, the driver did shout out pick up instructions but I just wanted to double check as it was back in the mists of time. I was rather hoping for a sign, "P&O Bus Goes from This Spot" but no such luck.

It was a twenty-five-minute walk to our hostel. Here they said they'd upgraded us to a four-bed room. "It's bigger," he told me. It wasn't bigger as it was filled with beds, one being a bunk bed and another a double bed. Upgrade, my foot! In addition, the room was on the second floor of one of those old tall Dutch mansions so it was quite a hike to the room with our heavy backpacks.

They had a new code system for the hostel room doors but you still needed a key card for the front door which hadn't yet been fitted with the code system. "Your job's on the way out," I thought, with regret, as the receptionist gave me the code. Many young people fund their travels by working in hostels so automation would dramatically cut down on the number of people employed at such places. In ten years' time, they'll probably even have robots changing the beds and doing the cleaning!

We had a walk past the impressive Erasmus Bridge, a single tower suspension bridge. Erasmus, the famous Dutch humanist, was born in Rotterdam so his name crops up absolutely everywhere. The locals are rightly proud of Erasmus, their famous son. We had a drink beside the waterway and watched the huge barges ploughing their way up and down the Nieuwe Mass.

The nearby old harbour was full of historic ships and barges that were home to some of the locals. Undies were strung out to dry on the decks that were decorated with colourful pot plants and bikes!

We passed the De Boeg (Arrow) Second World War monument, a sombre reminder of the horrors inflicted on Rotterdam. Most of Rotterdam was destroyed in the war and, as a consequence, the city decided to reinvent itself. Rather than rebuild the city in its pre-war image they experimented with some radical modern architecture, and probably the most unusual was the cube houses. These yellow cubes were striking to look at, but I could see why they never caught on. One window, at a 45-degree angle, had wine bottles leaning against it. It looked like something out of a "Crooked House" fairground attraction. Luckily, the White House, an art nouveau architectural gem built in 1898 was not destroyed in the war. At 10 storeys high it was once the tallest building in Europe.

We returned to cook dinner in the small and dingy kitchen. Initially it was full of French Erasmus students, so we had to return later but once we'd cooked our meal, we ate in the pleasant lounge-dining room full of quirky features like an array of different orange lampshades hanging from the ceiling.

OUR FINAL DAY!

O n our final day, we had the hotel breakfast in the pleasant lounge-dining area. It was a weird feeling not to be thinking about our next train journey! Our first day in Paris, three months earlier, felt as if it was centuries ago. There had been lots of clickety clacking on the tracks of Europe since then!

We had time to kill as our bus to the port didn't leave until late afternoon. We checked out at 11:00 AM and the hostel receptionist gave us two lockers in the basement to store our luggage.

We set off to explore Delft Haven, an area of Rotterdam that hadn't been destroyed in World War Two. It was a long forty-five-minute walk over there and whilst there were some pre-war mansions, we felt distinctly underwhelmed by the area. We returned via Het Park and Richard then chilled at the hostel while I walked up to the modern indoor market. It had been built with a huge arching ceiling, decorated with an attractive and colourful kaleidoscope of fruit, vegetables and other fresh produce. Nearby was the City Hall which was built between 1914 and 1920 in Dutch renaissance style. Miraculously, this huge building escaped the World War Two bombing. I had a look inside the entrance hall at the art nouveau stained glass windows of various figures, including what looked like

Neptune, which I guess is very appropriate in a city where much of the land is at or below sea level. Underneath a large Dome was a nude male in what could only be considered to be a rather provocative pose; one hand behind his head and the other on his hip!

I returned to the hostel where I went down to the kitchen to heat up the leftover pasta from the night before. It would have to last us until we got home early the next morning as we weren't about pay boat prices!! In the kitchen, I met Christian from Romania who worked in a distribution centre in Holland. He'd just been moved to a new centre in Rotterdam and was waiting for his agency to find more permanent accommodation. He'd worked for several years in Holland, returning to Romania to see his family every few months. "How do you get to Romania?" I asked.

"By bus," he said Christian.

"That must be a long journey," I commented.

"Yes, two days but working in the Netherlands pays four times what I would earn in Romania so it's worth it."

We chatted about my experience of travelling in Romania.

Next, I met a young couple from Taiwan. "Where are you from?" they asked,

"Britain," I replied.

"We have just arrived here from Edinburgh," they told me.

"Oh, I love Edinburgh," I said. "It's one of my favourite cities."

"We agree," they said.

"The trouble is," I continued, "it's full of Scots." They looked shocked. "I'm only joking, I love the Scots really," I reassured them. "I'm English. We have a love-hate relationship with the Scots." They looked confused but I had a boat to catch so I didn't have time to explain 400 years of history!

They told me about their plans for their eight-week trip, their first in Europe. "I've been to Taiwan," I told them. They looked shocked again. "Yes," I said. "Beautiful country but you won't meet many people who've been to Taiwan in Europe!"

Richard and I loaded our backpacks onto our backs for one last hike to the train/bus station. We got to the station at 4:20 PM so we were there in plenty of time, in order to catch the bus at 5:00 PM. We were feeling nervous because there was no public transport to the port so if we didn't get the P&O bus, we were stuffed! We would probably have to pay for an outrageously expensive taxi!

We looked around nervously to see if we could see anyone else waiting for the bus. "Do you think they're Hull Booze Cruisers?" I asked Richard, spotting a family in bright coloured clothes.

"Could be," he replied. They weren't it transpired, because they got on a Flexi bus to Brussels.

About fifteen minutes before the bus arrived, I went in search of people with Yorkshire accents. I found two. A woman and her son were returning for one night to go to her brother's funeral in Grimsby. "I've lived in Holland for 40 years," she told me. "I have six children and we always used to go over on the ferry, but I haven't been for 20 years."

"Do you speak Dutch well?" I asked.

"No," said her son.

Nearby was Mark, who was in his forties. Like me, he was nervous about being in the right place at the right time for the bus. In the end, the bus turned up ten minutes late but I wasn't too worried by that stage, thanks to the presence of fellow passengers.

Once on the bus, Mark told us about the purpose of his visit. He'd spent a week on a boat catching crabs. The six-man boat went to sea for seven days and pulled up 3,000 crab pots in sets of 100. Mark's job was to re-bait the pots ready to toss them back into the sea. "It was exhausting," he told us. "I think I'm going to sleep for a week." He knew one of the skippers on the boat who had offered him the lucrative work. "You get a share of the profits," he said. "The week before I did it, they got over 2,000 pounds. The catch was offloaded this morning and will be sent to Torquay where there's a processing factory. Three of the crew were Russians trying to escape being sent to war. Last night, the tracker on the boat malfunctioned so we were met by the police when we docked. One of the Russians couldn't find his papers and thought he was about to be arrested. Luckily, he managed to find them at the last minute!"

"Would you do it again?" I asked.

"I'm not sure" he said, "I need to recover from this trip! Ask me in a week!"

"You did it at a good time of year," I said.

"Yes," he replied, "we had waves the height of a house but my friend said he'd experienced waves that are twice the size of a house. In those conditions, they have to head back to shore or out of the storm area."

On arrival at Rotterdam Port, we ended up in a very long queue. In the six weeks whilst we'd been away, the holiday season had begun and there were coachloads of retired British, German and French tourists. I dreaded to think what it was like in the school holidays!

Richard and I sat in the waiting area with our bags, waiting for the queues to go down but Mark managed to get us moved to a different queue, away from the coach passengers who were checking in as a group.

A retired couple in front of us, who'd been on our bus, said they've been to Rotterdam and stayed overnight. 'What did you think of Rotterdam?" I asked. "We loved it," they both agreed. "Better than Amsterdam. Not so crowded."

"Better than Amsterdam?" I thought. Even if I'd been as fresh as a daisy in Rotterdam, I don't think I would ever have come anywhere near that conclusion; crowds or no crowds!!

Once on board, Richard and I dumped our bags and went up on deck to have a beer in the sunshine and watch the continent of Europe disappear as we set sail and quickly cleared the Port of Rotterdam.

BACK IN BLIGHTY!

It was a smooth crossing. On arrival back in the U.K., we gained an hour. At six in the morning when announcements began, I decided to make my way up on deck, hoping I'd see Spurn Point as we passed. In theory, we still had an hour and a half until we docked in Hull.

As I emerged onto the deck, it was the Humber Bridge that loomed large under the welcoming committee of thick grey clouds rather than Spurn Point. We weren't far from the docks.

I returned for half an hour's beauty sleep but by 7:00 AM, when there had been several announcements requesting car drivers and their passengers go to various decks, Richard was restless to leave the cabin. I gave in, just as there was a knock on the door encouraging us to leave.

After a few minutes in the lounge, we were directed to disembark. Passport control was swift and we were in the car park waiting for our friend to pick us up by the time the boat was due to dock. It felt a bit like a Ryan Air flight where they set the arrival time so late that they are always early or on time just so they can make their statistics look better than they really are in reality!

Tim, our friend and chauffeur who had kindly offered to pick us up, wasn't due until 8:00 AM. The woman from Grimsby and her son weren't being picked up until 8:30 AM.

Luckily for us, Tim is very punctual. At 8:00 AM, right on the dot, he drew into the carpark. "Has he been sitting around the corner so he can be on time to the second?" I joked with Richard.

Forty-five minutes later, I was sinking onto the sofa at home in Beverley. A moment, I have to confess, I had dreamt about for a few days, along with a fish supper and a glass of sauvignon blanc! It was a bit too early for wine so I had a strong coffee and posted messages on the Interrailing for the Older Crowd and Interrailing and Eurrail Facebook pages, thanking everyone for their invaluable help. As I said, "I couldn't have done it without you guys! Your invaluable help and expertise were much appreciated." There are a few jerks on there who have got nothing better to do than criticise and pontificate. A few even made me break my cardinal rule not to engage in a negative way on social media and just rise above it. One regularly posts a cyclostyled message about using google with a patronising link. When he posted this on one of my posts about a train route, my hackles went right up. One woman complaining about negative comments observed that it was mainly "older men". I agreed but pointed out that much of the excellent and detailed expert help and advice was also posted by other "older men".

Before I started to plan my next trip, I proudly posted our train statistics, so cleverly calculated by the rail app.
We had travelled 19,512 kilometres on 179 trains which had meant we had spent a whopping ten days, six hours, twenty-five minutes and forty-three seconds on trains! Being a geek, I'd worked out that the interrail passes had cost us €600 (in the half-price sale) but if we had bought the tickets individually, it would have cost us €4,457. A whopping saving of €3,857!

I find that when I return from a trip, it takes a while for me to process my memories of the journey which usually means all the good memories shine through and I conveniently forget the bad bits when I'm tired, frustrated, cold and hungry. I've always said that travel is the best education there is: forget the classroom, you've got to get out and about! With this in mind, I'd decided to take a leaf out of the Finns' book and count my blessings. I was very lucky to have the time and money to spend three months exploring our incredible continent!

And finally.....

The awards go to:

Most friendly people- The French (yep, I was surprised too)

Best trains- The Swiss

Most helpful in a crisis- The Swedes

Most hospitable- The Norwegians and the Finns

TOP TIPS AND HELPFUL HINTS!

Packing List/Tips

Quick dry clothes that dry quickly when on the go. Cotton/ specialist clothing from outdoor stores, for example, Millets, Mountain Warehouse and GO Outdoors are best. Wash clothes with shower gel or a bar of soap- there's no need to carry soap powder. I often wash clothes when I'm having a shower. Normal t-shirts and jeans are not quick dry so not ideal; you don't want to be packing up damp clothes that will get musty. Most of my clothes will dry overnight and be ready to wear the next day, even in colder climates. If I do have to pack up damp clothes, I don't shy away from getting my undies out to continue drying them on a train or a bus, or hanging them on the outside of my backpack but I realise this approach may horrify some people!

Research the weather for the time of year for your destination. If you are on a longer Interrail trip, you will probably find that you need to cater for more than one season/climate. At risk of stating the obvious, weather in Europe varies greatly according to geography and time of year. Layers are useful as you can wear a single layer in warmer weather and then layer up if it gets colder. You can't wear a thick jumper in hot weather.

Comfortable leggings can be used day or night.

Comfy walking shoes with a good grip. It's worth paying that bit extra! I'm in love with my Salomon walking boots and shoes but had to take out a second mortgage to buy them as they are the top end of the market. In the end though, they are good value for money as they last for so long and aren't falling apart half way up a mountain!

Travel towel or sarong that can be used as a towel/skirt/shawl etc

Multipurpose pen knife

Aero press coffee maker if, like me, you can't get started without a proper coffee

Water bottle and Robinson's mini juice cartons to flavour.

Nail scissors

Sun cream (U.K. tends to be cheaper than the rest of Europe)

Sun hat (I prefer a bucket hat with a wide brim for all round protection and a cord to keep it on in windy conditions or on a boat trip)

Sunglasses (I wear prescription glasses that are transition sunglasses)

Pain killers and other medication/small medical kit

Small sewing kit

Plastic sliders

Travel toilet

Small pack of toiletries- you will acquire soap and shower gel along the way so don't take too much.

Medium sized backpack. It's much easier to negotiate trains and stations than a suitcase.

Take a fold up day pack/ strong tote bag for day trips and shopping.

Take a power pack. You can also charge on trains/buses. It is very important to have charge on your phone to show your pass to a ticket inspector.

Personal Safety

Wear a money belt. I wore two. One had passports, spare cash and credit cards in it. This went inside my trousers in busy places such as city stations where gangs of professional thieves operate. The other was larger and contained a credit card and my phone, plus a small amount of cash to give anyone who held me up with a knife! I was held up at gunpoint in South America so I may be a little paranoid! Generally, instances of robbery are very rare in Europe.

Have a point of contact at home, for example, a relative or a friend and touch base with them on a regular basis, especially if you are a solo traveller. Europe is very safe but you just never know what may happen!

Interrail Tips

Join the Interrailing for the Older Crowd and Interrail and Eurail Facebook Pages. Read the posts to get general help and advice and use the search facility to find answers to the questions you have. If you have specific questions, you can get the benefit of people's experience and the expert knowledge of the 'rail experts'. Generally, people are amazing and give up lots of time to help strangers with queries, especially when you are 'on the go' and feel you are banging your head against a brick wall.

European trains are a metaphor for Europe itself. Every country has a different train system. In fact, in many countries, every region has a different train system! There's great variety in:
first and second class
rules for reservations

*availability of information/WiFi
facilities e.g. play areas for children on trains
attitudes of the train staff
your fellow passengers
the toilets
the stations*
At the end of the day, it's all part of the adventure!

Buy a first class rail pass, if possible, as it is far better value than a second class.

Use 1st class lounges at certain stations if you have a first class pass.

Get into the habit of adding your journey at least the day before so when you wake up you can activate your ticket. Take a screenshot because sometimes the pass won't load when the ticket inspector is checking. Only one ticket inspector in Finland refused to accept my screenshot so I had to turn my phone off and then back on!

Rail Apps for each country are useful. I double checked Rail App routes just in case they didn't have the most up to date information on the interrail app.

The Man in Seat 61 website is a wealth of information.

The Interrail Website has a very helpful vlog that talks you through how to use the electronic pass.

The ticket generated on the Interrail App is separate to seat reservations which can be on one person's phone if you are a couple. In France and Spain, reservations could only be made at a station so you have to wait until you are in the country. In Norway, you can make a reservation for free via an online chat and they will email you the seat reservation. Seat reservations seem to be the biggest bug bear for interrailers so it is worth doing your research so you understand how it works in each country.

Stay in one place on a train line for 3-5 days and zip up and down the line. This worked really well in the Loire, Dordogne and Switzerland (where we stayed in beautiful Vevey- a cheap alternative to the more famous places). It didn't work in the more remote areas, such as in Scandinavia where we travelled long distances between places.

If you are just passing through one of the big expensive cities and only using it as a stop on a longer train trip then stay in a cheaper town or city nearby, for example, Lille rather than Paris or Lillehammer rather than Oslo. You can also stay just up the line and commute to the expensive city, for example, Malmo for Copenhagen or Sodertalje for Stockholm.

Intercity trains in Scandinavia often have a family carriage with a play area.

Trains in Scandinavia, Germany and Holland normally have free Wi-Fi.

Talk to anyone and everyone you meet. It's one of the best parts of the journey!

Be prepared for the unexpected! There will be delays and glitches! Try to see it as all part of the experience!

Financial

We rarely used cash during our three-month trip in western Europe.

Take a credit that doesn't charge interest on foreign transactions or withdrawals at an ATM. We used a Chase debit card that gives 1% cashback for the first year and had backup cards e.g. Starling/Monzo. Beware of withdrawing cash from ATMs because the ATMs are increasingly charging commission even if you have a U.K. bank that doesn't charge fees. If paying by card and given an option of currencies, always pay in the local currency.

Bits and Bobs

Do your research. Google top sights- I like PlanetWare, Culture Trip and Crazy Tourist, to name but a few.

Use Google Maps and Rome2Rio to get journey times/routes.

Use TripAdvisor for reviews of accommodation and restaurants.

Trivago is a good accommodation comparison site. I mainly use booking.com which is great if all goes well but appalling if there are problems. I don't use Airbnb because I object to being reviewed when I'm a customer spending money to rent an apartment. In my experience most places advertise on all the main platforms.

Take GHIC (U.K.) or EHIC (E.U.) for emergency care. They are free so if a fee is being charged then it's a con! It's not a substitute for travel insurance. If you need to get medical repatriation, it won't be covered.

Avoid July and August in Europe if you can as it's busy and expensive. Schools break up in early June in Scandinavia and Scotland. September is good weather and most schools are back. May and October avoid university holidays and the weather can be good.

Stay positive! It's never as bad as you think it will be!

Eat well and sleep well in order to keep up your energy levels as you have to be resilient and ready to deal with the unexpected!

Relax on a journey or at the end of a long day with a book or a film.

Have a great time! You'll bring back memories that you'll be able to feed off for the rest of your life and, hopefully, most will be very good.

Printed in Great Britain
by Amazon

32575110R00215